AMON

Amon the Cowboy at Shady Oak Farm.

AMON

The Texan Who Played Cowboy for America

Jerry Flemmons
Foreword by John T. Montford

Texas Tech University Press

This book was set in Zapf Elliptical BT and ITC Newtext. The paper used in this book meets the minimum requirements of ANSI/NISO Z39.48-1992 (R1997).∞

All photographs ©copyright the *Fort Worth Star-Telegram*. Courtesy the Amon Carter Foundation.

Design by Melissa Bartz

Printed in the United States of America

Library of Congress Cataloging-in-Publication Data
Flemmons, Jerry.
 Amon : the Texan who played cowboy for America / Jerry
Flemmons ; foreword by John T. Montford.
  p. cm.
 New ed. of: Amon : the life of Amon Carter, Sr., of Texas. 1978.
 An expansion of the author's thesis (master's)—East Texas State
University.
 Includes index.
 ISBN 0-89672-406-9 (alk. paper)
 1. Carter, Amon Giles, 1879-1955. 2. Journalists—Texas—
Biography. 3. Texas—Biography. I. Title.
PN4874.C26F55 1998
070.5'092—dc21
[b]   98-24590
                 CIP

98 99 00 01 02 03 04 05 06 / 9 8 7 6 5 4 3 2 1

Texas Tech University Press
Box 41037
Lubbock, Texas 79409-1037 USA

800-832-4042
ttup@ttu.edu
Http://www.ttup.ttu.edu

For Amon's Army:
the men and women
of the
Fort Worth Star-Telegram

No man on this foot-stool can rise to git up and say I ever knowinly injered no man or wimmin folks, while all agree that my Show is ekalled by few and exceld by none, embracin as it does a wonderful colleckshun of livin' wild Beests of Pray, snaix in great profushun, a endliss variety of life-size wax figgers, and . . . the most amazin' little cuss ever introduced to a discriminatin' public.

—Artemus Ward

Acknowledgments

This is the way Amon Carter was. He was neither better nor worse, more nor less, but as he is shown here. For what he was, who he was and where he was, Amon Carter was a man of importance and distinction—and altogether a human one. I grew to admire him. I've attempted to show his full personality, and if I've failed, the fault is mine, not those who recalled the Amon Carter of their lives.

He began, for me, as a master's degree thesis and ten years passed before I set about to expand him into a book. In those years are countless people who deserve more credit than I can provide here. First and foremost, my deepest gratitude is for three frank, perceptive, gracious ladies, Ruth Carter Stevenson, Nenetta Burton Carter, and Katrine Deakins. They opened their memories, their files and their hearts, honestly and patiently answering hours of questions, many of which must have been painful for them. I must thank, too, Amon Carter Jr., who in many ways became more than his father, and other executives of the *Star-Telegram* who participated in the project and allowed me full access to the newspaper's files, and generously provided me with time to research and write. Jack Butler, Jack Campbell, Jack Tinsley, Phil Record, Bert Honea, Jack Douglas, Cal Sutton all have my grateful appreciation.

Sam Kinch Junior and Paul Rowan wrote earlier master degree theses that were invaluable for basic research on the lives of Amon and Jim Record. Hettie Arleth, the newspaper's librarian, and her reference room staff, especially Charlcia Bullard, allowed me to poke through the endless mass of clippings and were unflinchingly patient and kind to all my requests. Dorothy Hooper worked many hours searching for pictures. John Moulder, Z. Joe Thornton and Caleb Pirtle assisted with research and interviews. Dr. Jack Bell, Dr. Otha Spencer and Dr. Fred Tarpley, all of Texas A&M University at Commerce, with friendship and professional advice, guided me through the thesis and into this lengthier work. My friends, Pat and Bill Massad, provided counsel, editing and a proper writer's garret. Mike Nichols corrected my poor spelling and untangled grammatical snarls.

None of this would have been possible without the assistance of Amon's Army, the men and women of the *Star-Telegram*, all of whom are excellent storytellers. In no particular order, they are: Bert Griffith, George Dolan, Irv Farman, Pauline Naylor, Elston Brooks, Jim Trinkle, W. L. Redus, Ida Belle Hicks, C. L. Richhart, Leroy Menzing, Bess Stephenson, Charles Boatner, Mack Williams, Flem Hall, Alf Evans, Jim Vachule, Lou Hudson, E. D. Alexander, Al Panzera, George Smith, James Byron, DeWitt Reddick, Walter Claer, Claire Eyrich, Leonard Sanders, Ed Capers, Frank Mills, Bascom Timmons, Dean Blanton, Janice Williams and Jon McConal. Mary Crutcher, Jack Gordon, Delbert Willis and Willard Barr remembered their encounters with Amon Carter while working for the Fort Worth *Press*, Others who deserve credit are Congressman Jim Wright, J. Frank Norris Jr., Stanley Marcus, C. R. Smith, James Farley, Bill Loursey, Lon Evans, Davey O'Brien, Aaron Priest, Jimmy Durante, Bob Hope, Chester Shaw, Andy Fournier, Lawrence Wood, Don Woodard, Reverend Gaston Foote, and John Jenkins, who published the first version of Amon's life.

Special thanks go to Judith Keeling of Texas Tech University Press, who has infinite patience for a writer's always tremulous ego, and her design/editing staff—and Jeanne Warren Smith with her quick sure eye for grammatical blunders and missteps; she has an editor's steely resolve and a writer's soul. Errors in this work, of course, are mine and mine alone and cannot be attributed to anyone else.

Foreword

Even though Amon G. Carter is best remembered as the man
who invented the twentieth-century Texas cowboy and a city
"where the West begins," perhaps his most lasting contribution
should be as the champion of the people of West Texas.

Few early twentieth-century West Texans wore the hand-
tooled boots and ten-gallon hats the national media associated
with Carter. Perhaps none was determined, as was Carter, that
the mythic, freewheeling Texan occupy a permanent place in our
national popular culture.

These West Texans were hard-working, plain people who
planted dry-land cotton or raised sheep and cattle in a vast area
that encompasses two-thirds of the landmass of the state. At the
beginning of the century the power structure in Dallas, Austin,
and San Antonio paid little attention to their needs. In fact, the
state gave the Permanent University Fund more than 2,321,000
acres of West Texas land to support the University of Texas and
Texas A&M. At the time, the children of West Texas had two
small institutions of higher education in their region; both were
teachers' colleges. Few other state-supported amenities existed
in West Texas: parks, highways, and hospitals were unknown in
this part of the state when Carter came to understand that he
could change the face of West Texas through his personal influence and the editorial influence of the *Fort Worth Star-Telegram*.

Thus it came to be that Amon Carter and his wildly successful
newspaper brought national attention to the folklore of the Texas
cowboy, and state attention to the many needs of the people of
West Texas.

The most significant result of Carter's keen salesmanship and
relentless lobbying for West Texans was the creation of Texas
Technological College in Lubbock in 1923. The college of fewer

than 1,000 students when it opened in 1925 had grown into a university and health sciences center of nearly 27,000 students when Texas Tech celebrated its seventy-fifth anniversary in 1998. The 1,839-acre campus in Lubbock had expanded into health centers in Amarillo, El Paso, Midland, and Odessa and an academic center in Junction. The college, first created as the only "science college" in West Texas, had grown into a comprehensive research university with Schools of Law, Medicine, Nursing, Pharmacy, and Allied Health.

An editorial in the *Fort Worth Record*, soon to be merged into the *Star-Telegram*, set the motion in action in the fall of 1915. The editorial noted the lack of educational opportunities in West Texas and pointed to the West Texas land that the state had sold to build the Capitol in Austin. By 1916, Chambers of Commerce across West Texas had organized a movement to secure a new college. Amon Carter, an early, vocal supporter of the movement, took up the cause as his personal agenda. The *Star-Telegram* led the fight to gain recognition for the region's educational needs.

Success seemed somehow too easy when Governor James E. "Pa" Ferguson signed legislation creating a West Texas A&M campus in Abilene in 1917. However, when Ferguson was impeached soon thereafter, new Governor William Hobby set aside the legislation.

In 1921, the legislature passed a new bill to establish a West Texas A&M College. The bill was vetoed by Governor Pat Neff, who cited economic hardships in West Texas in his veto, declaring that this was not the time for such a bold venture in West Texas.

Amon G. Carter and the considerable sway of the editorial page of his newspaper seized the issue's momentum at this point. On April 4, 1921, four days after Neff's veto, a *Fort Worth Star-Telegram* editorial suggesting that West Texas take strong measures to achieve its goals concluded with this battle cry:

> A movement to get justice for West Texas, and an educational movement to acquaint the whole State, some West Texans included, with the extent of the existing injustice, will unite West Texas and raise up friends for justice throughout the State. Governor Neff's veto is only an incident. But if it will serve to awaken

West Texans to the fight ahead of them, it will perform a service of which the Governor never dreamed.

Reaction in West Texas was quick and decisive; virtually every West Texas newspaper endorsed Carter's message. Supporters organized a rally in Fort Worth, where Carter lambasted the governor in public and cajoled powerful groups in private to ensure a successful re-entry of a bill to create a college for West Texas in the 1923 session.

Carter and his friends in the legislature came to realize that a campus for Texas A&M in West Texas was not as powerful an idea as was the creation of a separate, new institution for West Texas that would capitalize on the need for technology to manufacture West Texas cotton and wool in a West Texas textile industry. The supporters for higher education in West Texas believed they had found a niche market the governor could not overlook.

On February 6, 1923, both houses of the Texas legislature passed Senate Bill 103 to create Texas Technological College. Governor Neff signed the bill into law on February 10 and soon after appointed Amon G. Carter as a member of the first Board of Directors.

Carter was elected chair of that first board; his energy and vision set the course for the rapid development of plans for the new college. In a letter to then Texas Technological College President Dossie Wiggins in 1949, Carter recalls that a high-placed official in Austin wagered with him in 1923 that Texas Tech would never enroll 1,000 students. I'd wager the official knew little about Amon G. Carter and even less about the people of West Texas.

Carter received Texas Tech's first honorary doctorate in 1930, the only college degree he ever received. In 1950, he commissioned, as a gift to the campus, a statue of Will Rogers and his mount, Soapsuds, which has become the school's most enduring and beloved totem.

He was so impressed with our come-from-behind Gator Bowl victory in 1954 that he diverted the team plane's return flight to his Carter Air Field in Fort Worth where he presented each player with one of his signature cowboy hats.

His unabashed support for Texas Tech led him to declare in a 1949 letter that "Texas Technological College is one of the great, outstanding institutions of the United States and affords great pride to the citizens of our own State and particularly to the people of West Texas."

Such support was not born out of his love for the bigger-than-life Texas cowboy figure he paraded before the media outside Texas. His support for the creation of Texas Tech was a result of a passion to see West Texas receive appropriate recognition as a vital and vibrant sector of the overall Texas economy.

It is with the most sincere appreciation of the legacy of Amon G. Carter that I write this foreword to the new edition of Jerry Flemmons's chronicle of the life of Mr. West Texas—Mr. Texas Tech.

John T. Montford
Chancellor
Texas Tech University
Texas Tech University Health Sciences Center

I never knew Amon Carter. He was seven years dead when I arrived at his *Star-Telegram*. Death, however, had not evicted his presence. He *was* there, and, to an arguable point, still is there, perhaps always will be. It was impossible not to be confronted by Amon, the quintessence of him, if not his physical presence. People spoke as though he had not succumbed to illness and old age but had just stepped out for a moment to give another cheer for Fort Worth. His name dropped easily and casually into conversations, and more often than not, "Mr. Carter" was uttered with a reverence and awe I could not understand. His reporters, who either worshipped or disliked him, told and retold favorite "Amon Carter stories." Because his name lay on so many public things in Fort Worth, it continued to pop up in print. Politicians and civic leaders conjured up his memory and deeds to emphasize this and that project. Amon Carter would not go away.

I saw him once as a dim image on a tiny Emerson television screen. He was inaugurating WBAP television, Channel 5. With hundreds of others come to witness that impossible invention, I crushed against the windows of a hardware store in Stephenville, a small college town west of Fort Worth. I was taken more with the medium than the messenger, but in my mind Amon still appears as an indistinct Lilliputian, gray-haired and portly, whose presence on that minuscule round screen was nothing less than witchcraft.

Then I was one of his boys, a *Star-Telegram* carrier, but did not associate that minikin figure with the newspaper. I did not live in West Texas. Stephenville was—is—in North Central Texas. The *Star-Telegram*, however, was dogged in its assertion that any piece of the state west of Fort Worth was West Texas. I thinking I was part of that vast Canaan. As were all *Star-Telegram* readers, I was told, and never doubted, that other Texas regions were inferior. From my small spot on the sandy farmland of North Central Texas, the newspaper assured me that nothing else on Earth mattered except West Texas and West Texans. (East Texans, living in all that suffocating foliage, could have been, for all we knew, a lost tribe of Israel; we felt only pity for them.)

I grew up with the *Star-Telegram*. The whole town did. It came daily, as constant and comforting as our families, and was not just a newspaper but *the* newspaper—a wise, theocratic authority that spoke of the world beyond West Texas as astrologers speak of distant planets. When words became important to me, I wished to write them for the *Star-Telegram*. No higher journalistic standard existed.

Later, I would learn that Texas had other good newspapers, and that really superior journalism was practiced elsewhere: New York, Chicago, in Washington and Los Angeles, even Kansas City and St. Louis. All else, I was told, was provincial, secondary to those newsprint Mount Everests. Interior American newspapers were too regional in their viewpoints, too local, to earn distinction. Those ideas, of course, were as misconceived as the *Star-Telegram*'s version of West Texas.

For its time and place, even endowed with a pardonable sugary chauvinism, the *Star-Telegram* was not just another good regional newspaper, but a great one. Perhaps not a crest of Everest, but very high up on the mountainside. By any measurement it was a better newspaper than the worst examples of Mr. Hearst, as good or better than his best. Within its wide territory and for its subject matter, it was as comprehensive, as authoritative, as scrupulous as the *New York Times*, as literate as the *Star* of Kansas City, certainly as dominating as Chicago's *Tribune*. It also could be exasperatingly dull, priggish and puritanical, boorish in its ceaseless role as ringmaster of the grand circus that is Texas.

Measured against today's journalistic yardstick, Amon's *Star-Telegram* would be short. It raked little muck, poked under few public rocks, supported too strongly the ruling bloc, ignored almost altogether the local social problems of the day. It would be considered racist, inside and out. Its boosterism voice was too strident, too constant. Newspapers, even then, reflected society around them, and for Texas, that was Amon Carter.

That early *Star-Telegram* cannot fairly be compared with today's newspapers, not even with its own modern self. It represented an historical period passed by, a time when regionalism had purpose, when growth and progress were virtues courted by all America.

In all important ways, the *Star-Telegram* honored its First Amendment franchise with complete and encompassing service to its readers. That made it a good newspaper. What made it exceptional was that it served fully and faithfully an area larger than the whole of New England, did it for so many decades, usually without the coercion of adequate competition.

Stanley Walker, the legendary city editor of the *New York Herald-Tribune* during the 1930s, returned to his birthplace in Central Texas after World War II, sick of newspapering and big cities. He lived out his remaining years as a rancher and sometime writer of books. Walker—a *Star-Telegram* rural subscriber—correctly assessed the basic weaknesses of Texas newspapers, as (1) a lack of boldness—all feared controversy, and (2) the Chamber of Commerce puffery that too often passed for news. *Lone Star Merry-Go-Round,* an anonymous pamphlet published in the mid-1930s, liked none of Texas's major newspapers, but gave grudging points to the *Dallas Morning News*'s editorial pages. Houston's papers, and San Antonio's, were dismissed with sneers. The *Star-Telegram,* then the southern United States' largest newspaper, was "the Bible of Texas's most bigoted section," and seemed, the pamphlet went on, to exist for no other reason than to promote Amon Carter and his boosterism schemes.

In defense, growth was *the* story requiring ongoing attention. Texas was rich in potential, poor in actuality, and filled with badly educated poor people. Growth desperately was needed, and newspapers stumped for it. Because of Amon Carter, the *Star-Telegram* was superior, even preeminent, at this game. The newspaper, which at times seemed like an out-of-breath town crier, gave its readers what they wanted and needed: hope and pride.

Readers' attitudes and needs and demands have changed, as have those of newspapers, including today's *Star-Telegram.* It was, like rumble seats, good nickel cigars, and our innocence, of another time, but of its era and place, it was a giant. Amon Carter would have nothing less.

I have gone on too long explaining the *Star-Telegram*, but it was the most visible and viable public evidence of Amon Carter, a living extension of the urgent zealotry with which he was stricken.

What the newspaper was, he was, but what he was not, was a newspaperman. He was a publisher, and publishers and journalism often are incompatible, may, in fact, be antagonistic to one another. He was not even a very good publisher. He had little time for the nuts and bolts operation of any business, especially a newspaper requiring daily, even hourly, tending.

Amon never had the "calling." He fell into the newspaper business. He was a salesman who in the beginning just happened to be selling newspapers. His journalistic education came initially from gentle, impractical Louis Wortham, the *Star-Telegram*'s first publisher, and later from editor Jimmy North, a knowing, generous man who set the newspaper's unerring course and kept in harness Amon's more impulsive conduct for more than fifty years. James Record, the managing editor, made the *Star-Telegram* happen twice a day and once on Sunday with snap and precision. Bert Honea, tall and angular and strapping, as lean in body as in his spending habits, kept the newspaper empire solvent in spite of Amon's audacious spending habits. Harold Hough, the circulation manager, daily placed the paper before readers as far away as the next time zone and developed radio and television wings of Carter's publishing house. Al Shuman filled the pages with ads.

These men—"St. Amon and the five apostles," mused a cynical reporter—created a formidable management cast; they built the *Star-Telegram* kingdom. They, claimed one observer, were "the best newspaper team in history." That is a much too generous appraisal, but doubtless they were the South's best. They proved that much.

While Amon had to be educated to the purposes of journalism, the newspaper's underlying philosophy was his alone: sell, promote, and build the city and region, and the paper will grow and prosper as well. "When the lake rises, the boat will rise, too," he was fond of saying.

No Caesar ever thumped his Rome as energetically as Amon peddled Fort Worth. Amon told William Randolph Hearst in 1924, "We have never seen the good in being a nagging kind of newspaper." Four years earlier, syndicated columnist Claude Callen wrote, "The *Star-Telegram* is alive, clean and full of news. It works for a quarter of Texas and strives to build itself without pulling others down." A fair appraisal.

Amon, however, created a unique problem. The publisher was the newspaper's principal civic news source and news maker. That alone was trouble enough. North believed that newspapermen, including publishers, should keep themselves out of print. His canon extended to families of newspapermen; Phil Record, nephew of North and James Record, won a grade school contest, and editorial board members convened to decide whether to publish the youngster's picture.

Ultimately, North gave up on Amon but the policy was in force for others, and in almost fifty years, little more than obituaries of *Star-Telegram* employees appeared in the paper.

If Amon making news was a headache for North, it was maddening for rival newspaper editors forced to provide space, often on their front pages, for a competitor.

Beyond Amon's conventional news making were his little antics, many of them page-one stories as far away as Europe. Nationally syndicated columnists wrote regularly of Amon. Many were published in the *Star-Telegram*. More were not. How does an honest editor ignore a man who fires a pistol through elevator doors during a national political convention? North did, but with nagging conscience; one almost hears his anguished sigh rumbling out of the past. The publisher's private files contained scores of columns killed and laid to rest by the ever-vigilant North. ("This seemed a little too bullish," he wrote atop a Westbrook Pegler column.)

For the final thirty years of his life, Amon Carter had more urgent interests than the newspaper, but he was identified as its voice and also as cheerleader for Fort Worth and much of Texas. He was recognized nationally as the foremost exponent of the best in Texas: the joyous, expansive, unrestrained celebration of life, the genuine unfettered friendliness, the sure and certain western independence and individualism. And also of the worst: the doctrine that everything in Texas is bigger and better, the loud, boisterous public displays, the practiced pretense of uncultured ignorance. Those who disliked Amon said he was an embarrassment, that he played a role no longer true of Texas. His supporters said he behaved as outsiders believed Texans were, so what was the harm? Not that the argument affected Amon. He did as he pleased. He did not originate Texas exaggeration, but he practiced it with a style and vitality never seen before or since.

There is a mutated gene of rustic rube in Texans that long ago was bred out of most Americans. Psychology explains it in terms of "ego-validation" and "the ontological verity of self-invention." It is what Texas writer Larry L. King called "playing cowboy." Others save the heirlooms of their past—their grandmothers' chiffoniers, their forefathers' rockers, their ancestral stoneware pitchers—while we preserve the cowboy character in an acting-out of what was. It comes in exaggerated dress—the boots of exotic animal skins, the wide-brimmed hats, the silvered buckles of ordinary businessmen who never rode a horse—a roiling balls-of-feet walk (the John Wayne canter), and in measured but emphatic hand gestures. The speech is a prairie patois, opulent in metaphor and simile, earthy and often profane, lazy and affable, often sexist, even racist, spoken nasally with ungrammatical self-deprecating humor calculated to hide any shred of cultural polish and education, an echoing of an era in Texas when book-learning was suspicious. It was not thought polite to let neighbors know you were smarter or richer than they—still is not—and many Texans hid well the fact that they had a metaphysical twist of mind. At its worst, the bucolic impersonation is self-parody, yet playing cowboy hangs on as a kind of good ol' boy *deus ex machina*.

We revel in our Bubba-ness.

Throughout its rather histrionic life, Texas has been a land bursting with glittery bombast. We have always been a braggy people. To camouflage the early misery, the ignorance, the uncomfortable circumstances in which Texans found themselves, they swaggered and boasted and overplayed their character to a world baffled, but always intrigued, by the pomp and noise rising from the Southwest.

Amon was *the* mythical Texan. He created the twentieth century image of the fictional Texan portrayed in movies and books, television and onstage.

It fell to Amon to arrive at a time when Texas was becoming engraved on the national mind. The 1920s and 1930s and 1940s were decades of Texanism's ascension, especially in Washington. John Nance Garner was vice president. Sam Rayburn was House Speaker. Young Lyndon Johnson stepped onto the American political stage. Aviation soared off the plains of Texas to commercial and military success. The automobile became a way of life, one depending on gasoline, and Texas had the most oil wells. In that time, too, Texans—particularly the younger, more restless Texans—fled the state. Texas, wrote Stanley Walker, was a place to get away from. Texans went everywhere, and everywhere they were a curious breed of people, more Texan among strangers than at home. They exaggerated their nasal brogue—the twangy *lingua franca* passing for English in West Texas—expanded their personalities into cartoon burlesque, magnified themselves until outsiders came to either smile or flinch whenever confronted with Texanism.

Amon Carter played the professional Texan with a perfection that would have shamed a Barrymore. He invented the cowboy, the yippeeing westerner that parodied the real thing but a character that was taken out and pranced before America with a master's proficiency for living theater.

Within Texas, he was a power, a force of politics, of civic boosterism, of industrial development. He was potent and important because he thrust himself into everything, partly because he was an insatiable meddler in the affairs of others, partly because he could effect success when no one else could and he knew it. He made dreams come true.

He ran Fort Worth. He loved it, lauded it, lavished gifts on it when it was good, punished it when it was bad. Amon was the ruling body of Fort Worth, yet he never held a public office. To oppose him was to live a lean existence outside the city's power base. He retained control almost until the end of his life, until after World War II, when all of America changed.

West Texas, as hungry for attention and self-esteem as a flogged orphan, easily and quickly became Amon's property. If Haskell township needed federal funds for a new hospital, city fathers jumped into their old pickups, drove to Fort Worth, and laid their problem on Amon's desk. A postmaster's position for Sonora? Candidates applied to Amon Carter. A state park for Monahans? New roads for Tulia? No problem. Amon Carter could do it all, and did.

He triumphed because for fifty years he primed the pump of friendship with men—industry leaders and politicians—who ran the country. He courted celebrities and movie stars and newspaper columnists. He reveled in the flashy prominence of his famous friends, but he wanted something from each of them—a business moved to Fort Worth or West Texas, money for his special projects, a written or filmed poem of praise for his town, his state. If refused, he simply asked again. And again. And again. Amon the Salesman never retreated. Thirty years passed between his initial efforts to collect a General Motors assembly plant and the day first dirt was turned for construction of a Chevrolet factory. The mammoth bomber plant was lost to Tulsa but Amon pestered FDR and the military until Fort Worth got its airplane business.

He was a stunning salesman who, someone said, could have sold Tupperware to Cartier's. He had the glibness of a snake oil peddler, the dogmatism of a saved-again evangelist, and the sincerity of a first-term congressman. The salesman was basic to Amon's personality, though his primary persona was that of a conservative businessman. He could be an outrageous Babbitt in municipal affairs. He was a philanthropist. He was a humble country boy awed by big cities and famous people. His theatrical Texan act—the cowboy—became the best known, best remembered, and most useful of his characterizations.

Those many Amon Carters were at work and play in the first half of this century, each separate and distinct, all tempered by his considerable emotional range. He was at any and all times ebullient, gracious, intractable, articulate, pompous, argumentative, egotistical, phenomenal, mesmerizing, dictatorial, and a genius. "Peripatetic," *Time* called him, and perhaps that is the best one-word description of Amon Carter. He was both a romantic and a realist, a sentimentalist of the past and a futurist. He had a mercurial anger that vanished as quickly and mysteriously as it arrived. He never forgot friends nor forgave enemies. He would be kind, magnanimous, overwhelmingly generous, and altruistic one minute, petty, greedy, spiteful, and selfish the next. Philosopher Wilhelm Hegel's lament, "Only one man understood me . . . and he didn't understand me" could have been written of Amon Carter.

Also an uncomplex man, the publisher never questioned himself. He was satisfied. Excepting the period when his son was a prisoner of war, those who knew him best couldn't remember a single moment of those self-doubts most of us experience. Doubts would have been a nuisance to him. Amon would not have understood the source or term, but he was ruled by the rationale of Nietzscheanism: aggrandizement and the will to wield power flowed out of him.

Autocracy is not an innately venal form of governing if the autocrat is benevolent, and Amon was—mostly. But one-man rule allows neither competitors nor successors, and when Amon died, Fort Worth suffered a business and civic recession. The city's leaders found themselves leaderless for the first time in almost fifty years. By dying, someone noted, Amon Carter committed his first disservice to Fort Worth because he was not, as suspected, immortal.

He was only seventy-four.

I have called Amon Carter "important," a vastly overworked and meaningless word. He was "important," without question, but never so much as he and his friends believed, or as legends now say he was. His old Democratic Party colleague, James Farley, who seemed to understand the frail control individuals hold on time and history, told me, "Amon had an importance. We all did, but not anymore." One of Amon's editors, Bert Griffith, claimed, "Texas has produced two men of greatness . . . Sam Houston and Amon Carter." A generous overstatement. Amon had a significance for a city and region and exerted some unmeasurable influence nationally, but he was, for history's sake, just a unique man of his time and place.

This is not an authorized or official biography of Amon Carter but this, I believe, is the way he was. Certainly this is the way he was remembered to me by hundreds of those who knew him, and the way he was portrayed by written materials in twenty-six file drawers and pounds and pounds of yellowed, brittle, newspaper clippings. I grew to admire him: his dash-ahead attack on life, the simple, joyous, outlandish flamboyance of his Texas cowboy persona. I know that Amon's cowboy merely was a modern reincarnation of what already was a mythological creature, but I do not want the legends of Texas, our mythology, to pass into obsolescence. We have run out of Amon Carters.

If I have failed to present the entire Amon Carter, if there are errors here, the fault is mine, not those who shared their memories of him, the newspaper, Fort Worth, and Texas. I thank them all.

The life and times of Amon Carter were many things: unpredictable, surprising, lively, grand, and exhilarating. Alf Evans, one of the legion of Amon's army of reporters, was there at the end, and though never a part of the frenzy around Amon Carter, he nevertheless had an intellectual's ability for analysis and was a skillful observer and collector of "Amon Carter stories."

"How Amon Carter and the newspaper are remembered in a thousand years is unimportant," said Alf. "But in the old days, everybody had fun. That's what everybody remembers about Amon Carter. They had fun."

And so they did.

Jerry Flemmons
Fort Worth, Texas

Early spring, 1939, Washington, D.C. The Mayflower: a hotel whose elegance is measured in marble floors and mahogany columns, the cathedral tranquillity of its lobby and public rooms, and the substantial graying and moneyed celebrity of its guests.

In late-day dusk, a westerner arrives at the Mayflower, his favorite hotel in Washington. He is a handsome, distinguished man, dressed in a white western hat and knee-length, bone-colored topcoat, the loose belt cinched in a square knot. He pauses and makes a decision. He will dine alone, though he dislikes being by himself for any reason. He enters the dining room, passes his hat and coat to an attendant. The maitre d' greets him enthusiastically—"Welcome back to Washington. We're honored to have you with us again."—and guides the man to his favorite table by a window.

The man orders dinner and watches strollers pass by outside in the darkness. Because Washington is an early town, the dining room is almost full, and quiet, with a rich, sepulchral ambiance.

Earlier, he had been in the White House, visiting with his friends, President and Mrs. Roosevelt. They chatted for an hour, speaking of their children, especially the man's daughter, who visited recently with the Roosevelts. The man told FDR a new joke and the president laughed appreciatively.

Then the conversation became serious. They spoke of the war situation in Europe and fears that America would be drawn into the conflict. The man soon would visit England, and FDR asked him to report on conditions there. The president sought the man's counsel on economy, attitudes of businessmen toward the administration, the wisdom of more taxes. The man mentioned a new national park for his state. FDR promised support.

At twilight, the westerner left the White House. Mrs. Roosevelt saw him to the door, called fondly, "Please come again." In response, the man touched the brim of his hat and stepped quickly through the gate, nodding to guards who called him by name with a deference shown only for important visitors.

Now he has eaten, finished his coffee. He signs the check and leaves a ten-dollar bill beside the plate. At the door, the maitre d' waits with the man's hat and coat.

He pauses, with a small grin, reverses himself and walks to the center of the room, stopping beside a table occupied by an elderly couple. He smiles at them. Indicating an empty chair, he asks, "May I? . . ." They appear quizzical, but each nods. The man slides out the chair and steps onto it.

Above the crowd of diners, he waits. Gradually, people notice the distinguished man standing on a chair. They stare and the room becomes silent. Good, be has their attention. He smiles again, raises a hand to his mouth and shouts:

HOOOOOOOOOOOO-RAAAAAY FOR . . . . . . FORT WORTH . . . . . . AND . . . . . . WESS . . . . . . ST . . . . . . TEXAAAAASSSSS!

The elderly lady drops her fork, a startled expression on her face. A head is thrust out of swinging doors leading to the kitchen. Toward the back, a man jumps to his feet. The room is in bewildered silence. Gradually, conversational murmur returns and a few notes of laughter rise above the murmur. Then there is scattered applause.

The man waves to everyone. He thanks the elderly couple. He collects his coat and hat and the maitre d' calls after him, "Good evening, sir."

"Good night," replies Amon Carter, grinning.

1

... and they [cowboys] were but creatures of circumstances, the
... circumstances of an unfenced world.
    —Anonymous cowboy

... [T]his place, this rural slum, this potential Utopia, this rolling
chunk of God's not-always-green footstool. ...
    —Stanley Walker, *Home to Texas*

West Texas is bound on the north by Colorado and Oklahoma, on
the west by New Mexico, on the south by Mexico and on the east
by Amon Carter.
    —*Amarillo Globe*, 1936

I went into West Texas one year and was never heard of again.
    —East Texas Senator Jack Strong, after a Democratic
      campaign tour of West Texas

The longhorn came from where every mean and marvelous thing of Texas came: the malignant, iniquitous brush country, the *brasada*, above the Rio Grande, and nothing ever believed of it was exaggeration. The *brasada* was a tortuous Eden, a natural savage wilderness without relief from the Nueces River to the Mexican border, and every living thing inside fought for its place.

There were mesquite, both brush and tree, with dirk-like thorns, and the Spanish dagger, walls of prickly pear cactus that to O. Henry seemed as "large fat hands," yellow blooming huisache, and the catclaw called by Mexicans "wait-A-minute" because it grabbed and held. Either dusted with a fine blowing sand or, said historian Paul Horgan, "beaten by deluges that hissed as they first struck the ground," the brush country was a haven for nature's angry misanthropes—the quill-backed peccary, the rattlesnake, the longhorn. Virtually waterless and endless to a man on horseback, the *brasada* was a labyrinth of interlocking thickets enclosing small clearings. There were wandering paths worn to dust by animals, but many dead-ended, and few men knew a safe route through. It was for this barbarism of a land that the first cowboys, who were Mexicans, devised leather leggings called chaps. Without protection, the brush would claw a man to pieces.

In its brush country sanctuary, the longhorn was an evil thing. Evolved from strayed Moorish cattle, the longhorn, J. Frank Dobie wrote, was the "parody of a cow." It had elk legs, could outrun a horse, was bony, high at the shoulders, low at the tail, shaggy-haired, gaunt-rumped, with a goat-limber neck holding a massive head from which grew horns curved like twin scimitars. In a wild state, cowboys claimed, the longhorn could nourish itself on wind and gravel. An adult bull weighed twelve hundred pounds of muscle and bone, and a few stood as tall as a man on horseback. Angered or wounded, it feared nothing, and once provoked, would attack anything, even the black bears that once roamed Texas. Should its victim escape, the longhorn followed indefatigably with its nose to the ground, sniffing the trail like a wolf.

The wild longhorn had no herd instinct but kept a few wives for whom he was a fierce champion. At sunset, he called his family together for the night, and his bellow, heard by cowboys camped in the *brasada,* was chilling and fearsome, the roar of a true wild beast.

The longhorn was never civilized. It was chased down, dragged to corrals, herded, branded, conditioned to a gentler environment, but never tamed. Man and longhorn, at best, held an uneasy peace. Gathered on the unfenced open ranges of South Texas, the longhorns foraged on sweet grasses, multiplied, spread over Texas, and became an industry. Soon after the Civil War, when Yankees cried for meat, ranchers began driving their longhorns to Kansas railheads. The longhorn's meat was sinewy and gamy, but northern appetites complained little.

"Them longhorns," said an Oklahoma cowboy of this century, "could live on nothing, and you could drive them to market and it didn't hurt 'em, 'cause they wasn't any good to begin with."

The American western experience began with the longhorn. Longhorns and open ranges. Tens of thousands of longhorns spread across the unfenced cosmos of West Texas. More longhorns, an estimated ten million, were driven north, still other millions shipped by rail. The age of the longhorn—never a breed, only a species—lasted fewer than twenty years. Then pastures were fenced and foreign cattle—the Hereford and Angus with plump meaty bodies and stubby legs but few survival skills on open ranges—were introduced. By the late 1880s, most longhorns had been bred away, chased away, or killed by ranchers to protect their precious, pure-blooded cows.

Many of those longhorns that escaped fencing and slaughter returned to a free wild life in West Texas, and a few existed well into the twentieth century. A Big Bend rancher killed one in 1910. As late as the 1920s, a rancorous old bull lived in a narrow canyon south of Lubbock. Around that same time, a Model T Ford encountered a bull longhorn in the eastern mountains of New Mexico, across the border from Texas. The longhorn stood on a rough narrow road, and the driver braked hard. The bull bellowed, pawed the ground, and charged the automobile. It bashed the machine, stepped back, and charged again. And again. Finally, a horn pierced the radiator and the bull actually raised the machine's front wheels off the ground, shook the car loose, and bounced it into a ditch.

The longhorn bawled triumphantly, then walked down the mountain and into the mists of time.

Before the longhorn fled into obsolescence, the cowboy had played his brief role in the American western drama and was offstage, a fragile anachronism within the drama of Manifest Destiny rumbling across the continent toward the Pacific. The longhorn created the cowboy, created the need for such a creature, and once present, he became the essence of legends and myths.

The original cowboy, or "cow boy" as the term first was written, was Texan—West Texan—but he took his profession from the Mexican vaquero. Though he is remembered as white Anglo-Saxon, the cowboy was brown or black and often spoke with a European accent. But whatever else he may have been, he was Texan and his life was far less romantic and adventurous than John Wayne led us to believe.

The cowboy neither built nor explored nor populated the American West but moved ever so briefly across it, as capricious and lonely as the blowing dust. Dime novelists and penny dreadful authors scribbled magniloquent lies about him for rapt eastern readers, but saw him only in town, often ending long cattle drives with a few desperate hours of extravagant carousal before returning to a life of social desolation. Like a cloistered monk of some distant forgotten monastery, he served his god—the rancher—and observed no religion but a Trinity of cow, horse, and land. Moving often from ranch to ranch, he made few lasting friendships. He was untutored and ignorant. For endless months he lived on the range, burned in summer, frozen in winter, as punished as the cattle he attended. He slept on the ground under "henskin" blankets, arose at 4:00 A.M., or earlier, and often was not asleep again until midnight. He was fed a constant diet of beans—"Pecos strawberries"—greasy stews and Arbuckle's coffee. His aches and sprains were treated with heavy coats of axle grease or prickly pear poultices. He lived in a society of men and made love to the only available women, the ubiquitous "soiled doves" and "fallen angels," almost on a seasonal basis, like some animal in heat. He smelled of the horse he rode, of the cows he tended, and of the dung of both. Miasmic as a nocturne, he was a neutered man, often profane, rarely profound, illiterate, itinerant, a harsh feral child who went crooked or stayed straight, or alternated, like an electric current. He hid his past behind such curious aliases as "Shanks" and "Pieface," "Muley," "Stormy," and "Joggy." For his always brief passage into towns, he exploded with drunkenness and venery, exchanging six months' wages for a few hours of release from his Trappist confinement. His was a "soulless, aimless" existence, wrote one of the few introspective cowboys who left the range when he saw it for what it was. But the cowboy, explained Paul Horgan, was the "last of the clearly traditional characters [born] from the kind of land he worked in and the kind of work he did."

His forefathers were the Spanish Conquistadors, his cousins the vaqueros and the mountain men who first ventured into the West. No American character has endured as the cowboy, though in reality he lasted little longer than the West, as few as twelve or perhaps as many as twenty years. Behind him came men with hoes and plows and women. He scorned the new arrivals but the farmer lasted, the cowboy did not. He went away to other jobs, he went away to other truths, and finally, he just went away.

If this were a logical world, the flatness called the Grand Prairie beginning east of Dallas would continue uninterrupted beyond Fort Worth, but it is not, and across the Trinity River, unexpectedly, are hills, gentle and mild and grassy, cut with seams of rocky creeks lined by groves of oaks. Those swells of odd geography billow outward to blend with a hundred-mile-wide band of good farming land called the Cross Timbers, on the far soft edge of which soil changes from rich browns and blacks to beige sands and pale red clays. Oaks disappear, succeeded by mesquite. Docile bossies of dairy farms are replaced by fatter, less tractable cattle. The land no longer rolls but becomes level, sloping upward to the sun, and at that topographical juncture, a few miles beyond the ninety-eighth line of latitude, begins West Texas, the fundamental dramatic stage for the American western experience.

The West's borders were about five hundred-by-five hundred miles, roughly the dimensions of West Texas, and within that austere compound evolved every blessed western thing we have come to hold sacred: the longhorn, the cowboy, the horse, the ranch, big hats, boots, lariats, chaps, spurs, kerchiefs, rustlers, the fruited plains, purple mountains' majesty, even the clichéd-but-immortal line, "They went thataway," as uttered by a sod farmer near Amarillo to a posse in pursuit of two cow thieves. ("Thataway," according to an early newspaper account of the chase, was northwest, toward Raton, New Mexico.)

West Texas was the West and later it would be *The West*, which is not the same thing at all.

As the land rises from the Cross Timbers, it becomes dustier, rockier, more of a dry savanna. Midway between the good farming ground and New Mexico's mountains is a blunt stone cliff called the Cap Rock, an eroded natural escarpment rising as much as a thousand feet. Above and beyond that stone palisade begins America's high plains, named in West Texas *Llano Estacado*. The Staked Plains. A true prairie once covered by tall grasses, level and seemingly as endless as the Russian Steppes, home to Indians, especially Comanches, and limitless herds of buffalo. Writer Willa Cather called it "the floor of the sky."

Far south of the Cap Rock is the *brasada*, and west, as the cliffs hook into New Mexico, are Texas's only true mountains and the nub-ends of Mexico's Chihuahua Desert. The Chihuahuan barrenness melds with the Sonora Desert and continues to the Pacific. That country's physiognomy is one of wildness and wilderness, of distance and space, colors washed and muted. In it are Texas's ventricous belly, the Big Bend, which sags onto Mexico, and tall crisp peaks rising almost nine thousand feet.

There was a prologue and an epilogue but generally the West was written in West Texas after the Civil War. The West ended when the first strand of barbed wire was strung between two cedar posts. Joseph Glidden's spiked wire stopped the West dead in its tracks. All after is but postscript.

Fencing meant the end of open ranges, the end of longhorns, the end of the nomadic cowboy, the end of his yondering spirit, his freedom. The West was gone and what followed was *The West*, and in *The West* the cowboy no longer was a serf for those prairie Caesars, the ranchers, but a kind of dauntless Cossack of the plains riding his white stallion across the prairie with the speed of summer lightning, delivering justice to an unjust world. *The West* is the Texas of official legend, a mythical country with its straight-line horizon and flat vacant space, the Texas of hard-bellied, lean-hipped Clint Eastwoods and Gary Coopers with dark, dangerous eyes. This is pulp magazine and paperback book Texas, Saturday matinee Texas, the *cine-vérité* state of celluloid heroism, six-gun valor, saloon-and-sarsaparilla true grit. Hollywood grew wealthy from *The West* and outsiders believed, perhaps still believe, the boots-and-jeans and shoot-'em-up stereotype, still suppose that *The West* lives on in the hearts of free men everywhere. God knows, we Texans have gone to preposterous lengths to preserve those vainglorious legends.

Fort Worth was a prominent geographical player in the American western experience. The city began in 1849 as a rough log fort on grassy bluffs along the west fork of the Trinity River, a dowdy, vermicular stream that either flooded or puddled and that, until 1913, served as a convenient garbage and sewage dump. The fort was built as a place of refuge for settlers from the frontier savagery of Indians. The army wasted its time. The first group seeking sanctuary was Indians, the Tonkawas, fleeing from other Indians, the Kiowas. No wild Indians ever attacked, and the army moved on, leaving behind the beginnings of a town.

Frontier Fort Worth owned all necessary ingredients for a place in *The West*. Sam Bass, a vigorous and successful North Texas bandit and train robber, bought his criminal supplies there. Luke Short, a deadly fast gun and adventuristic gambler who dandified his western garb with a stovepipe hat, held financial interest in the White Elephant Saloon. Wyatt Earp's consumptive friend, Doc Holiday, often was seen peering across the city's poker tables. Temple Houston—youngest son of old Sam Houston—a soft-voiced, eloquent trial lawyer and lethal gunfighter, periodically rode into town, usually wearing a dead rattlesnake for a hatband. Cattle trails—notably a branch of the

Chisholm—passed nearby and furnished off-duty cowboys for Hell's Half Acre—Fort Worth's marvelous shopping mall of sin.

Railroads in all directions, buffalo hunters, the cavalry, lynchings, red-eye whiskey, wagon trains, stagecoaches westbound to Yuma, stampedes, wild horses, gunfights—Fort Worth had it all, just as Dodge City and Abilene and Tombstone. Cowboys rampaged the streets, firing six-guns into the air, regularly plugging one another and occasionally private citizens who wandered into the line of fire. The Acre's whores always made news: "Another soiled dove crossed the river," reported an early newspaper, the *Democrat*, adding, "Yesterday another of the demimonde, weary of the trials and tribulations of her life, took a dose of laudanum and morphine. The last suicide of such nature took place about two weeks ago."

And someone nailed Good Sally, a pretty Acre girl with many admirers, to the door of an outhouse. Her crucifixion aroused reformers to have a go at shuttering Hell's Half Acre. The erogenous zone closed for awhile, then opened again but never with the élan of the bad old Wild West days. When Butch Cassidy and his lawless accessory, the Sundance Kid, arrived in Fort Worth in 1898, the Acre was reasonably harmless and sedate, but the district endured well into the twentieth century, when a religious fervor during World War I smited it out of business.

Fort Worth truly was a rough frontier city, but not the "Paris of the Plains" as claimed by early civic boosters. Fort Worth's problem was staying power. Boom or bust. It rose with the influx of western emigration, then fell as fewer settlers came. Good fortune arrived with the cattle drives, and poverty after. Railroads brought another period of prosperity. And the buffalo hunters. And stockyards. Between the booms, Fort Worth relapsed. Workers moved out. Failed merchants decamped to other, steadier economies. During a lesser period one newspaper declared that grass actually was growing in the sidewalks, and Dallas wits joked that their neighboring city was so dull they had seen a panther dozing in the street.

Late autumn, 1905, Fort Worth was prosperous again with slaughterhouses and stockyards, and the downtown Metropolitan Hotel was a gathering place for cattlemen and buyers, loafers and worn-out cowboys. During the next bust, the Metropolitan would become a moderately priced whorehouse but in 1905 it had a sturdy, if fading, elegance, a decent restaurant, and a large, airy lobby in which the cattlemen mingled for beer and lies.

Lan Twohig had been a real cowboy, a Texas cowboy, the original model. He was an economized man, thin and sinewy, with blue eyes over a flattish nose, a slit of a mouth, and a stubble of remaining hair. He used a cane, and the cause of his limp was one of the more remarkable lies told in the Metropolitan lobby. Lan claimed his story as truth, of course, and even brought out the horns for proof. They were huge, more than six feet from tip to tip, mounted on polished mesquite wood, and belonged, Lan insisted, to one of Texas's last outlaw longhorns.

When he was young, Lan always began his tale, he chased longhorns in the *brasada* for a living, for their hides and tallow, and he was the best man ever to hunt the brushlands, better even than the Mexicans, who felt a mythical kinship with the wild cattle. Lan bragged that he feared nothing within the *brasada*. He entered with a short rope and pistol, often on foot, in the densest thickets, or when the bull had come to a fighting place. He knew the bulls' souls, how each would charge, how low or high the horns would be carried, how the animal hooked, how desperately it would fight him. He remembered the *brasada* and its fierce longhorns as the best time of his life.

When the longhorns at last were hunted out, Lan rode as a drover in 1867 for an early cattle herd to Kansas, then wandered from ranch to ranch, cowboying for the Double Moon, the G-4 near Marfa, the Rocking C in the Panhandle. He was alone, often lonely, never married. In the late 1880s, as the era of open ranges ended forever, Lan settled onto a ranch beyond the Pecos, probably on the eastern fringe of Big Bend. He was the only gringo cowboy.

Lan bossed the Mexicans, tended to the docile cattle, and finally, about 1892, had the adventure he retold often in the Metropolitan's lobby. One day in a distant pasture, a longhorn bull suddenly appeared and lured away three cows and a heifer, running them into the bushy hills. Lan, sure that the huge blue dun with red flanks and wide flared horns, was the last wild long-horn in the world, followed.

The story Lan told was lengthy but, even for those who heard it often, enthralling. He trailed the longhorn until sunset, cross-ing Muke Water Creek and beyond Hog Mountain, to a gully cita-del filled with mesquite and cactus. Lan knew the bull had its nest within that brushy fortress. He waited all night. As the sun rose, Lan Twohig, rope in hand, pistol in belt, entered. He heard the bull bellowing. Depending on his audience—women would gasp and fan themselves during the bloodier passages—Lan shortened or lengthened the fight itself, but he said it went on for four hours, man and beast stalking one another, the bull charging and charging and recharging, Lan fighting in spaces too tight to swing a rope loop, twisting away at the last moment, using tree trunks and cactus piles as barricades.

Finally, man and animal were exhausted. The bull crossed a small clearing and disappeared into the brush. Weary of the chase, Lan dismounted behind a clump of mesquite, clutching the rope in his left hand, right hand on his pistol. He listened to the silence for long moments. Then Lan stepped into the dusty arena and began moving slowly across it. In the center, he paused, looking for a trail, when a savage roar came from his right as the bull burst into the clearing, head low, horns atilt, eyes black as coal chips, dust billows rising with the sudden rush. Lan was crouched in a half-turn when the bull reached him, hooking its head as it hit him, one horn swinging in low then snapping upward as the tip pierced the leather chaps and tore through the cowboy's upper right leg. Lan screamed with the pain and felt himself lifted high, hanging from the massive horn. The bull dipped, then slung its head and Lan remembered the agony of striking the ground, his leg bloody and twisted. The bull bel-lowed in triumph as Lan fell into unconsciousness.

A long time later, Lan opened his eyes. The bull stood across the clearing, head back, horns shimmering in the noon sun. The bull roared and pawed the dust. Lan watched the bull warily, then began crawling toward his horse, which stood back among the mesquite brush. His gored leg left a bloody trail over the sand and time seemed forever to him before he came to the horse. He used the right stirrup to pull himself to a standing position. The bull had not moved.

Behind the horse, Lan drew his rifle from the scabbard, laid its barrel across the saddle, and sighted in on the bull. He tightened his finger on the trigger. . . .

Lan always paused at this point, giving his audience time to absorb what they had heard, then he returned to the story of long ago. . . .

"I felt my finger on the trigger . . . but did not fire. . . ." He held still, one eye closed, the other unblinking, staring over the gunsight. The bull waited. Lan pulled the rifle butt tighter into his shoulder, increasing the pressure. His leg ached where the bull's horn had cut him. Lan closed his eyes and caught his breath. Then he raised the barrel slightly and fired. The bull spun away and disappeared into the brush.

Six months later, a Mexican hand found the ancient bull dead, a mile north of the creek. Lan took the horns and mounted them, hung the trophy above the ranch house fireplace for all to see. In 1903, sixty years old and tired, walking only with the cane, Lan left the ranch, lived briefly in San Antonio, then moved to Fort Worth to trade cows in the stockyards.

He told his longhorn story again that fall of 1905, the audience mostly old men, among them Will Drannon, who with Kit Carson had guided Fremont to California in 1845, and Uncle Tuffy Thomas, one of the first cowboys up the trail to Kansas. "An' I jus' told that ol' bull we'd do it 'nother day," Lan concluded, pausing dramatically, as usual, before asking the final question of his audience:

"Know why I didn't kill that ol' longhorn?"

Ordinarily, Lan answered himself, but that day a voice at the rear responded loudly:

"Yes!"

All heads turned to the speaker. He was a young man, almost six feet tall, built squarely. His nose and ears were prominent but blended smoothly with the olive complexion, deep black eyes, and infectious smile. The voice was sleek and glossy, convincing. He wore a heavy, dark suit, a striped shirt partially covered by a vest, and a fluffy bow tie, the obvious costume of a drummer.

Irritated by the interruption, Lan Twohig demanded, "Well, s'pose you just tell us why. . . ."

The young man smiled broadly, enjoying himself.

"Because that bull was a mean sonovabitch and you were a mean sonovabitch and mean sonovabitches respect each other," he said loudly.

He laughed and the others, even Lan, joined in. Still laughing, the young man left the lobby, walked quickly, very quickly, into Rusk Street, his shoulders hunched against the brisk autumn wind. He would meet Lan Twohig again in a year or two, and the old cowboy would show him the horns. The young man, a consummate salesman, would persuade Lan to sell the horns, and then for the next four decades tell the classic cowboy/longhorn tale to audiences from New York to San Francisco.

That day, Lan Twohig watched the young man leave and asked, "Who's he?"

"Name's Carter," someone answered. "Sells them streetcar signs."

"Knows his sonovabitches," mused Tuffy Thomas.

Amon Carter was all of the Texas Advertising and Manufacturing Company, occupying a second-floor cubicle office within Fort Worth National Bank. Amon sold a patented indexing telephone directory and owned the concession for street-car advertising cards. Business was slow, but he made a living for his wife, Zetta, and year-old daughter, Bertice.

Amon came to Fort Worth in May 1905 from San Francisco, where he had not done well as an advertising space salesman for Barnhart & Swasey. His salary there, one hundred dollars monthly, was too little to support his lifestyle, already grandly baroque. The family returned to native Texas, to Fort Worth, but Amon was unhappy with his business and bored with the life.

That day Amon returned to his office to keep an appointment with a typewriter salesman. Amon did not type but felt that the presence of a machine would impress customers. Awaiting the salesman, Amon napped on the office couch. Last evening he had stayed in the White Elephant Saloon, drinking and playing poker until long after midnight, and he had a mild hangover.

The salesman—a Mr. Shotts—arrived, awakened Amon, and began explaining his machine. Carter said the price was too high. Mr. Shotts, discovering that Amon did not type and wanted the machine only for ornamentation, closed the case and began talking about a new product being introduced in Fort Worth that day. Cow-chip fuel. The salesman believed that oil-saturated cow manure would be a moneymaking item bought by thousands of poor folks who could not afford other fuels. Fort Worth certainly had cow dung to burn. Its stockyards handled 250,000 head of livestock each year and were second in size only to those in Chicago. No one who ever experienced the aroma of downtown in a north wind had to be told that cow manure was bountiful in Fort Worth.

Intrigued, Amon collected his hat, coat, and Mr. Shotts. The men went to look at cow manure. The city's stockyards were—and largely still are—a labyrinth of cow pens and barns, rail tracks, and two new packinghouses, Swift's and Armour's, three miles north of the courthouse across the Trinity River. The two men arrived in front of the main auction barn as the demonstration began. Reporters were there, pens poised to tell the world of burning manure. Amon knew one—D. C. McCaleb, city editor of the *Record*. McCaleb introduced Amon to A. G. Dawson, correspondent for the *Dallas News*.

The pile of oil-soaked cow chips was lighted ceremoniously, and the audience crowded near to absorb the heat. Instantly, all were aware of an inherent weakness in the cow-chip fuel theory. Burning cow manure smells. Amon wrinkled his nose and decided not to invest. Dawson and McCaleb re-pocketed their pens. They stood together, backs to the fire, trying to ignore the pungent smoke. The two reporters began talking about their favorite subject: publication of a daily afternoon newspaper to compete with the *Fort Worth Tribune*. Neither had money, nor business experience, but each knew how to write, edit, and publish a newspaper.

Amon was interested. He had business experience. He could sell advertising. He had no money but knew where to borrow. The men became excited. A newspaper was possible. Then and there, they decided on a name, the *Star*, and sealed the pact with firm handshakes.

That moment rates, perhaps, a small footnote in American journalism history, for the *Star*—parent of the *Fort Worth Star-Telegram,* which would become Texas's and the South's largest, most-influential publication, spawning a multimillion-dollar communications empire, and almost incidentally would make Amon Carter the most famous cowboy Texan of his time—was the only newspaper ever conceived and founded over a pile of burning cow manure.

In hoc signo vinces.

Early Amon.

You may forget the singer, but don't forget the song.
　　—Traditional

No other city in America has anything approaching such a public citizen as Amon Carter.
　　—Will Rogers, cowboy humorist, 1931

Amon wasn't born. He was invented a little bit at a time and largely with his own recipe.
　　—Alf Evans, newspaperman, 1973

Texas is one great windy lunatic.
　　—Socrates Hyacinth, *Overland Monthly*, 1869

Well, it is not so hot as Death Valley, and, on the other hand, it is not quite so cool as Greenland.
　　—Answer to visitor's inquiry about summer temperatures
　　　in West Texas, about 1960

He died on a warm evening in June, a slow news day, a Thursday in 1955, the twenty-third day of the month, the second day of summer. Ever punctual, he passed on forty minutes in advance of the deadline for the two-star edition, which would be sent into every dusty nook and cranny of his West Texas empire. When death came, morning managing editor Herb Schulz was notified. Schulz told the men slouched around city desk, "He's dead. . . ."

An assistant editor turned to an ancient Royal upright typewriter and keyed out one sentence:

"Amon Giles Carter died at 8:20 P.M. Thursday."

The makeup editor collected the brusque sentence and trudged up dingy back stairs to the fourth floor, preparing to assemble the various mechanical remains of Amon Carter's life.

As was the newspaper's exacting, systematic practice, the *Star-Telegram* had killed off its boss weeks before he died. Amon's obituary was written, inspected for accuracy, set tenpoint double-column, then locked into a special galley lodged against the composing room's east wall. A scrawled sign guarding the precious hoard of type read: "Do Not Remove."

His death was not unexpected. For weeks Amon's critical illness had been an acknowledged fact of coffee-break conversations and his reporters and editors set about making the passing as professional and dignified as possible. The master plan was to announce his death with a scant eight hundred-word story in the most immediate edition. More space would be cleared in subsequent editions for the complete obituary.

The makeup editor visited the head dump frame, stooped, and reached for a type case marked "72 Pt. CAPS," a largish font kept in a dingy lower drawer like unsightly silverware too good to discard but useful only for formal occasions. The type size and style were considered gauche and tacky by the conservative *Star-Telegram*, which never cared to shout at readers. Its presence signaled great catastrophe, like a world war, rare whopping nota bene such as rain in West Texas, or, as in this case, the end of an epoch.

The editor slugged the obituary "P1, 8-72, ALL-CAPS, Amon Carter . . . ," composed and counted the banner headline: "AMON G. CARTER DIES AT HOME AFTER ILLNESS WHICH BEGAN IN '53."

Portrait of Amon

The headline violated a long-standing, unwritten, but strictly followed rule that Amon's name was never to appear in headlines—when he was awarded the air force's highest civilian commendation, the story's head said merely that a "Fort Worth Man" was honored. The editor scanned the terse obituary.

Noting that Amon Carter was publisher of the *Star-Telegram* and board chairman of Carter Publications, Inc., owner and operator of radio/television stations WBAP, the obit said he died in bed at his home, 1220 Broad Street, where he had been confined since returning late in April from the annual American Association of Newspaper Publishers meeting. He had been ill since February 23, 1953, when stricken by two heart attacks at home and a third in St. Joseph's Hospital. His final local public appearance was for the 1953 Fort Worth Exposition and Fat Stock Show at which he introduced Texas Governor Allan Shivers to a first-night rodeo audience. The remainder of the story concerned itself with a casual inventory of Amon's many honors and interests, hardly a satisfying final-word monument for Texas's best-known citizen.

An edition later and throughout Friday's daytime papers, the *Star-Telegram* eulogized its late publisher in a bare-bones biography spread over most of two pages. The full obituary imbued Amon with prominence and dignity, surveyed his fame, sketched his up-from-impoverishment beginnings, his major philanthropies, the showy mountaintops of his long career. It had an emotional vacancy, containing none of the unabashed breast-beating we have come to expect when a newspaper loses a family member. Decades later, one feels the awful weight of it and empathizes with the anonymous writer burdened by the assignment of encapsulating his boss's intemperate life with sober words, decorous phrases, and a few cleansing lies.

The obituary is a simple canonization of St. Amon.

At the very least one suspects the writer itched to sneak in a final long, loud, lingering "Yippee" for the man who invented the cowboy.

Perhaps not. Amon Carter was never very well liked by his newsmen, never real to them. They saw Amon as a phantasmagorical character, a character created by their written words, built like a Ned Buntline narrative, as fanciful as Pecos Bill. They viewed his neurotic quest for perfection as dictatorial, his eccentricities as gross egomania. For them, his genius was shadowed behind sulfurous mists of anger. The pixy, gregarious Amon was interpreted as a foolish rich man. His rabid promotion of Fort

Worth and West Texas embarrassed the newsmen. It reeked, they believed, of the smelliest kind of chamber of commerce journalism and was an abasement of their ethics, ideals, and talents.

Joseph Pulitzer, they argued from city room soapboxes, never welcomed a smokestack industry to town with a page-one banner headline. Horace Greeley had not published an eight-column photo of one hundred and thirty-seven visiting oil executives. The New York Times *did not devote its upper front page to an inspiring census report the day war began in Korea. Of course not, his supporters countered, and the* Chicago Tribune's *Colonel McCormick had not mailed the World's Greatest Newspaper free to any soldier. Nor had Harry Chandler's* Los Angeles Times *printed verbatim trial testimony covering as many as seven full, open pages, and done it for ten straight days. William Randolph Hearst had learned to turn pages of his newspapers with his bare toes and knew eighteen psalms by heart, but could he have driven a stagecoach down Wall Street? Yes, the Scripps and the Howards, the Copleys and the Knights, had comported themselves with dignity and regality while Amon stood on banquet tables and fired his six-shooters, but those men had only newspapers to sell, not towns, half of Texas, ideas, dreams, the future . . . glorious, magnificent, utopian visions. OK, but one cannot imagine The* Times's *autocratic Mr. Ochs pronouncing New York's highest elected official a "crazy sonovabitch" as Mr. Carter had of a Texas governor, and with an amazed audience looking on.*

But I submit to you, was not that governor a crazy sonofabitch? Of course, but. . . .

For reporters, especially younger ones who had not been there in the beginning, Amon Carter was never the deity to which they often compared him (not always kindly). For them, he was a tinseled widget, molded in the *Star-Telegram* factory, folded and tossed on Fort Worth lawns or mailed by second-class permit to distant hamlets of West Texas.

Thus, when second-edition copies came into the third-floor newsroom that tepid evening, few men around the horseshoe desk gave the obit more than cursory attention. They scanned the words for accuracy, digested their meaning, noting that the photo was one taken before illness had transfigured Amon Carter into a thin, feeble, old man.

No one knew, but the anonymous writer had written Amon's name incorrectly. At birth, he was Giles Amon Carter, but he detested Giles and with his first adult job had moved Amon to the forefront, reducing Giles to an initial. The despised Giles was hidden further when he banned even the initial from print because the *Star-Telegram* endlessly cited him as Among Carter. Finally, Amon banished Giles forever by naming his son, Amon Gary Carter Jr.

The black-bordered, three-column photograph published beside the obituary was of an older—not old—Amon Carter. He appeared relaxed and unhurried, looking less his age with an unwrinkled, possibly airbrushed, face, a strong nose, and prominent ears supporting white eaves of monk's fringe hair. As a *poseur* of consummate ability, the role he was playing for the photographer was that of a wealthy establishmentarian, which one part of him was. He wore a conservative smile and there was in it the merest suggestion of inner relief, as though he secretly was melting a Bisodal tablet under the tongue to combat his chronic indigestion.

Picture, obituary, and headline hung underneath Amon's favorite scrap of holy writ: Fort Worth . . .Where The West Begins. The phrase was his war whoop, his aphoristic article of faith, a mantra he chanted in all available ears. For almost fifty years the slogan rode the *Star-Telegram*'s masthead as a rallying call of the faithful. It became the city's official and highly metaphysical thesis and the nation's best-known, longest-lasting municipal epigram.

Mention Fort Worth in the opening half of the twentieth century and the audience responded by rote, "Where The West Begins." Amon had FDR repeating the litany in national radio speeches, Bob Hope joking with the phrase from theater stages. ". . . Where The West Begins" appeared on crude signs beside GI foxholes in the South Pacific zone of World War II and on the aluminum breast of a B-24 bombing Nazis.

Will Rogers quipped to a gang of reporters: "Fort Worth . . . Where The West Begins, and Dallas peters out."

School children from all over America wrote Amon Carter with the simple address of ". . . Where The West Begins," and their letters were forwarded promptly to Amon Carter's *Star-Telegram* office.

As health claims on breakfast cereal boxes, newspaper slogans must be read with some degree of myopia. In its early years as the *Star*, "Always For Fort Worth" was the masthead shout. Later, the paper experimented with "All The News While It Is News" and "Just A Good Newspaper." Those prosaic declarations were cast aside when Amon discovered ". . . Where The West Begins."

It became an enormously successful advertising tag line with, of course, very little truth in it. Amon lifted the phrase from a poem and hammered it into the nation's psyche until it was accepted as gospel. Wherever he went the phrase was trotted out, polished, and spoken with great conviction for the ignorant and unknowing.

Once Amon arrived in New York by rail, emerging from Pennsylvania Station at rush hour. Searching for a taxi to the Ritz-Carlton Hotel, where he kept a suite, he stood on the curb beside an English couple on holiday. All his life Amon Carter engaged innocent strangers in idle conversation. He disliked silence and anyone near him became an audience.

After a few moments, Amon opened with, "I'm from Fort Worth."

"I beg pardon," said the Englishman, leaning nearer.

"Fort Worth. I live in Fort Worth."

"Oh? . . . Oh! I see." The couple attempted to look uninvolved.

"Texas! Fort Worth, Texas!"

"Ah . . . Texas," said the man, uncomfortably. He edged away.

Amon tried again: "Where The West Begins."

Silence. The couple shuffled, embarrassed. Amon grumped at them, "Well, gawddammit, *The West* begins there."

His brow pinched with curiosity, the Englishman turned, asking, "The 'West' *what* begins there?"

Arthur Chapman was an Illinois-born reporter working for the *Denver Times* when he wrote for the ages and Amon:

Out where the handclasp's a little stronger
Out where the smile dwells a little longer
That's Where The West Begins

....

Out where the skies are a trifle bluer
Out where the friendship's a little truer
That's Where The West Begins

Chapman's mawkish phrasing vaulted him into Bartlett's and onto the *Star-Telegram*'s front page, even got him tucked into *The Congressional Record*, courtesy of Amon Carter, but he died a poor New York freelance writer unknowing of his immortal stature.

He wrote of a West that never existed, a sentimental duchy of the mind, and though Amon preached "Where The West Begins" as a gospel truth, Fort Worth had little more claim to that geographical and historical misdirection than Minneapolis, which briefly subscribed to the slogan. The West of Chapman and Carter was somewhere else, perhaps farther west or backward in time, but wherever it was, Fort Worth, Texas, was not its beginning.

The real West, and *The West*, however, were nearby. The West of old Lan Twohig and longhorns and ranches was out there in West Texas. If there was a starting point, it lay somewhat westerly of Fort Worth. That was not a problem for Amon, who subpoenaed Chapman's *ars poetica* and nailed it to the *Star-Telegram*'s masthead with all the imperiality of Luther issuing his theses. The city quickly accepted the phrase because the image was attractive, but mostly because Amon Carter wanted it that way. The *Star-Telegram* made it seem real.

More than those of most newspapers, its subscribers believed Amon Carter's *Star-Telegram*. They believed because it was *the word* in West Texas, a kind of newsprint *biblia pauperum* for folks out there. It, a rival newsman once joked, was in more West Texas outhouses than Sears-Roebuck. The real Bible and its surrogate, the *Star-Telegram*—each interpreted literally—were the two journals seen most often in West Texas homes, and the newspaper acquired an internal title, bestowed as much for its Victorian moral view as its unquestioned acceptance.

Reporters called it: *The Great Religious Daily.*

For most of fifty years, the *Star-Telegram* was the region's newspaper. It educated, amused, informed, protected, scolded, boosted, boasted, and gave pride to settlers of West Texas. The newspaper fought for and won roads and universities, two national parks, historical monuments, industries, called on new citizens, told farmers when and where to sell for better prices, and gave Mama new cake recipes, and Junior instructions for building his own crystal set. It nursed people and communities through sicknesses and calamities, lauded them in prosperity, consoled them in times of sorrow. Constant and comforting, the *Star-Telegram* came daily, not just a newspaper, but a wise, theocratic companion that spoke of life beyond West Texas the way a National Geographic Society explorer might explain the customs of Bantus in Africa.

The late Dr. DeWitt Reddick, the respected, nationally known journalism scholar and historian, once wrote, "The *Star-Telegram* was the best example of a newspaper so interwoven with the birth and growth of the country around it that people accepted it as part of their lives. It was a family member."

With as many as thirteen editions through a twenty-four-hour operation, the *Star-Telegram* covered an area from near Colorado to the Rio Grande and westward beyond El Paso, probably the largest geographic circulation in pre-electronic newspaper history. Three hundred and seventy-five thousand square miles.

By train, bus, truck, and mail, the newspaper went west daily on a delivery routing often composed with ingenuity. In 1907, it was in one instance delivered to a postmaster in Hale Center, a village of the Panhandle. The postmaster added it to other pieces of mail placed in a rusty tin bucket. The driver of the Stant-Rhea Stagecoach collected the pail and hauled it fifteen miles to an abandoned dugout on the plains, where he hooked it over a fence post. Subscribers rode in from their prairie homes to take delivery. When American Airlines established its first Fort Worth/Los

Angeles route, the Ford tri-motor planes detoured once a week to fly over a ranch near Guadalupe Peak, Texas's highest mountain. The pilot lowered his window and shoved out a bulky package of mail and *Star-Telegrams* for a ranching family, which lived a mere forty miles from the closest driveable road, sixty miles from the nearest town.

And sometimes the *Star-Telegram* did not arrive, always a distressing event for subscribers. West Texas, being a place of natural catastrophes—storms of rain, dust, or wind, and sometimes all three at once—caused delayed delivery now and then. In the early 1920s, there was a rash of intense public attention to "The Gumps" comic strip. The plot centered around Bim Gump's pending marriage to the fortune-hunting Widder Zander. Coming to his senses in time, Bim reneged. Widder Zander sued for breach of promise and everybody, including *Star-Telegram* comic-page readers, went to court.

West Texans followed each day's legal installment with rapt attention. Suddenly, a storm in West Texas. Days passed. A pleading telegram arrived at *Star-Telegram* headquarters in Fort Worth. It read:

> "Area flooded. No mail for ten days. Please wire at our expense verdict Zander vs Gump.
> [Signed] Seminole Chamber of Commerce"

Because no reader problem was insignificant, the *Star-Telegram* rolled into action. The verdict of Bim's exoneration was telegraphed immediately. The strips were dramatized and broadcast on radio station WBAP. And when waters subsided around Seminole, one of the first travelers slogging through the mud was a *Star-Telegram* man hauling a load of back-issue newspapers.

West Texans repaid such consideration of their needs by being a devoted constituency. They made the *Star-Telegram* the largest and most influential newspaper in Texas, with the highest circulation in the southern half of the United States (generally on a line below Washington D.C., Saint Louis, and Denver, from Atlanta to Los Angeles). It was beside the *New York Times* for daily reading in the White House, and could be bought at a score of newsstands as far away as Chicago, where interest in Fort

Worth was less than fervent. It, or certain pertinent clippings, regularly went to as many as five hundred of America's most influential businessmen, politicians, and columnists. It wandered everywhere, causing a Dublin, Ireland, publisher to inquire just how a newspaper could acquire a circulation equal to the population of its town. Did even small babies subscribe? And— no one has ever known how this occurred—a peasant of Samarkand, Uzbekistan, in central Asia, was inspired to mail the equivalent of twenty-one cents, his donation for a *Star-Telegram* fund-raising project to erect a mule memorial in Muleshoe, Texas.

The *Star-Telegram* was the most famous reading habit of West Texans and because it was, they, like the faithful performing a compulsory *hajj* to Mohammed's birthplace, made pilgrimages to the source of all that printed manna.

Especially in the early days, a trip to Fort Worth was long and hard and perhaps done but once in a lifetime—surely no more than annually for common folks. In Fort Worth, West Texans had three necessary stops. One was at the boxy behemoth Seventh Street headquarters of Montgomery Ward, colloquially called "Monkey Wards." Another was the jumbled basement of Leonard Brothers Department Store, where counters overflowed with bargain merchandise and aisles teemed with more humanity than the back alleys of Calcutta. And the third was the *Star-Telegram*.

Almost daily, old flivvers and rattling trucks arrived at the newspaper's front door on Seventh Street, unloading tribes of dusty *hajjis* come to pay homage. They climbed the steps, passing into the elegant lobby where they stood hushed and huddled, kids grasping Mama's dress or Papa's worn overalls, surveying that monument to truth. They might reach and touch a dark mahogany column, as though it could grant them wisdom and strength, and perhaps cure their poverty.

Employees of the business office learned to let West Texans wander as they wished and more often than not the father, his appetite for grandeur sated, would approach, cough for attention, and announce, "I come to re-new."

He could have resubscribed by mail or through the nearest district manager, but he was in Fort Worth with his cash-crop money and chose to do business in person. Bills would be passed over, Papa would tuck the precious receipt into his bib pocket, regather his brood, and lead them out.

The ragged Joads would pack again into their ancient vehicles, heading west for what might be a five hundred-mile trip home, assured for another year that their lives would be blessed daily by Amon Carter and his *Star-Telegram*.

West Texas—and *The West*—was another world, and even Amon Carter went there only when he had to.

None of this happened because Amon Carter placed *The West* where it never belonged. It was, after all, his *West* and he could do as he pleased with it. He owned *The West*, lock, stock, and barrel cacti. West Texas was his—his kingdom, his empire, his Xanadu, his sandy, thorny gadget to tinker with. He was West Texas's "Aesop of the Prairie," a fable-izer whose yarns made the land west of Fort Worth seem a garden of earthly delights. In his accounts of West Texas, the sand, the heat, the brushy complexion, became cardinal virtues or were ignored, and one felt it would be an honor, even a privilege, to live in such a place of beauty and abundance. West Texans often were amazed at Amon's and the *Star-Telegram*'s depiction of their homeland, wondering, as they counted their sunstroke-affected cows and watched unwatered crops fizzle, just where this mythical, fabulous paradise might be.

Because *The West* was his, Amon Carter felt a need to be part of it. He fashioned himself, his character, as he molded the fictional image of it, with camouflage coloration and clothing and sometimes outlandish behavior, to blend with the perceived scenic legends.

He became a cowboy.

Amon Carter, a child of the soil, had no credentials as a cowboy. He was a failed blacksmith's son. But *The West* seduced him as it later would ensnare generations of Saturday matinee children.

His yearning for a life of cowboying began early. At eleven, he sneaked aboard a freight train bound for what he believed was Montana and, as he later wrote, "that great west where cowboys and Indians predominated." The dream was brief. A brakeman halted the train and dropped Amon beside a dry stream, Salt Creek. He trudged back to the family farm.

As an adult, though, he could accommodate the cowboy fantasy, could step onto *The West's* fanciful stage, and surely did. He became West Texas's, therefore *The West's*, principal tub-thumping agent, dressed and acted out the role of—as he came to be titled—Top Hand of the Plains, Sage of the Sagebrush, and Mouthpiece of the Southwest.

Amon adopted what eastern columnists variously described as a "four-," "six-," or "ten-gallon" western hat. He stuffed the legs of his tailored trousers into handmade fancy boots, usually purple and white, the athletic colors of Texas Christian University, with little horned frogs chiseled into the leather. He strapped on hand-tooled double holsters and packed them with twin, pearl-handled pistols. Occasionally he added leather chaps branded "AGC," jingling silver spurs, and a bandanna knotted at the throat, held in place by an expensive pearl stickpin. In cooler weather, the costume was topped with an ivory-colored vicuna coat which, according to the *Washington Post*, resembled "a cozy bathrobe." For very special events of his later life, the cowboy rode a golden palomino, seated on a silver, five thousand-dollar saddle, a diamond pin stabbed into his silken kerchief.

Fully assembled, the Amon Carter cowboy looked like Friar Tuck playing Hoot Gibson.

Amon learned to yell "Yippee" and "Whoopee" without a shred of shame. He could bellow ridiculously, "Hoooooo-e-e-e-e! Round 'em up! Head off that lit'l dogie yonder!" for a New Orleans parade crowd, and tell a *New York American* reporter that the 1923 World Series "Ought to be a right smart set-to." He spoke such prairie-ized gibberish without blushing because, above all else, the cowboy enjoyed himself. He had fun. You and I were forced to give up our childish games at manhood. Amon Carter, who had no childhood, got to play cowboy all his life.

In action, the cowboy swaggered for his audiences, jingling his spurs, drawling in the fabricated West Texas accent, punctuating the comic dialogue by firing his pistols in the air and yippeeing joyously. The cowboy was a caricature, not a characterization, of the western Texan, but many outsiders never knew that. They thought he was art imitating life. The *New York Tribune* actually called Amon Carter "the father of the ten-gallon hat idea." Bob Considine, the Hearst columnist, who surely should have known better, wrote that the cowboy was "a rootin', tootin', sixgun shootin' . . . lusty, gusty . . . westerner."

The cowboy, however much a Texas aberration, was always memorable.

In the beginning, Amon invented his cowboy because the swaggering cliché of a Texan was necessary. As an impetuous, exultant man, the cowboy was his release for an ostentatious nature. It also masked a fragile, fifth-grade education, his early unsophistication. The cowboy could be as ignorant and graceless as Amon Carter wished to make him without people suspecting all was not an act. Once begun, however, he could not stop. Audiences came to expect and demand the cowboy, and an older Amon groused privately that he was unknown and unremembered for anything else.

For whatever other reasons the cowboy was invented, it was because Fort Worth and West Texas required a salesman, and no one who ever met him doubted that Amon was an extraordinary salesman, for himself, for the *Star-Telegram*, but especially for Fort Worth and West Texas. He was a walking, incessantly talking, fancy advertisement, a rodomontade without peer among hawkers of municipal chauvinism. Whether stalking an oil company headquarters, a government contract, or just the casual mention of Fort Worth by a syndicated columnist, the cowboy went after his quarry with the zeal of a fanatic. He sold a lifestyle, a frothy reverie Americans had come to believe was The Real Texas. He boosted a city, a region, and did it with genius showmanship.

"As a [Broadway] producer, you will pardon me if I envy you," Billy Rose once told Amon. "I build shows. Christ! You built a city."

Amon did build a city. At his death, fully half of Fort Worth's population worked for companies he had lured to town.

Amon Carter's cowboy made him, and Fort Worth, famous. He played the cowboy everywhere. Once he interrupted a Giants-Yankees World Series game by excitedly shooting his pistols into the air. His friend, Giants Manager John McGraw, left the dugout, strolled to Amon's box along the first-base line, and asked him not to do that again, please. The pistols fired starting shots for six-day bicycle races in Madison Square Garden, signaled for the downbeat of Paul Whiteman's baton, or just banged off indiscriminately for the pure hell of it.

The *Times of London* thought the cowboy "picturesque" and displayed him with an English bobby. The *London Evening News* described the cowboy as "an intimate friend of Will Rogers [and] a middle-aged Texan with a drawling western accent."

While in London, the cowboy was invited to dine at the home of Britain's press titan, Lord Beaverbrook. He was met at the door by a butler, who surveyed the cowboy's costume suspiciously. The butler left Amon outside while he verified the invitation with His Lordship. The butler returned, accepted the cowboy's calling card, and, never moving his eyes from the purple-and-white boots, stammered to the other guests, "Mr. Amon Carter . . . Fort Worth, Texas . . . Where The West Begins."

In Paris, the cowboy yipped and fired his pistols from a Ritz Hotel balcony. Management and police promptly suggested that the cowboy restrain himself.

The cowboy attended championship prizefights, formal dinners, nightclubs, groundbreakings, football games, most anything drawing a crowd. He led bands in parades, talked on national radio networks, attended rodeos.

The cowboy had various styles, being soft and gentle for women, rough and rowdy for men. Often the cowboy was farcical. In the early 1920s, Amon one day appeared at his office in his cowboy costume. He had bought similar outfits for several editors and told the men they had a special mission. Twenty railroad executives were coming by train to Fort Worth to discuss building a new terminal, which the city needed.

The bogus cowboys set out for the Oklahoma state line, where they flagged down and boarded the train. The rail executives were captivated by the cowboys, believing them to be true specimens of Texas. In the club car, the cowboys began a poker game with three of the Yankees. A dozen others crowded around to watch.

It was a high-stakes game. Amon was winning. One of his editors was losing. Outside Fort Worth, the editor turned surly. He accused Amon of cheating. Angrily, Amon denied it. Both men jumped up, kicked away their chairs, drew pistols and began blazing away. The editor grabbed his chest, gasped, and slumped across the table.

Amon looked around. The Yankees had fled the club car. He laughed all the way to the Fort Worth rail station.

Amon assembled all the necessary props for his role as the cowboy—collections of western guns, steer horns, cigar store Indians, an ancient stagecoach, horseshoes, just anything to provide him with the sense and feel of frontier days in Texas. He nicknamed his son "Cowboy." He became a collector of western art by Frederic Remington and Charles Russell.

"Did he die with his boots on?" a cynical reporter asked after Amon's death. He did not. Amon disliked boots. They hurt his feet. He preferred the $150 slippers handcrafted for him by a New York shoemaker. Spur rowels caught on furniture and ladies' long dresses and were a nuisance. He wrote friends, among them William Randolph Hearst, telling of his new palomino and noting that it was the first horse he actually had ridden in forty years. Amon never was unhappy to put away the cowboy and return to his more conventional self: the conservative, hardheaded businessman.

Kindly old J. C. Penney was more correct than he knew when he said, "Fort Worth is not 'Where The West Begins'. The West begins wherever Amon Carter is."

The cowboy was unselfish. He allowed his friends to play with him. He outfitted them in hats and boots, showed them how to swagger about his Shady Oak ranch house like cattle drovers come to Dodge City on Saturday night. Playing cowboy with Amon became a craze for many of the nation's most celebrated personalities, among them industry moguls and politicians who were tickled silly with their impersonations. Many never intended to stop in the cowtown west of cultured Dallas, but if someone of fame or influence passed near Fort Worth, he was pulled in to be entertained by Amon.

Jimmy Walker, the dandified mayor of Prohibition-era New York, meant to slide through Fort Worth enroute to the 1928 Democratic Convention in Houston. His private rail car, the Roamer, halted briefly to be switched to another train. Amon, who had spies everywhere, learned Walker was in town. He and Will Rogers, who was visiting Amon before going on to the convention, went to the private car in the early morning. They awoke Walker and had him dress and leave the car. Amon asked the mayor to spend the day in Fort Worth. Walker declined politely. Meanwhile, back on board, a porter—bribed by Amon—packed Walker's luggage. The bags were removed from the train and sent to Amon's suite in the Fort Worth Club. Angry but beaten, Walker agreed to spend the night.

The acerbic H. L. Mencken and Paul Patterson, publisher of the *Baltimore Sun*, were guests of Amon at the same time, and the Texan arranged a full schedule for the men. He took them to his Shady Oak Farm where, as Rogers wrote in his newspaper column, "[With] the champion host of the world, Amon Carter, we held a preliminary convention last night at Shady Oaks *[sic]*. It looks like a dry vice president." Amon had the men interviewed over a remote WBAP radio broadcast from the ranch. Walker fished in the well-stocked bass pond. Next day, Amon escorted the mayor to a civic luncheon where a glee club sang the song he had written—"Will You Love Me In December As You Do In May?" Walker became the luncheon's principal speaker, and told of his visit to the farm where, "I got bites while fishing. Chiggers. Chiggers, you know, unlike many friends, stick close to one. Some of them are deep-seated."

Before leaving, Carter gifted Walker and the others with western hats, liquor, and belts. For the happy mayor, the publisher had a special present: Lan Twohig's old scarred steer horns.

Doubtless Amon told the mayor of Lan's classic battle with the outlaw Longhorn and of buying the horns from the old cowboy. A *Star-Telegram* photographer snapped Jimmy Walker standing stiffly in front of Amon's Shady Oak Saloon. He wore brightly striped trousers and an enormous cowboy hat. The steer horns—the newspaper, incorrectly, grandly claimed that they were eight feet long—stood on one tip, towering above the mayor.

That evening, Walker continued to Houston. As the train pulled away, he stood on a rear platform, waving. He said something lost in a hiss of steam.

"What?" called Rogers.

Amon and New York City Mayor Jimmy Walker pose with Lan Twohig's legendary longhorn steer horns.

Walker cupped his hands to his mouth, yelling, "I said, 'HOOOO-RAAAAAY for . . . . FOOOOORT WOOORTH . . . and AAAAA-MON CAAAR-TER!"
Another convert for the cowboy.

3

He said he'd have to leave his home,
His Daddy'd married twice,
And his new Ma beat him every day or two;
So he saddled up Old Chow one night and lit a
shuck this way.
  —Verse 4, "Little Joe, The Wrangler"

The Origin of Amon G. Carter is shrouded in mystery. His discovery is a matter of record. William Randolph Hearst, strolling through his beautiful gardens one dewy morn, paused in admiration before an exceptionally large cluster of violets. Underneath was the Baby Amon. . . . Since then his family silver has been marked with a shrinking violet as the Carter coat of arms.
  —Menu legend, Sherry's, New York City, May 7, 1928

Perhaps there is significance in the fact that Fort Worth's second telephone, installed in the *Democrat,* was but a single line leading to the fourth telephone located in the Club Room, a saloon two hundred feet away across Main Street. Perhaps not. Editor Buckley B. Paddock wrote that he ordered a lemonade to test the new service.

The portly Paddock, once a Confederate Army scout, literate, an excellent journalist and more than a little Victorian, was weary of fighting sin, specifically as practiced in Hell's Half Acre, Fort Worth's red-light district where back-sore whores and card slicks serviced ranch hands and itinerant cowboys with competency and perfidy.

With his *Democrat,* Paddock had crusaded to close the Acre and for a while customers stayed away, which cut the trade of legitimate businesses. Angry merchants demanded that Paddock remove his blue nose from the cribs and gambling joints. The Acre returned to its former busy activities. Vice was a growth industry in late nineteenth century Fort Worth.

The town's first newspaper was the *Chief,* founded in 1849 by the slightly dotty Anthony Banning Norton, an impassioned supporter of Henry Clay in the 1844 presidential election, which was won by James Polk. Norton vowed neither to shave nor cut his hair until Clay became President. Norton has no rival as the hairiest newspaper editor in American history.

The *Chief* and Paddock's *Democrat* withered and died as newspapers seemed to have done in early Fort Worth. Fully forty publications came and went before 1906, when Amon Carter and the *Star* wandered into that journalistic cemetery. Only two papers existed as Amon sniffed the manured air and agreed to become advertising manager—actually, the entire ad staff—for the *Star.* C. D. Reimers edited and published the *Telegram,* the *Star*'s afternoon competitor. Clarence Ousley owned and edited the morning *Record,* a reincarnation of the short-lived *Register.*

Amon, when presented with the newspaper dream of A. G. Dawson and D. C. McCaleb, had little cash. His small business paid bills but could not be stretched to support his rather vigorous nightlife style. He had borrowed $250 from American National Bank, pledging as security a small, diamond ring. Most of that money was lost by a mistaken investment in three aces against a high straight. Amon steered Dawson and McCaleb to Paul Waples, who had made his fortune in wholesale foods. Waples, extravagantly addressed as "Colonel," a common though specious male title of the period, gathered $50,000 from friends as seed funding for the *Star*. Dissatisfied with Dawson and McCaleb, Waples brought in Louis Wortham, yet another "Colonel," as publisher/editor.

Colonel Wortham was a puckish-faced, large man with middle-parted hair. He was impractical, windy, gentle, drank too much and had little notion of how to operate a daily newspaper. Amon liked him immediately, and immensely. They became close friends and allies against Dawson and McCaleb, both of whom left before the newspaper's first anniversary.

The first *Star* arrived on the eve of Groundhog Day, February 1, 1906, two weeks late but with great exaltation inside the twenty-five-foot-by-twenty-five-foot newsroom located at Sixth and Rusk streets, underneath the Eagle Lodge Hall and behind the Senate Bar, a saloon of some upper class distinction (its bar mural was that of a pudgy but solemn-faced nude Venus). That afternoon, the *Telegram* bragged on its front page of 11,156 paid circulation.

The *Star* was a typical, typographically dull publication with seven columns, stacked headlines, and few illustrations. It had sixteen pages, but subsequent issues were only eight pages because the crippled flatbed Bullock press could print no more in a single run. The ancient press was propped up on one corner by an iron brace. There were three rickety Linotype machines and an antique stereotyping pot of molten lead with a metal dipper. The men stood at shelves around the walls because the newsroom was so crowded.

Predictably, there were few local ads, and the *Star* seemed a kind of inventory sheet for the patent medicine industry. Dr. Shoop's Rheumatic Tablets owned a prominent spot, and Hostetters's Stomach Bitters, and the always popular Dr. Thurman's Lone Star Catarrah Cure. ("Doubtless one of the most aggravating, disgusting and destructive diseases to which human flesh has fallen heir.")

Sprinkled amid the truss and hemorrhoid commercials was a modest supply of current news. Fort Worth skies were cloudy, swept by a twelve-mile-per-hour winds. Charging "intolerable cruelty," a forty-year-old mother of twenty-seven children petitioned for dissolution of her two-decade-old marriage. C. W. Post, a former Fort Worth resident, was back in town promoting his Grape Nuts as a medical cure for every known disease. Prohibitionists condemned Alice, daughter of Teddy Roosevelt, for serving wine in the White House. The Boll Weevils, a baseball team, opened spring training. In St. Petersburg, Russia, the emperor warned peasants to stop annoying large landowners. Standard Oil was accused of stifling competition. In the West Texas town of Brownwood, Charles Hale was "terribly burned" when he struck a match to inspect the innards of his new gas-powered automobile, and at nearby Abilene, a pair of cowboys interrupted a ranch dance to fight with pistols and knives: "Two women were slashed right and left, inflicting severe, if not fatal, gashes on their bodies."

For entertainment, there were reviews from the Edison Family Theater ("Appeals to the Masses and not to the Classes") and Greenwall's Opera House, with "Mrs. Wiggs of the Cabbage Patch," featuring the original New York cast. The Majestic Theater presented, live on stage, "Don Carlos . . . seen in a cage with a lion which he has trained to jump from place to place and which he catches hold of and throws across the cage and in fact handles with almost as much freedom as though it were a common tame cat."

Among the few local advertisements were sale announcements on "Ladies Dip Hip Corsets, 29 cents" and a "special lot of ladies Union Suits, in gray and ecru, 25 cents." Butter was thirty cents a pound, paint seventy-five cents a gallon, valentines one cent each, and Pullman train tickets to California twenty-five dollars. F. O. "Painless" Cates charged just fifty cents per extracted tooth.

Readers got all that for only two cents—or a nickel on trains and out of town.

Amon sold every ad, seventy-one column inches total, representing an income of $387.30 for the fledgling paper. In fact, he sold too many ads, and a somewhat ungrammatical boxed apology explained:

> The response to solicitations for advertisements
> was so much greater than anticipated that it was
> a physical impossibility for the *Star* to get out
> an issue on this date with all the advertisements
> that should be in the issue in it.

As a new employee, Amon's first duty, as he saw it, was to tell everyone how to operate the newspaper. He named three rules for Colonel Wortham: (1) there would be the same rates for all advertisers; (2) the circulation would be guaranteed, no matter how small; and (3) the newspaper would indulge in neither contests nor premiums to secure subscribers. "The advertiser must use the newspaper because it is beneficial to his business, not because the newspaper grants him special favors," lectured Amon. Later, he added a fourth doctrine: the *Star* would sell its own national advertising and save paying agency commissions.

Those four inviolate principles would, by all accepted reports, make the later *Star-Telegram* America's most profitable newspaper—"Territory considered," Amon always alibied, when confronted with his paper's profitability.

To promote the *Star*, placards were distributed proclaiming it ". . . clean, conservative, conscientious, enterprising and independent . . . with more local news than any other in the city."

Fort Worth was not very interested in the *Star*, or anything else. In 1906, it was a somnolent town of forty thousand people; fewer than five thousand even bothered to vote in the last election. Packinghouses, a natural extension of the stockyards, were the largest businesses. As Amon settled into his new job, Fort Worth possessed a few fancy stores but far more plain shops, more dirt streets than paved boulevards, streetcars, an interurban trolley to Dallas, a large and well-visited selection of saloons, more outdoor privies than indoor bathrooms, more horses than automobiles, a new eight-story skyscraper called the Wheat Building, thirty passenger trains daily, and a society composed of too many families on the outskirts of poverty and beyond middle-class respectability.

At age fifty-five, Fort Worth was more rural frontier than western, but for Amon Carter it was the grandest city of Texas. Why, it was there, he would later recall with wonder, that he had first ridden a marvelous new contraption called an "elevator." He stepped onto the platform and rode up seven floors. At the top, he asked the operator, "How much do I owe you?" The man smiled at the boy's naïveté and said there was no charge.

"Then I will ride down with you," said Amon.

For the thrill of an elevator ride, Amon had come from Bowie, sixty-five miles northwest of Fort Worth, as blind baggage on a passing freight train, a regular activity for little Amon.

Another boxcar once had taken the young vagrant Amon north to Wichita Falls because he had heard of the capture by Texas Rangers of two bank robbers, Kid Lewis and Foster Crawford. Amon, who would be lured toward celebrities all his life, wanted to see the famous outlaws. As he arrived, a mob placed nooses around the necks of Lewis and Crawford, and stood the men on wooden boxes. Burk Burnett, a ranger captain and one of North Texas's largest ranchers, asked the bandits if they had any last messages for friends and families. Lewis kicked Burnett in the stomach. Burnett pulled away the boxes. Lewis and Crawford dangled until dawn, when their bodies were cut down and stacked in the bank's doorway. Early customers stepped over the corpses. An enterprising member of the lynch party, Amon later wrote admiringly, swapped the nooses to a bartender for a gallon of whiskey.

Amon regaled Bowie citizens with the hanging story. They had never experienced anything so exciting. The best Bowie could offer were the drunken high jinks of old Dan Waggoner's cowboys. The Waggoner hands enjoyed tossing rope loops around the legs of black train porters and swinging the terrified men upside down from store signs. The porters, justifiably, were cautious when passing through Bowie. From the trains they could see the friendly city-limit sign: "Nigger, Don't Let The Sun Go Down On You In Bowie." That warning was standard roadside reading in many western Texas towns of the last century.

Bowie, in the mid-1890s, owned the congenital blandness of a thousand other Texas hamlets, characterized by a weathered clapboard grayness and simple, unornamental silence interrupted only by yawns from front-porch swings and the squeak of buggy wheels. Bowie had memories of Indians, by then shuffled off to Oklahoma reservations, who had scalped settlers and burned cabins in the 1870s. Nearby were fading remnants of the Chisholm Trail, once a super highway for ten million longhorns driven to railheads in Kansas. When Amon Carter arrived in Bowie, the famed cattle trail was a literal cow path.

What passed as childhood for Amon was a hardscrabble lonely life in frontier Texas. His father was William Henry Carter, some-times a farmer, sometimes a blacksmith, always distant and indifferent toward his only son. Early photographs show Father Carter to have been a small, solid man, muscular, almost hand-some, his longish face adorned with a drooping mustache. He was, most certainly, as ignorant as the mules he shod. Josephine Ream Carter, Amon's mother, was pretty with dark curly hair and aesthetic features. She had lived at La Reunion, an experimental French commune beside the Trinity River near Dallas. She had some musical talent and taught Amon to peck out a one-fingered piano version of "Jesus, Lover of My Soul" and encouraged his singing, which was and would remain earnest but awful.

Amon was born December 11, 1879, in a log cabin that his father built near the community of Crafton in Wise County, arriv-ing in the near-gale force of a numbingly cold norther. In later years, Amon claimed that his log cabin birth was a status shared by too many others to have any social status in Texas. His mother wrote to a cousin, Mary Bundrad, about little Amon: "Tell Aunt Nancy I do reckon I have the finest boy you ever saw. He can crawl but . . . I can't kep him on'na palet nor hardly in the house." [That was a complaint his three wives later would echo.] Josie concluded her letter with a prophetic observation about Amon: "He is the worst rounder I ever saw."

Josie died in 1892, soon after giving birth to a daughter, Addie. Papa then married Ella Patterson and very soon, thirteen-year-old Amon was sent away. He never explained his conflict with his stepmother, but in 1920, five years after William Carter died, she wrote to him for money. Amon replied that already he was supporting a dozen relatives in addition to his immediate family and reminded her of "the time you ordered me to leave my father's house." Nevertheless, Amon, ever generous, sent her money—he always addressed her as "Mrs. Carter"—each month until she died in Macon, Georgia. Amon was not listed among her surviving family members.

Without a home, Amon trudged to nearby Bowie, to the rear door of the boarding house operated by Millie Jarrott. She fed him and gave him work as a handyman, chambermaid, and janitor, giving Amon room and board and paying him $1.50 weekly. She also mended his ragged clothes. Amon considered Mrs. Jarrott his second mother, and later in life he supported her, finally buying the boarding house to make her last years financially secure.

Amon's young life in Bowie was one of endless work, a kind of Horatio Alger odd-job survival course. He sold peaches. He assisted a doctor. He worked in a confectionery shop peddling ice cream and candies. He made soda pop in a bottling plant. He operated a refreshment stand for weekend horse races. He was a wagon-yard roustabout. He collected and resold empty whiskey bottles. Amon was a born entrepreneur.

It was there, hauling buckets of drinking water to Z. T. Lowrie's wholesale grocery store, that Amon became involved in what the *Saturday Evening Post* would one day tickle its readers by calling Amon Carter and The Great Snuff War. Railroad Snuff and Levi P. Garrett Scotch Snuff were fiercely competitive in 1890s America. Each sold snuff in square bottles of the same size for twenty-five cents. Railroad fired the first shot heard 'round the snuff-dipping world by cutting its price to twenty cents. Levi P. Garrett regarded the discount as crass commercialism and maintained its two-bit price, but sneaked a nickel under the cork of each bottle. Stalemated, the two snuff generals rested their armies, plotting the next flanking maneuver.

Amon learned of the nickels hidden inside the Garrett snuff bottles. One spring dawn, Lowrie's grocery store burned, and by mid-morning, Amon had waded through smoldering ashes straight to the snuff department. The nickels were too hot to handle but he dug them out with a stick and stored the coins in a number-two tomato can. Amon collected about six dollars, the most money he had ever possessed at one time.

His most successful and lasting venture, however, seemed to have been the peddling of chicken sandwiches to passengers on trains stopping in Bowie. He made a deal with the Widow Brodie. For $2.50 weekly, she would provide Amon with room and board and cook one chicken daily. Amon bought the chickens for twenty-five cents each, and sold the resulting sandwiches for ten cents, netting about two dollars a day. When young Amon, already a spendthrift, had no money to buy chickens, he made late night henhouse raids, which lowered his overhead considerably. Or he substituted rabbit meat in the sandwiches. Soon, other Bowie boys took up the business and Amon gathered five friends—John Black, Mose Johnson, Shorty Ryan, R. J. Sandefur, and Tan Turner—to form a cartel and squeeze out competitors. The Carter monopoly did well, and they became well known as The Chicken and Bread Boys on the Fort Worth and Denver run through North Texas. Decades later, Franklin Roosevelt paused his presidential campaign train in Bowie, and an adult Amon Carter boarded with a basket of chicken sandwiches. He handed a sandwich to FDR and asked for ten cents. He accepted the coin and grinned, "Thank you, sir!"

In his late teens, Amon branched into more adult businesses. He and a railroad brakeman, O. G. Hurdleston, bought a knife-board concession in Lindsey's Saloon. The board held knives stuck in whiskey corks. Coins were glued to each knife. Customers paid to try their luck tossing wooden rings over the knives. The old carnival game appeared simple but was not, especially for drunks. For one thing, the rings would not fit over knives guarding fifty-cent coins. A deer-foot knife stabbed through a five-dollar bill was turned in such a way that it was impossible to ring.

The knife board prospered until a part-time house painter and pool hustler nicknamed Shadow arrived one evening. Lanky, loose-jointed, and long-armed, Shadow could—and did—ring any and all knives, including the five-buck deer-foot. Amon was fascinated with Shadow, partially because the man had a double row of upper teeth and smiled like twin piano keyboards. Shadow broke the knife-board bank, so Amon did the only honest thing—he barred Shadow from ever playing again, then hired him for five dollars a week to drop in each evening and show the suckers how to win. The knife board's profitability increased dramatically.

Shadow suggested that Amon allow the deer-foot knife money to be ringed at least once a month, so Amon now and then turned the handle to a winning angle. A farmer was the first winner and the news spread quickly throughout Bowie: Adolph Fincher had beaten the game. Ring tossers lined up three-deep that evening. Weeks later, Fincher brought a bale of cotton to town. He spent all his cotton money trying to ring the deer-foot again.

Ignorant of Shadow's business arrangement, Bowie's peg-legged city marshall, Charlie Bray, offered to run the house painter out of town. Amon declined. He had grander mischief for his shill. Amon financed a train trip to Dallas during the annual State Fair of Texas, where Shadow could beat any game the carnival folks offered. They split the profits. The young men then wandered by the Oriental Hotel poolroom, and the gangly Shadow played like a country rube—until local hustlers suggested a friendly game for money. Amon took side bets. The pair returned to Bowie with more than a hundred dollars each.

Amon spent a portion of his profits on his first grown-up clothes, disembarking from the train dressed in a white suit, high-collared silk dress shirt, narrow red-and-white bow tie, black derby (Texans called the round, narrow-brimmed hats "chili-dippers"), and bile-green Selzswab Piccadilly shoes with toes as sharp-pointed as fence palings. Amon would admit later in life that his appearance caused some excitement in Bowie. Children laughed, dogs growled at him, his saloon chums slapped knees and guffawed loudly.

Town parents understandably felt Amon was an inappropriate companion for their children. Hooking rides on freight trains, hustling farmers in saloons, midnight chicken thefts, the curious sartorial inclinations—his lifestyle gave him the social standing of a transient spot welder. (Amon's youthful transgressions would be forgiven and forgotten six decades later when Bowie was naming its town lake for him and bestowing other honors on its most famous son.) Nevertheless, Mrs. Arch Turner felt sympathy for the socially awkward young man and granted him the concession of Sunday dinners at her home. Several other young people gathered each Sunday around Mrs. Turner's table and it was there, presumably, that Amon met and wooed Zetta Thomas, the tall, gaunt daughter of a prominent family. After several years of wandering, Amon would return to marry her.

Eighteen-year-old Amon Carter was described by a contemporary biographer as "Almost six feet tall . . . of medium build. He had black eyes, rather large ears, a prominent nose, dark brown hair, and an olive complexion. His facial features were strongly formed with a pleasant, benign expression that easily showed either a lopsided grin or a broad smile. Carter greatly resembled his mother, Josephine, whose picture later hung near his desk in the *Star-Telegram*."

In 1898, having ridden elevators and worn green shoes and become a worldly man, Amon left Bowie, itching to travel and see America. He went most of a hundred miles north to Indian Territory and what now is Norman, Oklahoma. A cousin found him a job in Davis's Confectionery Shop paying thirty dollars a month. He boarded at Grand Central Hotel and worked from 5:00 A.M. until almost midnight six days a week. He made friends with a grocer's delivery wagon driver, Bill Ince. They bought a gross of pipes and tobacco and acquired a taffy-pulling machine, preparing to join a traveling circus.

Before they could hook on with a circus, however, Amon met a Mr. Phillips at the barbershop. Mr. Phillips represented the American Copying Company of Chicago and was that very morning hiring young men to travel and sell patented, colored portraits. Amon signed on immediately and left Ince with the taffy machine.

The portrait dodge was one of the great scams of nineteenth century America, no more legitimate than Amon's knife board. First, a crew of boys called on small-town and country families, telling mothers they could have oil paintings made from their children's photographs at very little cost. The gimmick was that the paintings were odd-sized, fitting no known or available frames, until one day a dapper salesman—that was Amon—a rrived with perfectly matched plaster-of-paris frames, which sold for as much as three dollars each—at least a week's wages for most working men.

Amon made the framed portraits seem like Rembrandts, and within a year he was the company's top-producing salesman. By 1901, he was American Copying's sales manager in Chicago, with a salary of three hundred dollars monthly, a magnificent sum for a young man hardly twenty-one years old. He traveled to every state in the union and enjoyed life on the road, but he understood that his future was limited. Ed Swasey, whom he had met in Portland, offered Amon a job with Barnhart & Swasey Advertising Agency in San Francisco for one hundred dollars a month. Delaying long enough to marry Zetta Thomas in Bowie, Amon accepted the job and pay-cut and left for the West Coast. He remained there until 1904, when boredom sent him home to Texas, and Fort Worth, and the first edition of the *Star*.

Before leaving Chicago, Amon acquired from American Copying a letter of recommendation that read in part: "We believe Mr. Carter has few equals and never a superior in his representation of us."

Amon thought the statement underestimated his abilities. He couldn't remember any equals.

4

We were failing, so we decided to expand.
> —Amon, explaining why the small, bankrupt *Star* bought the larger, successful *Telegram*

When the lake rises, the boat will, too.
> —Amon's philosophy on why his newspaper's prosperity depended on the progress of Fort Worth and West Texas

I got tired of being married to the chamber of commerce.
> —Nenetta Burton Carter, on why she divorced Amon

The sky is high and wide and blue,
And you say to strangers, "Howdy-Do."
> —"Cactus Jack," a song inspired by Vice President John Nance Garner, 1933

The *Star* flopped, a loser from first edition to last.

Without the support of large, local advertisers, the *Star* produced too little revenue to pay its bills. Soon Amon, who had no financial interest in the newspaper, was pawning his rings with Oscar Wells, cashier of the Fort Worth National Bank, to meet each week's payroll.

He traded an interest in his patented telephone directory for a peach orchard near Arlington, midway between Fort Worth and Dallas. During the day he sold advertising and solicited orders from grocery stores for his peaches. After work he would board a streetcar to the orchard, pick and pack the peaches, and return them to Fort Worth, usually arriving about midnight. He was up again at 5:00 A.M. to deliver the fruit before striking out on his advertising rounds.

Amon produced one early scoop for the *Star*. He was hanging around the Cotton Exchange on April 18, 1906, when the wire operator received a flash that fire and earthquake had destroyed San Francisco. Amon copied the sparse details and rushed to the newsroom. In his wallet Amon still carried a map of San Francisco, which showed artist representations of the Ferry Building, Palace Hotel, city hall, and other structures. A wood cut was made of the map and printed on the *Star*'s front page beside the meager story written from Amon's notes. The *Star* published its first extra. Amon snatched a bundle and dashed into Sixth Street. Later he hauled a load of extras to Dallas. The *Star* sold twenty-four hundred copies before the *Telegram* even learned of the disaster.

By early 1908, the original $50,000 was gone and so was another $27,000. Dawson and Amon never got along. Amon threatened to "knock his block off" during an argument over a proposed special-edition romanticizing the West Texas cattle industry. Wortham reduced Dawson to a mere reporter and he quit. McCaleb also resigned, to accept a political writing job in Austin.

By autumn, Wortham knew the *Star* was a gray corpse but Amon refused to give up. He suggested a preposterous thing: The bankrupt *Star* would buy the successful *Telegram*. It was an audacious proposition, but typical of Amon—"We traded up," he

Amon and first *Star-Telegram* publisher Louis Wortham in Fort Worth's stockyards, c. 1905.

was later to say. For the ruse to work successfully, Amon counseled Wortham, they would have to pay more than the *Telegram* was worth—but not too much more. They went underground.

Amon enlisted help from O. P. Thomas, secretary of the Abilene Chamber of Commerce. Thomas bid for the *Telegram*. It is generally understood that Publisher C. D. Reimers knew from the beginning who really was buying his newspaper, but all parties played out the charade to the end. The selling price was $100,000, with $2,500 to be deposited on Monday morning, November 16, 1908, and the cash balance of $92,500 due in ten days. A $5,000 note to Goss Printing Press Company was to be assumed by the new owners.

To obtain the $2,500, Amon returned to Oscar Wells and left on deposit in Fort Worth National Bank "1 diamond ring, 3 31/32 K; 1 diamond ring, 5/8 K; 2 smaller diamond rings, one diamond and pearl scarf pin." Amon told Wells if he could not obtain the remaining $92,500 in ten days, he would give up and accept a job offered him in New York.

A young Amon at his early *Star-Telegram* desk in a joke pose with fireman ready to douse his cigar.

Amon again approached Paul Waples, who quickly saw the advantage of a monopoly afternoon newspaper. Waples solicited investment money from W. G. Burton, who operated the Burton-Peel Dry Goods Company, and from department store owners H. C. Meacham and W. C. Stripling Sr. (Amon met Will Stripling when each was living in Bowie.) Grandly, Waples offered corporation shares to Amon and Colonel Wortham. Each took 10 percent. Waples agreed they could buy the balance as they wished, at cost plus 6 percent—a generous offer that one day would provide Amon with full control.

Amon, as usual, had no money, but he borrowed a "piece of swamp land in Fort Myers, Florida" from an old Chicago friend as security for his share. Amon was a newspaper owner.

So, on January 1, 1909, the amalgamated *Star* and *Telegram*—the linking hyphen was not added until two weeks later—arrived at Fort Worth homes. It didn't seem much more than its parent papers, but interesting times were coming.

In later years, Reimers bragged that he cheated Amon because the *Telegram* was sold for twice its worth, but Amon replied that the *Telegram*'s real value had been a million dollars. Amon was probably right. The *Fort Worth Star-Telegram*, conceived over burning cow manure and secured by Florida swamp land, became a $100,000,000 newspaper property.

As Amon stepped from the Fort Worth and Denver train to astound Bowie with green shoes, a boy named James North dreamed of becoming an attorney. Without college funds, however, North had to settle for work at the *Sherman Democrat*, where one of his regular duties was to trudge into the back shop and cut G. O. Hunter's hair out of the old Cottrell Press.

Hunter and his brother, E. C., owned the newspaper. Hunter wore his hair pompadoured and long. When the press rolled each afternoon, he stood behind the machine, reached in for papers, and counted loads for his young carriers. Too often, he leaned in and the gears would grab his hair, sometimes jerking it out in clumps, sometimes just snarling it while the press ground to a halt. Jimmy, a carrier, used shears to free the *Democrat*'s co-publisher.

North was born in Jefferson, a steamboating town on the East Texas/Louisiana border. His family moved to Sherman and he began delivering the *Democrat*, marveling at the sight of G. O. Hunter being snatched bald by the antagonistic press. North advanced to be a kind of junior circulation manager and foreman of all the carriers. Then, with money saved from this job, went off to the University of Texas.

He returned each summer to work as a reporter and had advanced to a ten-dollar-a-week salary when his family developed financial trouble. He never returned to college. In the fall of 1905, North read of a new paper to be published in Fort Worth. He applied for a reporting job at the *Star*.

As Amon went on the road to peddle odd-sized portrait frames, James Record was a young baseball player in Paris, Texas. Like North, he dreamed of becoming an attorney. Record played left field for Paris's YMCA team. The day he left baseball forever was during a crucial game with Sulphur Springs's YMCA nine.

Sulphur Springs was two runs behind. Late in the game, with bases loaded, a Sulphur Springs batter knocked a long fly ball toward left field. Catch it, and Paris would win the Northeast Texas championship. Miss, and Sulphur Springs had the title. A switching engine had parked in the railroad yard behind the left-field fence. As the ball arrived in Record's glove, the engineer blew the train whistle. Startled, Record dropped the ball. He walked off the field and never played baseball again; sixty years later he still was complaining about that humiliating day.

At seventeen, Record entered the University of Notre Dame. A serious scholar, he won the school's medal for proficiency in Greek and Latin during his freshman year. Two years later, he transferred to the University of Texas Law School but soon left because of illness. Recuperating in Paris, Record took work as a reporter for the *Advocate*.

One of Record's stories reached Jimmy North, by then city editor of the *Star*. The story told of a hot day in Paris when the temperature heated a nail until it set a fence afire. Flames jumped to a nearby barn, from which sparks ignited a house. North didn't believe a word of it, but admired the reporter's imagination.

Record decided against returning to law school. He applied unsuccessfully for reporting positions in Dallas, then wandered west, to the *Star*. North, remembering the hot nail, hired him.

In 1907, A. L. Shuman, a former traveling notions salesman who had worked in the back shop of the Marshall, Missouri, *Daily News*, stood on the steps of the Continental Bank Building enjoying Fort Worth's spring warmth. Amon bounded up the steps, passed Al, then called back, "Want a job?"

"Suppose so," answered Shuman.

"All right, $17.50 a week. Mine's $20 and I ought to have a little edge on you."

Shuman became an ad salesman for the new paper. He joined handsome, athletic Bert Honea, who had arrived from Palestine in East Texas to become classified ad manager and bookkeeper for the struggling newspaper. Already, Honea knew he had made a mistake.

As a teenager, Harold Hough and three friends monopolized newspaper delivery in Oklahoma City. One day, crossing some rail tracks, he was struck by a train, which severed his right lower leg. The accident caused him to miss a planned camping trip with his friends. Days later, the other three boys' massacred bodies were found. Two had been scalped. The murders were never solved.

Using crutches, Hough returned to work but quit when the first man to whom he sold a newspaper "looked at my [missing] foot and handed me a quarter tip." He had a wooden foot fitted and learned to walk again, then joined the *Daily Oklahoman* as assistant circulation manager.

In 1909, while browsing through a trade publication, he read that a Fort Worth newspaper needed a circulation manager. On a whim, he boarded a train for Fort Worth and asked Amon for the job.

"What kind of circulation plans do you have for us?" questioned Amon.

"Oh, just get the papers to readers when it's handy for them to read it," replied Hough.

Amon liked the answer. He hired Hough, and the *Star-Telegram* management team was in place.

Harold Hough was a frump of a man, folksy, blessed with a whimsical bucolic wit, an ingratiating introvert with a studied disregard for himself. There was about him the casual physiognomy of an awkwardly assembled rag pile. He dressed with a blind man's sense of color. A new tailored suit on Hough instantly mutated into a Salvation Army discard. A hat—he never removed his hat, indoors or out, and reporters suspected he even slept in it—became a deleterious thing crouched on his head, the brim casting a perpetual shadow over the little man.

Hough was unassuming, kind, congenial, and something of a public relations and circulation Merlin.

Hough was as unmindful of his car's appearance as his own, and his auto in the early years was a clanking, smoking, coughing Chevy, seemingly on its last wheels. The very sight of it was enough to send Amon into spasms of anger; the car embarrassed the publisher and he demanded Hough replace it with a new one at company expense. The jalopy suited Hough and he refused. Amon simmered.

One day Hough's flivver was missing. He reported the theft to police but it was never seen again. Hough bought a new Chevy; Amon was happy. Years later, Amon admitted he had driven Hough's clunker to the Trinity River and sunk it in ten feet of water.

The newfangled automobile was an intrinsic piece of the early *Star-Telegram*'s success. Many early promotions centered on the automobile which Amon, ever the futurist, predicted would transform American life. For him, cars were marvelous doodads and the *Star-Telegram* enthusiastically encouraged their use. Al Shuman sold the South's first full-page ad in 1909 to Overland Automobile Company—later to become the Willys Jeep manufacturer—for Texas's first auto section, an extension of the state's first regular auto page.

The newspaper sponsored endurance runs to Waco, ninety miles south, led by a *Star-Telegram* pace car, "The Spizzerinktum Special." A Chalmers-Detroit roadster won the first run, during which, the paper reported, a driver was thrown from his car and remained "in a somewhat critical condition," although he had "regained nearly complete consciousness."

Jim Record, who did not drive, was the newspaper's automobile expert, and edited the weekly car news page. He rode with numerous professional drivers on test drives, including T. F. Abbott, who gunned a ten-horsepower Maxwell up the Tarrant County Courthouse steps, then bounced the auto and Jim Record back down.

In 1912, the Maxwell company proposed a race between its car and a train, and Hough, always aware of the need to increase circulation in West Texas, proposed the speed contest be from Fort Worth to Abilene, 150 miles into the western wilderness. Record was assigned as lookout and navigator.

The road was hypothetical, little more than buggy ruts often disappearing into the mesquite thickets or dipping into dry creek beds, and Record, dressed in bug-spotted goggles and white duster, coughed and bounced and kept pointing westward. There were repeated delays to repair punctured tires or to refill the boiling radiator from cattle tanks, and once to placate a startled bull. Twice, the road intersected railroad tracks and the Maxwell jumped across only moments before its surging, competitor train, the engineer jeering at the terrified reporter and his driver companion. Even with frequent stops, the Maxwell averaged forty miles an hour and arrived in Abilene ahead of the train.

Badly unnerved, Record dismounted from the Maxwell, removed and neatly folded his dingy duster, and returned to Fort Worth aboard the next eastbound train. When he reached the office, he turned the auto editorship over to another reporter.

Amon was pleased with the auto/train promotion, mostly because it involved West Texas, which already he considered his. Early within the *Star-Telegram*'s mergered rebirth, Amon understood that afternoon monopoly in Fort Worth still limited the growth of his newspaper. It needed a larger circulation base and the only direction for expansion was out there, into the nothingness of West Texas.

That way lay madness, for West Texas was not just rural and barren. It was wild and primitive.

Isolation and distance gave the franchise of West Texas to Amon and his newspaper. There was no larger town between Fort Worth and the Pacific Ocean, almost 1,300 miles west. When Amon slipped into the newspaper business, there were sections of West Texas without one person in a hundred miles. Amarillo had moved beyond its modest plat-of-tents origin into flourishing township status, but was decades away from becoming the largest city on the high Panhandle plains. El Paso was a huddle of crude homes, five hundred highway miles away, if there had been a highway. Any road was rudimentary. As late as the 1920s, Frank Reeves, the *Star-Telegram*'s legendary ranch editor, often slept under trees on the prairie because he could not move from one hotel to another, or one ranch headquarters to the next, in a single day. Even in 1930, the north-south highway from Texline (near Colorado) to San Angelo was almost five hundred miles long and had fewer than fifty miles of hard-top paving, much of that around Lubbock and Amarillo. Into the 1940s and 1950s, people routinely drove a hundred miles to see a movie or drink a beer and thought nothing about it. Distance was endemic to West Texas.

The new urban innovations of electricity, sewer systems, telephones, and gas for heating and cooking were late coming to the region, and electricity and indoor plumbing were not common to remotest West Texas until after World War II. It has been claimed that electricity did not reach the last remaining unwired community until 1952. West Texas was always behind the rest of Texas —and America—in every significant way: education, medical services, public utilities, industry, jobs, transportation.

Politicians ignored West Texas. Industry spurned it. Those who went there, for business or to visit, got out as soon as they could. The middle-class population was sparse. West Texans, poor and isolated and largely ignorant, hungered for attention. Amon Carter merely stepped in, assumed the mortgage on West Texas's future, and became its Paladin, carrying the tattered banner to all America.

West Texas is important! Amon Carter said so! See! It's right here on the front page of the Star-Telegram!

West Texans were prisoners in a country that punished them with heat and dust, took everything, and gave little. For every cattle baron, there were hundreds of beaten-down cowmen. Every rich cotton farmer had dozens of failed homesteaders to look down on. The cattle business, and farming, were cyclical ventures. Cows that brought wealth one year went begging for buyers the next. A season of rain, good grasses, and abundant crops was followed, perhaps, by years of drought. A common joke was: "It got so bad one year that this ol' boy stole a bunch of cattle, trucked them to Fort Worth, sold them, and lost money on the deal."

No matter what happened, though, West Texans carried on. They coped. Texas was settled by migrational flows from the mid-South, from Tennessee and Kentucky. One historian has suggested that the gentler farmers and merchants remained in East Texas and the malcontents—the unsociable men with hard eyes and searching souls—continued west to do battle with that unfortunate country, untouched by civilization's flow, living anonymously with their poor choice of homestead, enduring the ungodly weather and the lonely distance. They shouldered their burden and hoped it would all change as quickly as the *Star-Telegram* kept promising them it would.

Most West Texans lived lives that contradicted *The West's* legends. Stanley Walker, who returned to his native Texas late in life, wrote, "Many outsiders have the idea that the marks of Texans are buoyance, optimism and bustling energy. The average Texan is a tired man, and has been ever since he can remember. . . . A quiet defeatism is the rule. They are stoics, never excited over their petty victories, and at the same time never crushed by adversity. Most of them can take an honest blow of fate without wincing much. Let a man's beautiful daughter elope at the age of fifteen with a bum, let the grasshoppers eat his pasture, let the bugs destroy his oat fields, let anthrax lay low his herd of cattle, let the screwworms decimate his sheep, let illness ruin his bank account, if any, let Republicans reach high office in the nation—whatever happens, the Texan is not greatly astonished."

He survived.

In West Texas, there were floods and famines, wolves, coyotes, rattlesnakes, tarantulas as big and black as derby hats. There were range wars and blood feuds without end, diseases and deaths, Indian raids and loneliness—eternal loneliness.

And always, the West Texan, by God, survived.

When the West ended and became *The West*, the rancher, his empire behind barbed wire, needed less land. He sold some to sod farmers. The farmers discovered something ranchers never knew. The crumbly beige soil was abundantly productive when watered. Using irrigation, large farmers made the prairie rich with crops, especially cotton and wheat. Families with smaller pieces of land could not afford irrigation and had to trust Providence to water their crops; the trust largely was misplaced.

A few men, digging for water, found oil, though not all appreciated what they had discovered. Old Dan Waggoner ran his considerable nerve and luck into sixty thousand cattle grazing a half-million acres covering much of seven counties. He died in 1904. His son, W. T., dug for water but found oil. "Dammit!" legend says he shouted. "Cows can't drink that stuff!" W. T. plugged the wells with cedar posts and later moved, as many ranchers and oilmen did, to Fort Worth, where he and Amon resumed a friendship formed earlier in Bowie. "Pappy", as W. T. was called, would become a handy lode to mine for Amon's little ventures requiring money. Pappy had lots of money. In the 1930s, Amon negotiated with Pappy on behalf of Phillips Petroleum, which wanted the old man's oil. Amon reported back that Pappy would not accept Phillips's offer of $50,000,000. At his death, his estate valued at more than $500,000,000, W. T. Waggoner was Texas's richest man. His children knew what to do with oil and the money it produced.

Somehow the early inhabitants of West Texas endured and became a hardy, taciturn, patient people imbued with a lengthy index of social qualities. They were warm-hearted, openly friendly to travelers and passing strangers, independent, individualistic, conservative, proud, frank, honest. (My grandfather never locked his farmhouse when leaving—neighbors might need to borrow something while he was gone.) They were deeply, fundamentally religious. Social sinning was broadly condemned— smoking and dancing Methodists were considered by Baptists to be bound for hell. Doubtless, they were racially intolerant. There were few blacks and West Texans had only Mexican Americans ("Meskins") to look down on—it was a very short glance.

West Texas was the origin of much of Texans' exaggerated boasting. People dared not tell the truth about their country so they made up extravagant stories poking fun at their predicament—"It rained in Loving County yesterday but I didn't have time to drive over and watch it."

Amon had a collection of "facts" he loosed on audiences. These were generous overstatements and a few outright lies, written for him, I suspect, by Boyce House, a *Star-Telegram* reporter who collected all those Texas brags and published them in a dozen best-selling books.

Amon's talk always began with the shout: "TEXAS FOREVER! FORT WORTH NOW AND HEREAFTER!"

He told audiences: "If Texas was chopped off loose from the United States, it would float into the ocean, as it rests on a vast subterranean sea of fresh water. . . . The chief occupation of Texans is trying to keep from making all the money in the world. . . . If a Texan's head was opened the map of Texas would be engraved on his brain, and also his heart. . . . You do not belong to society as constituted in Texas unless your front gate is 18 miles from your front door. . . . If all Texas steers were one big steer he would stand with his front feet in the Gulf of Mexico, one hind foot in Hudson Bay, the other in the Arctic Ocean and with his tail brush off the mist of the Aurora Borealis. . . . SOME STATE!"

Amon never stopped reminding other, less-fortunate Americans that Texas was a sovereign nation reduced to statehood.

In serious moments, he restructured his data into more palatable truths:

"West Texas is an area greater than that of New York, Massachusetts, Pennsylvania, and Maryland combined, peopled with 2,000,000 thrifty folks, courageous builders. . . . Oil produced in this area is nearly one-half of all the oil produced in the world."

Through his efforts, the West Texas Chamber of Commerce grew to a membership exceeded in numbers only by the United States Chamber of Commerce, a statistic that hardly flattered the region and one that caused old Sam Rayburn, the U.S. House Speaker, to shake his head and mutter, "Any town big enough to have a chamber of commerce is beyond saving."

The survivors of West Texas had children, then grandchildren, who got an education of sorts. Given learning and a somewhat wider view of the world, the young left home, often at a dead run. Mostly they came to Fort Worth, which accounted for its twenty-fold growth in the early years of the twentieth century. That always was the essential difference between Fort Worth and Dallas. Dallas received the mercantile men, ambitiously seeking fortune; Fort Worth got the half-grown children from West Texas, not coming to town in search of fortune but to escape. Failed farmers and ranchers fled to Fort Worth for work in the slaughterhouses and other muscle industries and, with the larger migration of the early 1940s, to man the bomber plant's assembly line.

Wealthy families came, too, maintaining second homes in Fort Worth because the town, bragged the *Star-Telegram*, was "The Queen City of the Plains." A resident once complained to his city councilman that streets around his east side home were unimproved and dusty, while the west side had brick avenues and tall light poles and curbing. He was told that Amon Carter wanted it that way. West Fort Worth was that part of the city seen first by arriving West Texans.

Always West Texas. Amon's chaw-bacon, rube cowboy believed, and often said, that West Texas was "the most beautiful backyard a city ever had."

Perhaps he was right. There is a time out there when softness comes to the plains and mountains. Bluebonnets and Indian paintbrush and the lavenders of sweet William and wild verbena flow over the pastures. The pampas flatness is coated with clovers and tall buffalo grasses become golden, as in Spanish Andalusia. The air is cool and clear and clanking windmills rise as sentinels over the long landscape.

The land truly is epic and grand and *The West* undeniably still is there, as glorious and indomitable as Amon Carter always wished it would be.

Isolated by miles, West Texans were insular, unknowing, often uncaring, of what went on beyond their world, and they welcomed the *Star-Telegram* as a kind of lighthouse beacon pointing the way to safe harbor.

Amon and his newspaper, as was his master plan, grew with West Texas.

By 1913, the *Star-Telegram* was the fourth-largest newspaper in Texas, having grown from fifteen thousand to forty thousand daily circulation in four short years. December 15, 1912, the company celebrated its success by issuing what it called a "Progress" edition of two hundred and fifty pages, then the largest single newspaper edition ever published. Amon sold seventy-four full-page ads, an accomplishment that he bragged was a world record, and may have been.

Also in 1913, William Capps, a Fort Worth attorney, purchased the morning *Record* from Clarence Ousley. Capps knew nothing about the newspaper business, and the *Star-Telegram* simply ran away in the circulation race. The newspaper's graph line for sales, and income, and circulation rose dramatically in the next decade. From forty thousand circulation and the state's fourth position in 1913, to fifty thousand and second place two years later. In another three years, there were sixty-six thousand subscribers and the *Star-Telegram* was Texas's largest newspaper, a position it would not relinquish until the 1950s. By 1923, Amon was able to advertise in *Newspaperdom* that his paper was the largest in the Southern United States with 115,000 circulation—thirty thousand more than the *Dallas Morning News*, forty thousand ahead of the *Houston Chronicle*, and twenty-five thousand beyond the *Atlanta Journal*.

In 1920, Amon moved the newspaper into what *Editor & Publisher* considered the "Finest Newspaper Plant in [the] Southwest." It was a "million-dollar" four-story squarish building at Seventh and Taylor Streets with terra-cotta cornice work and candy-stripe window awnings. Inside were elegant marble columns and mahogany lobby counters, an employee restaurant, kitchen, three elevators, and a library club with sofas and cane-backed rockers. There even was a separate "rest room for women employees" and in the basement, space "with toilets" for newsboys to remain "out of the elements." The building was air-cooled and had its own artesian well.

Six years later, in a two hundred-page anniversary edition, the *Star-Telegram* boasted of its accomplishments in just two decades: from 4,500 circulation to 125,000 (Sunday); $25,000 capitalization to $1,000,000; 25 employees to 343; one press to four; three Linotype machines to twenty; no correspondents to 600; first issue receipts of $387.30 to "considerably more."

In that second decade of ascendancy, Amon Carter was busy inventing his cowboy persona, busy boosting Fort Worth, busy traveling the country servicing the *Star-Telegram*'s national accounts, busy becoming semi-famous, busy yippeeing the virtues of his dusty Valhalla: West Texas.

Amon's artistry at grandiloquent puffery, and his brilliance for spreading all that bogus good news, was to haunt him. Outsiders began to believe when he boasted that Fort Worth would become a grand Paris and West Texas really was a place of splendor. Roy Howard, his friend, listened, then offered to buy the *Star-Telegram*. Amon refused and suddenly he had the *Press*, the newest Scripps-Howard paper, to live with. The *Press* opened in 1921 and Amon was irritated because he knew Fort Worth was no more than a two-newspaper town, and already he was competing with the morning *Record*.

Even more alarming was the sudden arrival of William Randolph Hearst.

The Lord of San Simeon, said an observer, came to Fort Worth like a knight in rusty armor, his journalistic reputation yellowed by decades of questionable ethics and high-handed meddling into national affairs. But his newspapers were a nationwide network and a worrisome power wherever they existed—so nettling, in fact, that an informal organization of competing publishers met now and then to discuss the common enemy Hearst had become. Fort Worth was the smallest city in which Hearst ever was to publish a newspaper, and he came more to punish Amon than for the town's rich promise.

As early as 1918, Hearst proffered a bid for the *Star-Telegram* as a means of buying Amon Carter. The offer was part of a five-year campaign to bring Amon into the San Simeon stable. Amon always seemed to consider the offers, though actually he only was playing with Hearst. He never seriously considered selling the newspaper or becoming a Hearst man, but he flirted with the offers, often replying that he would "think it over for a day or two."

He wrote of the Hearst hiring campaign in an autobiography begun then aborted late in life, and his correspondence files portray Hearst as a man believing he was dealing with a Texas rube ready to lay down his hoe and come to town. So perhaps Amon's carrot-and-stick act was justified.

Soon after Hearst's first offer to buy the *Star-Telegram*, Joseph Moore, the Hearst organization's treasurer, asked Amon to become publisher of the *Atlanta Georgian* at $36,000 annually, plus a share of the profits. Amon scuffed his unshod rural toe in the dirt and reluctantly said, "No, thank you." Moore countered with an offer as publisher of the *Chicago Examiner*, which Amon was challenged to "put ahead of the *Chicago Tribune*." Again Amon thought awhile, then declined. Would Amon run Hearst's Baltimore paper? No.

January 1, 1919, Hearst wired a simple message to Amon: "I wish we had you."

A month later, Moore urged Amon to "cash in on your wonderful work in Fort Worth and move on into the big tent." Moore offered Amon full control of the *New York American*, then the

New York Herald-Tribune—"Forget the 'piking' amount [$75,000] we talked about the last time you were here. Stop clinging to small propositions rather than getting out into the big show."

Hearst wearied of playing Amon's game. He could not understand why a man would remain intentionally in such a bobtail, ragtag place like Fort Worth. The reason was simple: Amon remained in his one-horse town because he was the horse.

So, Hearst decided to run Amon out of town. Late in 1922, he bought, sight unseen, the *Fort Worth Record.*

The *Record* had passed through two unexceptional ownerships after William Capps bought it from Clarence Ousley, and with each change it declined in circulation, income, and reputation. For his $150,000, Hearst bought the name and little else. Across town, J. Frank Norris, a nationally known Baptist fundamentalist preacher whose newspaper, the *Searchlight,* was circulated coast-to-coast, chortled in print: "Amon has plenty of enemies in Fort Worth. The complaint is that Amon irritates quick. He has a violent dislike for some . . . citizens, who return it with usury. The Anti-Amonites look forward with great joy to Amon's impending ruin at the hands of the Hearst organization. The big show is on. When newspapers fall out, the public always gets a square deal. One newspaper [Star-Telegram] owes a million dollars. The other has a hundred million dollars. It won't be long now."

The confrontation of Amon/Hearst had elemental clichés of those Saturday-afternoon westerns of so long ago. Amon actually spoke that classic line so thrilling to fans of Tom Mix and Lash LaRue, the precipitous words uttered before the big shootout: "The town is not big enough for the two of us."

Moore replied, "If the town is so bad off as you indicate you should be glad to have a live publisher come in and revive the city."

Amon hurried to New York and a meeting with Hearst at the press lord's Riverside Drive mansion. Amon asked Hearst to stay out of Fort Worth. Hearst said the request came too late, he had paid $10,000 for an option on the *Record.* Amon offered to buy the option. Hearst refused and asked once again that the *Star-*

Telegram be sold to him. Angry, Amon returned to Fort Worth to oil his six-guns.

April 1, 1923, Hearst began publishing the *Record* and that day Amon printed on the Star-Telegram's front page an editorial titled: "WELCOME, MR. HEARST." The editorial—it was a rhetorical gesture; Hearst was in Fort Worth spiritually, never in person—proclaimed the press lord's arrival as "unqualified proof of the greatness of Fort Worth and the whole Southwest." Privately, he gawd-dammed the whole situation and beat his fists against his desk.

The American Association of Newspaper Publishers convened in New York, in the old Waldorf. Amon met with other men whose newspapers competed with Hearst. A Colonel Blethen called the meeting to order and asked Amon what he had done when Hearst came to Fort Worth.

"We published an editorial welcoming him," answered Amon. Other publishers guffawed.

"You are a sap," said Blethen. "We have been giving him Hail Columbia and eating his fanny out."

The shoot-out deserves a proper dramatic conclusion, but has none. Clearly out of his league, Hearst never had a chance. What was applauded in larger, particularly northern, cities would not play in provincial Fort Worth. Hearst published only a newspaper. The *Star-Telegram* was a lifeline. The *Record* stuck with a daily diet of national and international news, unaware that to West Texans, Washington, Berlin, and Tokyo were not of immediate concern, not so much international as totally alien. Chinese court intrigue was not as crucial as Lubbock's mayoral election or the coronation of a 4-H sweetheart at Mineral Wells High. The Hearst paper quietly dug its own grave while Amon the Undertaker looked on, patiently waiting for the body to grow cold and stiff.

Amon, wrote Alva Johnston in the *Saturday Evening Post*, "smothered the Hearst paper with kindness." Not really. It is true that when Hearst sent columnist Arthur Brisbane to town to perk up reader interest and demonstrate the *Record*'s importance, Amon hosted a banquet to honor "the world's greatest journalist." Amon did that with a smile. And no doubt he smiled when he sent word to his merchant friends that Hearst was "an outsider" and not to be trusted. *Record* men found it difficult, if not impossible, to sell advertising in Amon's town.

To hype its image, the *Record* resorted to several deceits. It carried on its masthead as "star reporters" the operators who handled wire machines. It also printed—and dumped—thousands of extra copies daily to boost circulation numbers. Hearst lost $35,000 to $50,000 monthly.

In May 1924, Hearst asked to see Amon in New York. Once again, Hearst offered to buy the *Star-Telegram*, suggesting "$500,000 cash and $100,000 a year for five years at 6 ½ percent interest." Amon was to remain as publisher for $100,000 a year.

Still playing with Hearst, Amon replied, "It would take $600,000 cash to satisfy my associates alone." Plus, he added, $150,000 a year for six years.

"That's at least $300,000 too much," Hearst protested.

"That's all right," countered Amon, smugly. "You'll lose that amount in the next twelve months and we can make $125,000 in that time."

Almost as an afterthought Amon said, "Sell me the *Record* for what you have in it."

Hearst accepted instantly. Hearst's moneymen came to Fort Worth, to room 1316 in Hotel Texas, and the *Star-Telegram* merged with the *Record* like a toad with a fly.

At the 1924 AANP convention, Amon again met Colonel Blethen and asked, "How are you getting along eating Mr. Hearst's fanny out?"

"We're keeping it up," Blethen boasted. "How are you doing being nice?"

"Wonderful. We just ran him out of town."

Not only was Fort Worth a one-horse town, there was just one stall for the horse.

That Mr. Carter is the voice of the Administration in the Southwest, there is no question.
—*Lubbock Avalanche,* 1934

He madded up sudden.
—A contemporary, describing Amon's "mad spells."

What Verdi reached for in arias and Nijinsky in entre-chats, Amon mastered in cussing. Lyrical poetry. Peerless, multi-loquent cussing of illimitable depth and sensibility.

He was never a general, all-purpose cusser—Amon had only contempt for the courser idioms—but a specialist in "goddamn" and "sonofabitch" and his variations on those themes soared and rang with artistry. Being what we now term as a man with old-fashioned ideas, Amon mostly hid his cussing from women and children, and though outrageously profane, he was never consid-ered vulgar or obscene.

In a state aswarm with effusive cussers, Amon Carter was pre-eminent, because of the emotional scope he brought to the art. Given his passion of expression, he could make "goddamn"—his cowboy spoke it as "gawddam"—seem as virtuous as "amen" or he could warp trees with the vexed intensity of it. "Gawddam" from Amon's lips was gentle, humorous, sympathetic, stinging, or venomous.

Once he strolled through his editorial offices late at night turn-ing off lights. A reporter working in a corner protested, "Mr. Car-ter, I can't see to type!" Amon turned a cool eye on the man and said evenly, "You can gawddam sure squint, can't you?"

Told of the death of one of his newsmen, he cried out sorrow-fully, "Oh, gawddam. . . ."

"Gawddam" was staccato punctuation, or like punishing lashes, or spat in disgust. Unannounced one dawn, he appeared at the home of *Star-Telegram* oil editor John Naylor, punching the bell impatiently. He woke Naylor's wife, Pauline, a part-time society writer for the newspaper. She asked Amon to wait while she roused her husband. Amon at first was astonished that Nay-lor was still in bed at that predawn hour, then angry because the editor was taking too long to dress. As Pauline returned to the liv-ing room she found Amon pacing rapidly, muttering over and over, "Gawddam, gawddam, gawddam, gawddam, gawddam, gawddam. . . ."

The New York columnist, O. O. McIntire, wondered if the "G" of the publisher's name meant "goddam," and referred to the publisher as "Amon Goddam Carter."

Amon's enraged voice was as the taste of hemlock made audible and he did his best cussing when infuriated. Portly, humorless

Ross Sterling was elected governor in 1932 with Amon's support on the assumption anyone was preferable to Ma Ferguson—the other major candidate and a Carter antagonist. It was an era of oil-field scandals and Sterling sent National Guard troops to enforce Texas's prorating laws and to halt illegal production in East Texas.

Sterling's action, concentrated in East Texas, a foreign country, was unimportant to Amon, and in fact the *Star-Telegram* applauded editorially. Then the governor turned his troops loose on the Panhandle plains, on Borger, virtually a lawless oil-boom town. That was meddling in Amon's West Texas. The *Associated Press* issued a bulletin announcing Sterling's foolish sortie into Amon's world.

The publisher did not often come onto his newspaper's third floor and into its editorial offices, but when he did he came like Caesar entering Rome. That day, he burst out of the elevator clutching the AP dispatch, mouth drawn to a bloodless cleft, eyes awash with fury. He marched to the telephone switchboard, commanding, "Get me the governor!" and spun toward the city desk. As he whirred past reporters, all work stopped. City deskmen froze. Jim Record popped up from his managing editor's tilt-back chair, hurrumphing to attention. The telephone rang. Amon clutched it by the throat and shouted, "Sterling?"

The giant room was silent.

"You crazy sonovabitch," he yelled into the phone, "what the gawddam hell you think you're doin' in Borger?"

The staff was awestruck.

Amon listened, then snapped, "Well, gawddammit, I'll think of somethin'." He jammed the receiver into its cradle and stalked from the room. Reporters stared at the retreating mass of wrath then at one another in disbelief. Twenty minutes later, AP clattered out an Amon-dictated bulletin stating that National Guard troops certainly would not march on Borger; Governor Sterling, by Amon's order, blamed the whole mess on a Guard commander, who had acted without authority.

Editors and reporters were benumbed by the raw power of Amon's language and that he dared speak that way to Texas's most important elected official, but ever blunt and impetuous, a man honest to his emotions and convictions, he spoke his mind to anybody.

Elliott Roosevelt lived in Fort Worth when he divorced a wife to marry Ruth Googins, a pretty young socialite. It was considered a minor scandal, and national reporters followed Elliott to Nevada for the divorce, then descended on Fort Worth, tracking rumors that the president's son would marry a Texas woman. One early morning, FDR telephoned Amon at home, interrupting the publisher's thrice-weekly osteopathic treatment to ask about the woman that newspapers were linking with his son.

"Ruth Googins's only scandal is being mixed up with the Roosevelts," Amon told the president of the United States. Later, Eleanor Roosevelt, accompanied by American Airlines President C.R. Smith, came to Fort Worth to talk privately with Ruth Googins at Amon's Shady Oak Farm. Newsmen learned of the intended meeting and Amon whisked the First Lady on to Los Angeles where she and her future daughter-in-law could talk without interruption.

Amon Carter was a complex man with uncomplex ways. Once the formula was understood, his every reaction to any situation could be predicted. He was impulsive but rarely surprising, compulsive but always within the borders of his highly anomalous personality. Very much a man of his time and place, Amon was rarely out of character.

Nenetta, his second wife, recalled Amon as "A marvelous father, the worst husband." In her divorce petition, Zetta, the first wife, charged that Amon "traveled much. . . sought public esteem and personal adulation, grew censorious of plaintiff and her . . . humble methods of living."

In turn, Amon was more attentive to his ex-wives after they were divorced. Nenetta was included on guest lists for his parties, introduced to his famous friends as "the mother of my children, Amon and Ruth." Following her divorce, Zetta moved to Chicago where she sold magazines door-to-door to augment her small regular income. In the early 1920s, Amon drilled a successful oil well which paid out about $100,000; without legal

The Carters (left to right): Ruth, Amon, Amon Jr., and Nenetta, dressed in Amon's famed vicuna topcoats and hats.

obligation, he gave half to Zetta. A relative borrowed Zetta's money and lost it to a bad investment, so Amon gave her more. She had a small piece of property willed by her father. Amon had it drilled for gas. The drilling was successful and Zetta had an income for life.

His children, Amon Jr. and Ruth, and the older Bertice born before he and Zetta moved to Fort Worth in 1905, were special passions. For his namesake, Amon mounted an engraved plaque in St. Anne's Hall of St. Joseph's Hospital: "Amon Carter Junior was born in this room, December 23, 1919." That piece of paterfamilias hung in place until the building was razed in the early 1950s.

Ruth was born prematurely, a forceps delivery. The instrument cut her face. Amon, who could not abide pain and suffering, in himself or others, and paled at the sight of blood, stood beside his new daughter's crib sobbing loudly, anguished, questioning whether Ruth "ever will be OK?" He told little Amon "the old stork dropped Ruth and cut her" and lectured the four-year-old in a stern voice, "You will have to stand up now, you have a sister."

His children's illnesses distressed him and even the minor events of their tonsillectomies incited an extreme anxiety. He refused to go to the hospital but paced his office floor, wringing his hands, tears flowing over his cheeks, telephoning Nenetta every few minutes, "Is it over yet?"

He called little Amon "Cowboy" and Ruth "Sugar Pie," pampered and spoiled both, but was a "little hard" on his son. "He would give Ruthy twenty dollars to take a dose of medicine and Little Amon a lickin' if he didn't," said Nenetta. A consummate sentimentalist, Amon saved his children's first report cards and their Baptist Sunday school quarterlies. Among his office papers was a yellowed envelope inscribed: "Change from Amon Junior's first newspaper sale"—two age-tarnished pennies. Given a flower by three-year-old Ruth, he pressed the petals and entombed them forever in his files. Amon printed the children's baby pictures on *Star-Telegram* Christmas bonus checks and named new presses bought in 1920 for Bertice and young Amon.

Bertice was said to be most like her father—brilliant, with a decisive, penetrating mind and forceful manner, Bertice lived with her mother in Illinois, however, and Amon knew her least of all. He visited with her irregularly, sent an allowance in her younger years, and later gave her stock in the publishing company. In return, she worshipped her father, but the fawning attention embarrassed him. A big-boned, heavy woman, twice married, Bertice became a broadcaster for WFAA radio in Dallas. She died in 1952 of alcoholism-related kidney failure as Amon sat beside the hospital bed, holding her hand throughout a long night, sorrowing deeply for the tragedy of his first-born child.

Amon Carter, who portrayed the coarse, blustering cowboy frontiersman for outsiders, loved flowers, especially heavy-scented hyacinths, lilies, and red tulips. The boy who slept on tow sacks and wore cast-off clothing grew into the man who treasured luxuries: silk, monogrammed pajamas and sheets, tailored suits and handmade shoes. The child who lived in log

cabins and drafty rooming houses without plumbing, who emptied bedpans for nickels and dimes, became the multimillionaire
with meticulous personal habits. Each day he scrubbed the lava-
tory after shaving, the tub after a bath, perching on his hands and
knees, scouring the porcelain basins like a common scullery maid.

He bathed in a Matchabelli oil costing twelve dollars a bottle
and afterwards doused himself in cologne, both of which he
bought by the case and about which, said Nenetta, he felt "if a little bit is good, a lot is better. You could smell him comin' and
goin'."

Star-Telegram newsmen knew when he had been in the elevator because Amon's heavy musk permeated the tiny cubicle.
Roscoe Brown, the black elevator-operator, joked of the saccha-
rine aroma, "You know 'Evening in Paris?' This is 'Night in Fort
Worth.'"

An effetist in creature comforts, Amon nevertheless had a core
of Texas good-ol'-boyism. He craved plain foods. Meat and pota-
toes, nothing fancy. Fried chicken and corn cooked in bacon
grease, black-eyed peas and cornbread. Barbecued beef and beans.
He ventured into turtle soup, Nenetta shamed him into sampling
cucumbers, and a national columnist marveled that he ate
Roquefort dressing on grapefruit, but mostly exotic foods confounded him. O. O. McIntire repeated many times in his syndicated column the tale of Amon's first encounter with a potato
soufflé at Ciro's in Paris: Amon pushed away the dish, vowing, "I
won't eat that 'til I know who blew it up."

He ate as he did almost everything, too quickly, gulping his
food, and by middle age was pained with chronic indigestion,
which he eased by constantly eating Bisodal tablets. When no
guests were in the house he dined at the simple kitchen table and
usually with the radio for companionship, chuckling at Amos
and Andy, Fibber McGee, and his old friends, Edgar Bergen and
Charlie McCarthy. And to Nenetta's endless consternation, he
brought Ike and Lindbergh, J. C. Penney and FDR into his home
through the servants' rear entrance, as though they were yard-
men coming for their victuals and pay. Often after supper, he
rushed his children off to a movie where, being Amon, they sat
where he wished to sit, always halfway down on the right side

where screen images moved irritatingly aslant. Amon, not surprisingly, favored westerns.

Blatantly nonintellectual, he rarely attended theater or ballet or opera and, said daughter Ruth, "if he ever set foot in a museum, I don't know about it." But he became Fort Worth's largest contributor to the arts merely because he thought them necessary for his town's completeness. In all of his life, *Time* reported, Amon never read more than a dozen books.

Amon collected anything and everything: people, memorabilia of his childhood, autographs of famous friends, menus, letters. His cache grew so large that much of it was moved to a warehouse. Nothing was discarded. Once American Airlines retired a DC-3 passenger plane, and officials organized a brief ceremony. As the company's chief stockholder and a connoisseur of public rituals, Amon was present. A short pole flying the company flag was mounted on the plane. The ceremony ended with the flag being lowered by a thin string and Amon approached public relations manager Buck Marryatt, asking, "May I have the flag?"

Amon Carter Sr. with Charles Lindbergh at Amon's Shady Oak ranch house.

"Certainly, Mr. Carter," answered Marryatt. Amon turned to leave, then paused.

". . . uh . . . Buck?"

"Yes, sir?"

"Can I have the string, too?"

He assembled large stores of string, crammed into desks at home and in his office. When the drawers overflowed, Nenetta and his secretary, Katrine Deakins, simply threw away the precious hoard. Amon began gathering again. He lay by paper bags and rubber bands, old odds and ends, scraps of paper with indecipherable scribblings. He subscribed to a clipping service for news of himself and Fort Worth and those clips, often as many as thirty copies of an identical story, were squirreled away in file cabinets. After Amon's death Katrine and Jimmy North burned thirty fifty-gallon barrelfuls of his pack-rat treasures.

Amon was excruciatingly punctual, always five minutes early, and hostesses who invited him to their homes learned to be dressed and waiting at the precise hour because he already would be punching impatiently on the doorbell. And his world was ever atilt. The sight of a picture hanging crookedly or a twisted lampshade gave him the fidgets and he went through life putting everything in exact symmetrical order, even compulsively shuttling objects on tables until they had a geometric harmony.

He loved gadgets, the toys denied him as a child, and he bought whatever caught his eye. A New York antique dealer told Nenetta that Amon was "the answer to an auctioneer's dream. He'll buy anything." Endlessly, he purchased what he believed to be beautiful art objects, but few ever matched any decor and Nenetta hid them. For months after he toured the Orient, packages arrived in Fort Worth containing Mandarin robes, rich brocades, fancy underwear, jeweled letter openers, carved ivory and jade figurines. He bought dozens of pistol-shaped cigarette lighters and in South America almost was attacked by soldiers when he attempted to present one of the flaming guns to Eva Peron.

Captivated though he was by the magic of doodads, nothing mechanical ever worked correctly in his hands. He could not type. He cut his fingers on can openers. Pencil sharpeners fell apart at his touch. Amon simply could not be trusted with machinery, especially automobiles. He was an awful driver and even his children were afraid to ride with him. He drove too fast and on whichever side of the road he chose and he regarded stop signs and signal lights as other drivers' responsibilities. Twice daily he drove the two miles between home and the *Star-Telegram*, always in second gear. Amon was much too busy to waste his time shifting gears.

Mounted to the driver's door of all his automobiles was a leather holster packed with a gleaming six-shooter. He owned many pistols, one of which he broke in 1912 pounding for immediate service on a Baltimore bar top. Another—a Remington .45 given him by Nelson Rockefeller—served as an impromptu gavel at Shady Oak parties. And there were the twin pistols worn with his cowboy costume. And Frank James's old cap-and-ball .45.

No evidence exists that Amon ever fired a live round of ammunition through any of his pistols, and there is credible testimony that he was at least uncomfortable around the real thing. Bud Fisher, the "Mutt and Jeff" cartoonist, joined Amon at a baseball World Series game in Philadelphia. As Fisher wrote in the *Saturday Evening Post*, Amon boasted loudly about Fort Worth and Texas.

"No one is considered well-dressed in Texas without a six-shooter," bragged Amon, "and I'm such a dude I wear two of them."

Later the pair returned to New York and Amon visited in Fisher's apartment, continuing to bluster about his rough Texas heritage. In defense, Fisher produced a pistol given him by "Pancho Villa after shooting the original owner."

"Look," said the cartoonist, "here's a pistol I have and it shoots and everything."

Fisher loaded one shell, took aim at a blue china cuspidor across the room, and fired. Noise and acrid fumes filled the room. Amon blanched, stammered a hasty goodbye, and rushed out. "I didn't see Mr. Carter again for a year," Fisher wrote.

By Fort Worth standards, the large house at 1220 Broad Street was a mansion. On the grounds were a greenhouse, a garage often used for parties, and open gardens where Nenetta and later

Minnie, the third wife, cultivated Amon's aromatic flowers. There, too, was a large vault, the steel door of which came from W. T. Waggoner's defunct bank, and in which Amon hid important treasures: his liquor and his children's Sunday school quarterlies.

In early years, the home was surrounded by open acreage at the city's western outskirts and the family kept cows and chickens, cats, rabbits, and dogs. Amon loved animals, especially a bulldog named Boomer, and Blue Boy, Fort Worth's first French poodle—another of Amon's doodads. Blue Boy was a car chaser and one day unexpectedly caught a mail truck. Furious, Amon attempted to have the mailman fired for maiming the poodle, but the postmaster only transferred the carrier to a route far away. Once Amon bought Nenetta a blooded kitten, Lady Jane, and paid for the animal by cutting $250 from pots of a poker game in his home. Other players complained about the kitty tax, but Amon dismissed their grumbling as sour grapes.

The menagerie naturally had losses over the years, and for the death of each pet, Amon and the children staged elaborate funerals. Invariably, Amon cried during services.

He was a splendid gambler—at poker, at dominoes, at hundred-dollar racetrack windows, playing as he lived—aggressively. He "won more than he lost," admitted Bert Honea, who nonetheless felt Amon spent too much time gambling.

In 1931, Amon emceed an American Association of Newspaper Publishers dinner in Chicago. Colonel Robert McCormick, the *Chicago Tribune* publisher, asked for a biography. Amon replied by letter "I am tall, raw-boned, thirsty and possess an excellent appetite as most newspapermen do when the dinner is free. I am married, have 2 children. Fortunately, both of them take after their mother. In addition, I neither drink, smoke, swear nor stay out nights and take no interest in feminine society. I play a little indifferent poker and some bridge, mostly by ear. . . ."

After his marriage to Nenetta began deteriorating, Amon stayed more and more in Suite 10G of the Fort Worth Club where, amid the sodality of men, he drank and played poker, often forty-eight hours without a pause. He was a superb womanizer and tireless carouser, but gambling occupied his attention most at the club.

He ran over less-bold players with his money, and there was a curious stain of charity, not all of it benevolent, in his poker style. During one game, a player lost more than he could afford and Amon, the big winner, privately returned the man's losings with a lecture on the folly of gambling beyond one's means. In another game, Amon purposely lost money to a friend deeply in debt.

Amon turned back winnings in other games, but those generosities were influenced by his schemes to help Fort Worth. Josh Cosden, of the oil family, lost $15,000 in a craps game. He paid by check, which Amon refused to cash. A Standard Oil president lost $1,200 at poker, and Amon would not accept the money. Later, he asked civic favors of both men and they paid their gambling debts, but in Amon's coin.

With a Robert Burns panatela clinched in his teeth or waved in an expressive hand like a symphony conductor's baton, Amon was a fast talker, his crisp voice swaddled in a soft accent that broadened into a caricatured twang when he played the cowboy or told jokes or disappeared altogether on solemn occasions. He walked fast—very fast—as though fleeing bill collectors or a posse, his gait almost a trot. Everybody complained they could not keep pace with him.

The double-time step reflected the energized Amon, a man capable of working eighteen-hour days or playing around-the-clock without rest. He was able to recharge himself with instant twenty-minute naps, but those were rare. He mostly went through life on the run, without pause. Once friends invited him to West Texas for a quail hunt. A photograph shows Amon on the plains beside an old car, dressed in shirt and tie and broad-brimmed hat like a man on his way to a business luncheon. Afterward, his hunting companions complained around the Fort Worth Club that Amon "walked down all the dogs" and kept the men awake by drinking and talking all night. He collected the dead quail and took them to his Shady Oak Farm. He was never asked to go hunting again.

His friends teased him about the bird hunt until he tired of the jokes and growled angrily at them. Everything paled before Amon's anger. Of all his personality quirks, the "mad spells," as

Katrine Deakins named them, most affected those around him. Amon, an overachiever in all ways, had monumental fits of anger. He was neurotically impatient—with himself and with others— and he demanded precision of an imprecise world. The shortest delay or slightest error brought on his furies. He would puff up, redden, shout, cuss, even stamp his feet, and those near him were either mesmerized or terrified. No doubt the mad spells were a bullying influence on civilians and reporters alike, and there were otherwise strong-minded businessmen in Fort Worth who would agree to anything rather than face an angry Amon Carter.

"Amon the Terrible," said a newsman, reflecting on his publisher's rages. In a tantrum, Amon was unreasonable, intimidating, and simply steamrolled anyone who dared step in his way. Told by a secretary in New York that her boss could not see Amon, the publisher brushed her aside, burst into the man's office and demanded to know "why in the hell you're puttin' me off?" In the 1920s, when the *Star-Telegram* building was sparkling new, Amon became enraged over a trifle, jammed on his hat, and headed for the Fort Worth Club. In the lobby, a *Press* newsboy talked with several *Star-Telegram* carriers as he sat on a counter, kicking his heels against the shining mahogany. Amon the Angry swept into the lobby. He saw the boy and his thumping heels and burst into the circle of carriers. He grabbed the *Press* boy by the scruff of the neck and seat of the pants. He hauled the kid outside and abruptly dropped him on the sidewalk, continuing without a word to the club. Within hours, Fort Worth was gossiping of how Amon Carter had attacked a small boy.

When angered, Amon demanded immediate retribution. His parking space was under a tin-roofed shed reserved for *Star-Telegram* executives, but outsiders often sneaked into the handy slots. One morning Amon found an old Ford parked in his space and instantly went into a fit. Motorcycle patrolman Lawrence Wood passed and Amon yelled for him to stop.

"Give this car a ticket!" ordered Amon.

Wood protested, "I can't, Mr. Carter. It's on private property."

"I don't care, give it one anyway. That's my parking space."

"Honest, Mr. Carter, I can't. I'd get in trouble."

Amon simmered at the Ford for long moments then told Wood, "Ride around the block." Wood rode, circling very slowly. As he turned the final corner, there was Amon pushing the old Ford into the street, blocking traffic in both directions.

"Now it's on public property. Ticket it!" growled Amon.

As volcanic as the mad spells could be, they most often disappeared as suddenly and mysteriously as they appeared and Amon would be contrite and seemingly embarrassed by his behavior. In the early 1950s, he was force-feeding taxpayers on the merits of a bond issue to build what would become known as "The Amon Carter International Airport." The *Star-Telegram* daily published on page one highly optimistic stories praising the proposed air facility. Jim Vachule was summoned to Carter's office to receive "facts" for the next glowing report. Amon dictated and Vachule scribbled notes.

"Read that back to me," said Amon. Vachule read.

"Where's 'triumphant?'"

"Triumphant?"

"Yes, 'triumphant,'" said Amon, irritated. "I was talking about how the airport would affect us and I said it would be a 'triumphant display of the city's future.' You left out 'triumphant.'"

Vachule consulted his notes.

"It's not here," said the reporter.

"I said 'triumphant!'" yelled Amon.

"I'll write it in but I don't think you said it, Mr. Carter."

Amon detonated. The publisher ranted, stomped back and forth in front of the newsman, lectured Vachule on the need for accuracy. Stunned by the suddenness and force of his boss's anger, Vachule was speechless. Finally, Vachule escaped, shaken by the experience.

At 1:00 A.M. the telephone rang and the sleeping Vachule groped for the receiver.

"Jim?" said the voice. "Amon Carter here."

Vachule instantly was awake. "Yes, sir?"

"I've been thinking about it," said Amon, "and I don't believe I said 'triumphant' at all."

They talked for a few moments and Vachule returned to bed, puzzling over his enigmatic employer. He arrived at work the next morning and found an envelope rolled into his typewriter. Inside was a crisp one hundred-dollar bill. Amon was apologizing.

For those closest to him, the mad spells were both irritating and often humorous, and they reacted by returning the anger or teasing him into a good mood or ignoring the outbursts. Amon and Bert Honea argued endlessly while James North or Katrine stood in the middle as mediators, pacifying both. Nenetta and Katrine mostly ignored him.

For almost forty years, Katrine Deakins experienced Amon's mad spells daily, and remained as unperturbed at the end as she was in the beginning. An earlier job ended when her boss made an indecent proposal and she hit him with an ink well. She came to work as Harold Hough's secretary. Still another of Amon's secretaries quit in tears and Hough asked Katrine to move into the second-floor suite to serve the publisher. Until his death, she attended the galvanic Amon in spite of his anger. She was as tough as he was, contending, "You had to stand up to him or he'd make a mop out of you." He fired her regularly, especially every New Year's Eve, on general principles, and she ignored him.

Amon warned Katrine never to clean his desk or office, both of which he considered sacred ground. She waited until he left town and cleaned anyway, then patiently bore the mad spell when he returned.

In the heat of a fit, Amon often would strike out at the nearest hard object. At home, he once beat his fists against a wall until blood flowed. He pounded his office desk so hard he broke a diamond ring. Curious about a loud thumping from Amon's office, Katrine peeked around the door one day to find her infuriated boss loudly and determinedly beating his head against a wall.

Amon's doctors repeatedly warned that his tantrums would kill him but he outlived both the mad spells and the doctors and happily was ranting away at this and that on his deathbed.

There was an innate gruffness to Amon. Part of it was contrived but more was only the wrapping of his style. He could be, and was, kindly gruff or grouchy gruff and few could distinguish the tones. He practiced a fine, pungent sarcasm and owned almost no tolerance at all for what Harold Hough characterized as "social horse pooky." He loved nothing better than skewering the affectations of others.

Once a culture-voiced grand dame, diligently hiding away the cotton-sack twang of her early life, telephoned Amon in the early morning, cooing, "Oh, Amon, have I awakened you?"

"No," he grumped. "You woke me up."

A Washington columnist reported Amon was toured through the baronial manor house of the capital's most ardent snob. The proud host stood Amon before a canopied bed, boasting of its pedigree back to the seventeenth century French court.

". . . and it cost me $200,000," the man bragged.

"You get the mattress and springs thrown in for that?" asked Amon.

6

He was the only person I ever saw who was rumpled all over.
—Alf Evans, newspaperman, describing Harold Hough

For kindly acts, his 'Hired Hand' he always is
a-blamin',
But those who get beneath his hide all know he's
dear old Amon.
—Menu legend, Ritz Hotel, New York City, 1928

It is quaintly interesting that when the WBAP dynamo broke down in midst of a program, Mr. Carter mounted to the roof and broadcast a speech with no other facilities than those vocal organs the good Lord had given him, and that coils were burned out in receiving sets five hundred miles away.
—Menu legend, Sherry's Restaurant, New York City, 1928

$\mathbf{R}$adio, in 1921, was only a gadget, a funny little black box that talked, and Amon, the consummate gadgeteer, was intrigued by the new medium but more than a little afraid because a New York friend warned him the little box would kill newspapers.

One day he asked Harold Hough, "What do you know about radio?"

"Hardly anything," admitted Hough.

"How much?"

"Well, nothing."

Amon sent Hough off to investigate radio, grouching "if this thing is going to be a menace to newspapers, maybe we better own the menace."

He advanced Hough three hundred dollars to catapult the *Star-Telegram* into the nether world of radio.

What Hough knew about radio was that a friend sometimes listened to a Dallas station, WRR. The friend operated an electrical supply firm and Hough asked for a radio.

"How far do you want to listen?" the friend inquired.

"Listen? I don't want to listen. Amon wants to talk."

That was when Hough first knew talking and listening were different in radio and with that useful knowledge he found a broadcasting unit in Dallas, a homemade rig put together by a tinkerer, W. E. Branch. Hough bought the flimsy transmitter, packed it in an old tomato crate, and transported it to the *Star-Telegram*, where he installed the thing in Louis Wortham's office, mostly because Wortham was out of town. An aerial wire was strung through the window, over Taylor Street, to the roof of a nearby building. Someone read a news story. The *Star-Telegram* was on the air—illegally and poorly, but nevertheless broadcasting with the power of five homemade watts.

A few days later a woman in Mineral Wells, fifty miles west, wrote that her radio had picked up the station's loud and clear signal. Amon read the letter and decided the gadget had promise.

Throughout the summer and fall of 1921, Hough experimented with the funny black box, spending the three hundred dollars and more, most of which came from the petty-cash drawer. He determined that a more powerful, professional transmitter was needed and contacted Western Electric. When the new broadcast unit—the sixteenth manufactured by Western Electric and the first installed in the South—arrived, Hough applied to the Department of Commerce for a license. Herbert Hoover, then the Commerce secretary, assigned the call letters WBAP, saying they stood for "We Bring A Program."

May 2, 1922, with two seventy-foot-tall broadcast towers rising from the *Star-Telegram* roof, WBAP became a functioning and law-abiding radio station. W. T. Waggoner, who lived a full two miles from the transmitter, telephoned to report that reception was good. He requested a song—"Wabash Blues."

That was the pattern of early radio, including WBAP. Music by local trios and orchestras, church choirs and neighborhood bands. There also were fire-call reports, a little news (read by Hough or off-duty reporters), and a bedtime story for kiddies, but no commercials. The station even broadcast one of the first "hillbilly" programs, featuring Confederate veteran and fiddler, Captain J. M. Bonner, backed by Fred Wagner's Hilo Five Hawaiian Orchestra.

WBAP began with ten watts of power. Within a year it increased to 1,500 watts, then 10,000 in 1928, and ten years later became one of eight national stations with 50,000 watts of clear channel power. Half of the station was sold in 1936 to the *Dallas Morning News*, and at the same time Amon bought KGKO in Wichita Falls, moving it to Fort Worth.

Within two years of that first feeble broadcast, Hough was taking his transmitting equipment outdoors, to rodeos and football games, baseball games and groundbreaking ceremonies. And by 1928, WBAP was affiliated with the National Broadcasting Company.

Hough was virtually the station's only announcer, dragged into the role one morning when a cub reporter failed to arrive for work. He substituted, and remained at the mike to become the Southwest's most popular broadcasting personality.

In those days, announcers signed off with their initials. Listeners liked "H. H." and wrote asking the name of the man with the droll voice. "I'm just the Hired Hand, up from the basement," was Hough's reply. Fan letters became so numerous that Hough was forced to provide pictures. He posed in overalls, checked shirt, and long-billed railroad cap, holding a broom and cowbell. The bell became the sound symbol of WBAP.

Amon Jr., Amon, Harold Hough, and James North at Channel 5 television 1949.

Listeners liked the Hired Hand's wry wit, such as his Radio Truth Society, for which he ran a legal—if not too serious—campaign for governor. He filed for the office, pledging to campaign entirely in El Paso—Texas's western-most city, so distant and remote that politicians ignored it.

"I believe the people of El Paso deserve more political amusement than they get," the Hired Hand said.

"Truth—Save it from abuse & overwork" was the Society's slogan. Adventures of the Hired Hand's struggle to seek "truth" in all things jumped over into the *Star-Telegram*, appearing as a series of cartoons, which then were reprinted as a booklet for readers and listeners. The *Star-Telegram* artist was V. T. Hamlin, who would go on to create the classic comic strip, "Ally Oop."

Ultimately, Hough hired "fellows with lace on their tonsils" and took himself off the air, explaining, "I'm the only announcer who ever fired himself for being no good."

In 1963, the National Association of Broadcasters named Hough "Dean of American Broadcasters," declaring him the "grand old man of American broadcasting." Throughout the prestigious award ceremony in Washington, D.C., Harold Hough sat quietly at the head table, wearing his ubiquitous rumpled hat.

Amon often talked on his radio station, emceed variety shows, and manned the microphone for remote broadcasts, especially those originating from Shady Oak Farm where he featured his famous visiting friends. Radio was made for a compulsive talker like Amon, and he loved the gadgetry of it all. Television was the next logical step.

WBAP-TV went on the air in the early fall of 1948 as, crowed the *Star-Telegram*, the first television station south of Saint Louis, east of Los Angeles, and west of Richmond, Virginia. The initial broadcast was remote, with one camera focused on Harry Truman as he made a railroad campaign whistlestop in Fort Worth. A few days later, the station officially signed on with a thirty-minute dedication given by Amon, followed by an old movie, followed by—nothing. An automobile had struck a nearby power pole and knocked WBAP-TV off the air.

Planning for the station, Amon and Hough decided that a grassy hillock east of downtown was perfect for the transmitter site. They went to inspect the property, climbed through a barbed wire fence, and began walking. A young bull was in the pasture, eyeing the men. Hough was apprehensive. Amon admonished, "Forget the gawddammed bull. He won't bother us." The bull pawed the ground irritably. Hough turned to leave, saying over his shoulder, "I'm gettin' out of here. I've got a wooden leg and that bull don't know who you are." The bull charged and the men scrambled to safety under the fence.

WBAP-TV sent out its first color broadcast in 1954, as usual ahead of its time because Amon was fascinated with the gimmicky splash of it. Hough had recognized the future of color television and sold Amon on investing in the expensive, necessary equipment, though the peacock representing NBC's Living Color seemed to most a white elephant. Amon and David Sarnoff, Radio Corporation of America board chairman, jointly pulled a switch converting WBAP into a peacock subscriber. That first color broadcast lasted three hours, but it hardly mattered. In all of Fort Worth and Dallas there were fewer than one hundred color television sets.

With the addition of television, Amon owned the full circle of communications in Fort Worth, and virtually all of it was aimed into the remoteness of West Texas. The monopoly's propaganda power was enormous, so much so that Alf Evans, looking back, commented, "Letting someone like Amon Carter have his own newspaper, radio and television stations is like letting Billy Graham have his own church. The only sermon you hear will be his."

Throughout the Hearst affair, Amon ignored the *Fort Worth Press*. From its beginning in 1921, the paper was never very important in Fort Worth, never successful, never much competition. It was a feisty little thing, a snippy terrier chewing on bones tossed aside by the *Star-Telegram*. Why Amon did not put it out of its misery is a mystery. He had no respect for it, believed it was a cheap, claptrap piece of journalism, but never moved to pronounce its death sentence.

"In his lifetime," wrote Gary Cartwright, one of its alumni, "Carter could have killed the *Press* with a flick of the finger, but he allowed it to exist, possibly because it reminded him of something out of his childhood, a disfigured monk or maybe a mangy cat."

For most of its fifty-odd years, the *Press*, smallest and shakiest branch of the Scripps-Howard family tree, had the social standing of a man living in a trailer house behind a filling station. It was tossed in poor neighborhoods and folded on dashboards of redneck pickup trucks and, after it became a racy tabloid in the early 1950s, a favorite luncheon companion because it was small enough to prop against a glass of tea. The *Press* considered itself the voice of the people but, denied access to corporate boardrooms and society ballrooms, it was left to serve those for whom wrecks, rapes, and robberies were life's only grand adventures.

The *Press* worshipped the scoop and the ominous headline and the quirky angle missed or ignored by the *Star-Telegram*, and it chased fire engines and murders with fervent urgency. After the *Star-Telegram* absorbed the Hearst's *Record,* the anemic *Press* was the only competition in town and it struggled to stay alive. Amon was ambivalent about the little paper, either ignoring it or siphoning away ad dollars. He kept bank call advertising from the *Press,* and aborted many special sections by letting friends know he would be unhappy if they bought space. After a *Press* salesman solicited special advertising from Montgomery Ward, Amon wrote its president, Avery Sewell, "The *Press* has been operating here for the past 12 years. Its name has been mentioned in the *Star-Telegram* but twice—when it opened and when it moved into a new building. During this period they *[sic]* have devoted a big majority of their time and effort trying to run down the *Star-Telegram* or . . . embarrass its publisher." He asked Sewell not to advertise in the *Press.*

Each time the *Star-Telegram* raised its ad rates, the *Press* lost business because advertisers who could not afford to increase their budgets simply cut lineage in the smaller paper.

Amon confounded the *Press.* His little promotions and deals invariably became news events that the *Press* was forced to cover, and how to treat the rival publisher was a question it never was able to answer. At one time there was a policy to publish Amon's picture each time he appeared at a public function on the theory that people would get sick and tired of seeing him. In other years the *Press* refused to print either his name or his picture.

From its middle years, the *Press*'s editor/publisher was Walter Humphrey, a portly, pipe-smoking, congenial man whose idea of a newspaper crusade, said a former reporter, was soil conservation. Amon, at best, was intolerant of Humphrey. Though he was able to introduce from memory a head table of fifty persons without stammering a name or title, Amon called the *Press* editor "Humphreys," leading *Star-Telegram* reporters to suspect the mispronunciation was deliberate.

In 1949, the Trinity flooded Fort Worth and several thousand families lost everything. The disaster proved the necessity for taming the river and a citizens' committee, which included Amon and Humphrey, was formed to devise a flood-control program. At the first meeting, Humphrey proposed that reporters be present.

"Hell, no," shouted Amon. "We're not goin' to have any gawd-dam reporters at any of these meetings."

Amon ranted for almost five minutes, denouncing the idea, scolding Humphrey for daring to suggest such a silly thing, finally growling, "Sometimes newspapers do more harm than good." Witnesses said Amon's denunciation of "Humphreys" was received with embarrassed silence.

"Carter cut him to pieces. Walter just looked hurt," said one of those present.

Amon's animosity toward Walter Humphrey perhaps was caused by more than his editorship of the ragtag *Press*. Humphrey also wrote and produced the annual *Texas Gridiron Show*, an evening of satire and song parody in which newsmen skewered politicians. The production brought out most state officials, many national figures, and all local prominent citizens. Except Amon. Uncharacteristically, Amon never attended the reporter roasts; his newsmen believed he was too thin-skinned to watch himself portrayed as Fort Worth's Machiavellian powerbroker—always his role in Walter Humphrey's *Gridiron* sketches.

One skit had a reporter playing Mayor Edgar Deen. His only duty was standing on stage and listening for a loud voice to call, then mimicking fear, answering meekly, "Comin', Amon . . . comin', Amon . . . comin', Amon." In one of the last shows before Carter's death, a reporter chorus sang a Humphrey hymn parody, the final reverently intoned word of which was "Aaaaa-mon."

Being poor and powerless, the *Press* never made money. It served as a tax write-off for Scripps-Howard and by necessity Humphrey's fiscal policy toward his small staff was stingy. Salaries were minimum, raises unique. Newsmen needing a new copy pencil had to exchange the stub of an old one. The newspaper was housed in an ancient building, dark and without air-conditioning, behind which was the New Gem Hotel, a flophouse used by black prostitutes. Often the hookers propositioned *Press* reporters on the adjacent parking lot. In the dank newsroom, black soot poured down from the floor above through an opening workers called "the coal chute."

Despite poor pay and even poorer working conditions, the *Press*, surprisingly, maintained a core of capable, loyal newsmen and editors who competed well against the rich *Star-Telegram*, perhaps because they were underdogs, the mom-and-pop grocery store clerks against the A&P. Through the years, as Cartwright recalled, the *Press* not only nourished "honest young writers and reporters" but was a "sanctuary for freaks, for idealists, for demonologists, for outcasts, for drunks . . . and curiosity seekers."

There were Puss Ervin, a retired postman who sometimes wrote his bowling column while wearing only his undershirt and sick Charley Modesette, who overcame Hodgkin's disease and regularly drank himself into such a stupor that he lost his car for days. Nat Lehmerman, who would double-park his taxi and rush into the *Press* to write a quick sports story, C. L. Douglas, whose lunch often was green peas speared one at a time with a toothpick from an open can, and Jack Mosely, an excellent but anxious reporter who once became so excited over a murder story that he fainted.

When the *Press* was good it was very good, and if not it always was outlandish and startling. During the tabloid years, a deer was struck and killed by a police car. Cops butchered and barbecued the animal for their annual picnic. Ever vigilant for the exotic angle, the *Press* discovered that the deer had been a child's pet and Bud Shrake composed an immortal headline: "POLICE EAT KID'S PET."

Virtually all *Press* reporters eventually encountered Amon Carter, and few of the meetings were placid. Mary Crutcher was a pretty young woman fresh from college and assigned to cover the 1936 centennial exposition, an Amon Carter production from start to finish. Amon brought Vice President and Mrs. John Nance Garner to the show and Mary set out to interview them. The publisher first took Cactus Jack away to speak with *Star-Telegram* reporters, so Mary began talking with Mrs. Garner. Amon saw the two women and "jumped between us and shoved me backward," recalled Crutcher. She got off the ground, dusted herself, and continued interviewing Mrs. Garner while Amon fumed.

Jack Gordon, whose black pencil mustache and slicked-back hair gave him the mien of a ladies' fancy underwear salesman, was the *Press*'s entertainment columnist. His beat was celebrities, and all Amon's friends were celebrities. Once Amon brought

Will Rogers to Fort Worth for a benefit performance. Gordon was assigned to interview the humorist for an early edition. Amon planned a downtown parade and the streets were lined with spectators. Gordon was waiting when Rogers arrived by train but Amon brushed the columnist aside and ushered the humorist into a waiting open sedan.

The parade began with Rogers and Amon in the convertible, followed by horses and clowns. Becoming impatient about his deadline, Gordon jumped on the sedan's running board and began interviewing Rogers. Furious, Amon shouted, "Get the hell off!" Gordon ignored him. Amon stood, shaking his fist at Gordon as hundreds of people cheered from the sidewalks.

"I said get the hell off there!" Amon yelled again.

"Aw, Amon," drawled Will, who was enjoying Amon's tirade, "leave the boy alone. He's just trying to make a livin'."

Gordon rode the running board throughout the parade to complete his interview.

Amon hosted Jeanette MacDonald for an early-morning press conference in his Fort Worth Club suite and the actress asked reporters not to smoke. Gordon, a dapper, gentle man who chain-smoked black cigars, arrived late. He entered with the usual glowing stogie clutched in his hand.

Amon ran across the room, grabbed the hand gripping the smoking cigar, and pulled the bewildered columnist into the bathroom. Carter held Gordon's hand over the commode, shook it until he dropped the cigar into the water, then walked out without a word.

As a tabloid, the *Press* was bright and brassy and brazen and no one took it seriously, not even its own sports staff. Blackie Sherrod, a bear of a man and a strict disciplinarian, commanded a four-man staff, the antics of which perplexed straight news reporters and editors, especially Walter Humphrey.

Sherrod and his boys had reverence for nothing but good writing. There was Jerre Todd who, arriving to apply for a job, took a long run down the newsroom center aisle and performed a perfect baseball hook-slide into the corner of Sherrod's desk. Blackie looked down at Todd and said softly, "You're hired." Bud Shrake moved over from the news department and wrote fictional sports

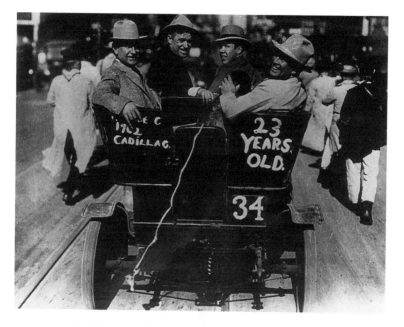

Amon with Will Rogers (front left), riding in Fort Worth parade.

stories better than the real thing. Dan Jenkins became a kind of utility man and sports columnist whose best stuff, said Cartwright, "had to do with how hard it is to open a package of crackers or buy gasoline." Humphrey never understood how crackers could be the subject of a sports column. Cartwright came from the morning *Star-Telegram* police beat, where conventional writing and reporting stifled his imagination.

Never ordinary, Sherrod's boys read aloud to each other from the writings of Mark Twain and S. J. Perelman, polished and wrote leads days in advance of a sporting event, were literate and literary, and wrote sports stories that never read like sports stories. They had water-pistol wars and chinning contests and broadjumping competitions, and gathered often at Shanghai Jimmy's, a Mexican food cafe, to plot against the *Press* and *Star-Telegram*. One of the schemes involved Crew Slammer, a mythical sportswriter they invented and promoted into the finals of a national Sports Writer of the Year contest.

When the staff broke up and scattered, as it had to, Sherrod became one of America's premier and most honored sports columnists for the *Dallas Times Herald* and later the *Dallas Morning News*. Jenkins, Shrake, and Cartwright became successful novelists, especially Jenkins, whose *Semi-Tough* was a national best-seller and popular movie. The trio wrote movie scripts together. Jenkins and Shrake became associate editors of *Sports Illustrated*. Several of Jenkins's sport-based books became movies, while Shrake wrote the best-selling golf instruction in history using golfing tutor Harvey Penick's diary. Todd, meanwhile, opened one of Fort Worth's largest and best ad/public relations agencies.

By the time Sherrod's boys reinvented sports writing, the *Press* had become thoroughly limp and ineffective. Time had killed the spark. Its brightest days were the 1920s and 1930s, when it competed so well that the *Star-Telegram* felt obligated to kill off its rival's Pulitzer nomination.

That the lowly *Press* should have been nominated for a journalism Pulitzer prize over the dominant *Star-Telegram* is not surprising, given the story's subject: oil scandal. To spread Fort Worth's oil-lease swindle shame before the world was, to Amon and the *Star-Telegram*, unthinkable. One did not air one's dirty linen in public.

Before 1917, Ranger, one hundred miles west of Fort Worth on the brink of West Texas, was a somnolent farming and ranching community, yawning and unambitious, and choking in the dust of a yearlong drought. Then Texas Pacific Coal Company chanced a wildcat oil well. It was a gusher, and overnight Ranger became a boomtown. Nearby Fort Worth was the oil-well supply center and a partner in prosperity.

At the peak of the petroleum frenzy, Amon's city gained five thousand new citizens a month and ranked seventh nationally in new construction. Amon was ecstatic.

Riches, however, brought the slick-shoe guys—hundreds of oil-lease swindlers. Theirs was a business of pyramiding greed, and business was good. Armed with leases on a few worthless drilled-over West Texas acres, a promoter would mail hundreds of thousands of promising letters to potential investors. Once the suckers paid their money, the swindler would close his office, only to open a week later under a new corporate name. Of 2,300 known oil-lease swindling firms in Texas, 2,100 were in Fort Worth.

Into this maelstrom of oily avarice came Dr. Frederick A. Cook, the Arctic explorer whose claim as discoverer of the North Pole was debunked by the National Geographic Society in 1909. The society ruled that Naval Commander Robert Peary was the first man to reach the North Pole. Cook spent the next decade unsuccessfully defending his claim, and by the early 1920s was in Wyoming, broke but not without inspiration. Cook spied the Ranger oil boom, and opened the Texas Eagle Oil Company in Fort Worth. Within a year, Cook merged with 413 other companies, none, as Texas Eagle Oil, owning a single oil well. Claiming he wanted only to make all Americans rich, Cook mailed millions of promotional letters and let the cash flow in.

In 1921, Henry Zweifel was appointed United States attorney in Fort Worth and immediately set out after the oil-lease swindlers. Two years later, his work made considerably easier by a series of stories on Doctor Cook in the *Press*, Zweifel had indictments on 535 persons. Doc Cook was sentenced to fourteen years and nine months in Leavenworth.

For its part in crushing the swindlers, the *Press* was nominated for a public service Pulitzer Prize by the Associated Advertising Clubs of the World. It did not win but only later was Fort Worth to learn why.

The Pulitzer Prize committee had questioned the *Star-Telegram* on the *Press*'s worthiness of the coveted award and the letter of inquiry found its way to Byron Utecht, a longtime political writer. Utecht promptly gutted the *Press*.

In his reply, Utecht claimed the *Press* had little influence on any of the oil-swindle prosecutions. Utecht quoted Zweifel as saying, "The *Press* had nothing to do with bringing about prosecution of Cook or the many others. . . ." The *Press*, Utecht noted in an aside to the Pulitzer jury, "has only a small street circulation."

The *Press* did not win its Pulitzer Prize.

A copy of the condemning letter somehow arrived in the *Press*'s office, and on July 17, 1924, the paper bannered an intriguing headline: "HERE'S A LITTLE 'INSIDE' STUFF, FOLKS!—IT'S

ABOUT THE *PRESS*, PULITZER PRIZE, *STAR-TELEGRAM* AND THE OIL STOCK CROOK."

Utecht's letter was printed in full.

Sweet revenge, but only momentary. For all of its feistiness, the *Press* never was a challenge to the *Star-Telegram*—never more than a minor irritant, like a bunion.

It self-destructed in 1975, finally written off forever by Scripps-Howard. It had endured twenty years beyond Amon Carter. Once when he cussed the poor *Press* in one of his mad spells, someone asked him why he hated the rival newspaper so much.

"Because," he snapped, "their gawddam delivery boy walks across my yard."

In the very earliest years, Fort Worth newspapers had a kinship with their more cosmopolitan cousins. Single copies were sold by boys and men who actually shouted "Extra!" and "Read All About It!" just as actors did in all those Pat O'Brien reporter movies.

The street urchins generally were a motley bunch, mostly poor, life-hardened, wise, and young, playing a hardscrabble game of survival on the pavement. Those corner gladiators schemed and fought to gain, then hold, the busiest and best positions, protecting what was theirs and, without conscience, beating out a lesser boy or older man for an improved location. Territorial disputes were resolved with strong talk, fists, and at least once, clubs, and were grand forms of public entertainment, much as Europe's street acrobats. The weakest and oldest were pushed outward from downtown until, just as Indians settled the problem of their infirm and elderly, they were left to die in warehouse districts and slums where newspaper street sales were as rare as hope.

Amon Carter allied himself with the little newsboys. He saw in the often-savage corner corsairs the poverty and combativeness of his youth. He kept his office door open to them and in later years, sought out the more successful graduates to speak lovingly of the good times. There were many alumni of those street guerrilla wars. A chief of detectives. The director of New York's cotton exchange. Merchants and millionaires, scholars, oilmen, ranchers, and bums. With an enviable left jab and swing-from-the-heels right hand, a thin Ben Hogan commanded a select corner bunker before moving his skinned knuckles to the caddy lot of Glen Garden Country Club, where he competed for golfing coins with another Fort Worth youngster, Byron Nelson.

For his boys, Amon staged annual dinners at which he praised their salesmanship and handed out silver dollars to each. There was a newsboy baseball team and during World War I, drill squads. The boulevard foot soldiers performed the manual of arms with broomsticks and practiced other army skills just in case America stumbled and the Kaiser's troops laid siege to the *Star-Telegram* building. Carter fondly called them the country's Second Front and often, after the forced marches, he joined the boys as they awaited another edition to peddle.

Carter asked their opinions about the *Star-Telegram*, which stories sold papers, what the readers liked and disliked. Because of a newsboy suggestion, he instructed Harold Hough to place the multicolored comic section outside the large Sunday edition. The move made street customers instantly recognize the *Star-Telegram* among competing newspapers and incidentally showed that West Texans were more interested in "Mutt and Jeff" than Watch on the Rhine.

One boy, DeWitt Reddick, told Carter of another sales gimmick. In black sections of Fort Worth, newsboys flipped the Sunday comic sections to the "Bringing Up Father" strip whose Maggie and Jiggs were a favorite of black readers.

Carter never forgot his newsboys, even when the vendor system was outdated and youngsters on bicycles delivered papers to homes. He gave each a money gift at Thanksgiving and Christmas, and provided in his will for the holiday cash to continue years after his death.

The newsboys were his pets and he forgave them any wickedness. Once, as he arrived at the *Star-Telegram*, a newsboy shot him in the nose with an air rifle. Possibly it was a stray shot. Probably not. Carter stumbled into his office, clutching a handkerchief to blot flowing blood and tears, bellowing, "Gawddammit, get that boy!"

The sniper was gone for, collared, and dragged in front of the publisher's desk. Amon glared at the awe-stricken boy. He began yelling, beating his fists on the desk, shouting about the mighty sin of shooting the nose of one's employer, the words falling like whip ends on the terrified youngster. The boy began sobbing, crying of how sorry he was to have shot Carter, of how he supported his family. Amon sighed deeply.

"All right . . . all right," Carter said peevishly, "just don't do it again."

He handed the boy a silver dollar. The kid fled. Amon dabbed his bloody handkerchief to his wounded nose and mumbled, "Gawddammed boy. . . ."

Daily, as *Star-Telegrams* came off presses, the news hustlers massed to fight for stacks of papers, to be first on the street with the latest editions, and reporters gathered to look on the melee in wide-eyed wonder. A mite of a lad, fatherless, and the only support of his mother and sisters, seemed the fastest and most aggressive of the boys.

His name was Monroe Odom. He had an urgent punching technique, bluish-gray owl eyes, was at best semiliterate, at worst, mildly retarded. He spoke with a slurred voice, a speech defect he later used as a valuable selling tool. Time has obscured Monroe's arrival as a *Star-Telegram* newspaper hawker, but legend says he was five or ten—the story was told with both ages—when he asked Amon for a job. Amon assayed little Monroe.

"Here," said Amon, passing over twenty papers. "Sell these in an hour and you have a job."

Fifteen minutes later, Monroe was tugging at Amon's coattail. His pockets hung heavy with silver dollars. Monroe had dashed to the nearest saloon, reasoning that drinkers would buy anything from a small boy with a speech impediment. For less than two bits worth of newspapers Monroe had collected eleven dollars. Amon hired him instantly, and for the next fifty-three years, Monroe Odom peddled the *Star-Telegram.*

At first he was a rover. Then he fought and held the better corners. Ultimately, he settled at the Worth Hotel's front door where his stand was a pinewood fruit box. Amon awarded him the position. When the Worth opened in 1927, Amon selected Monroe to snip the official ribbon. There he stayed for the rest of his life, outliving the news vendor system and outmaneuvering the soulless coin machines. Not until his death did the *Star-Telegram* place a coin-operated vending machine outside its own building because it would have encroached on Monroe's territory.

Monroe was king of the block. His stand faced Seventh Street, was within a block of four banks, a federal-center complex, dozens of oil company headquarters, opposite the posh Petroleum Club, beside the even posher Fort Worth Club, adjacent to the Worth Theater, and across the street from the *Star-Telegram*. Amon could look down from his corner office and watch Monroe at his news-peddling beat.

Monroe was there, rain or shine, in cold and heat, and he claimed he was the best newspaper salesman in the world. Possibly he was. His customers included bank, oil company, and college presidents. Most bought a paper daily from Monroe, and paid a considerable tip, although they also received the *Star-Telegram* at home. Amon rarely left his office without the latest edition in his pocket, yet he bought a newspaper from Monroe each time he passed. He paid a dollar a copy.

Monroe was not an official *Star-Telegram* employee. He was an independent merchant who bought wholesale and sold retail, plus tip. He rarely accepted the printed price of a nickel. If one bought from Monroe, one paid premium rates. A new reporter once strolled into the hotel coffee shop for a late lunch. Monroe called, "Paper, mister?"

"I work for the *Star-Telegram*," the reporter explained.

"So what?" mumbled Monroe.

Weeks later, the reporter wrote of a lost boy. At lunch, Monroe came to the newsman's table, sat and began complimenting him. "Kids sell newspapers," said Monroe. "You see a copy yet?"

"No, not yet."

Monroe handed the reporter a newspaper with the lost boy story on the front page. The reporter had no change. He gave Monroe a fifty-cent coin. Monroe shuffled out with it.

The reporter had been "Monroed." Most every reporter and editor was "Monroed" at one time or another. It was a common and active verb meaning that Monroe once again had sold them one of their own newspapers.

Editors learned to cross the street on poor news days rather than face Monroe. His judgment of story values was based on street sales. Disaster was marketable, routine was not. Editors called that "The Monroe Doctrine." Once, a major Washington official was fired and the story ran on for days while a board of inquiry investigated. Monroe hooked an editor on the street.

"This Washington stir was real good the first day," he advised, "but the investigation stuff is gettin' thin. Let's go with something else tomorrow."

As all good businessmen, Monroe changed with the times. In later years he learned that people no longer wanted news shouted at them. "Extra!" died with high paper costs and time-and-a-half wages. Monroe began mumbling the news in his indistinct, impeded voice. His peculiar style also included the right to select the story subject to be sold. A headline need not be on the front page for him to promote its message.

One customer heard Monroe mumbling about "World War Three." He bought a paper but found nothing on the front page about war. He returned and challenged Monroe. "Page 10-A," Monroe answered, and there, printed under a one-column headline was a four-inch story quoting a government official as saying that WWIII was unlikely in an age of nuclear stalemate.

Monroe tailored his pitch to fit the customer. If an oilman approached he would pick up on a petroleum industry story. At noon, when hundreds of federal employees hit the streets, Monroe had a civil service headline ready for them. A businessman passed the hotel one day after his daughter's wedding and Monroe captured him with "Debutante Weds." In the 1930s, when the Sino-Japanese conflict was a page-one item, the Japan Cotton Trading Company had offices in a nearby building; as the Japanese office staff emerged for lunch, Monroe had news from home.

Years of standing on concrete sidewalks caused him to limp badly. He spoke with that slurred voice and it became permanently hoarse. His working uniform was a canvas change apron, wrinkled khaki trousers, worn shoes too comfortable to throw away, and a plastic-billed military-style cap. From his stand, he hailed his customers, or collected. Monroe gave credit. Beeman Fisher, president of Texas Electric Service Company, began paying Monroe one dollar weekly, collectible each Friday. Whenever Fisher passed, Monroe handed him a newspaper. Soon Fisher was paying two dollars, then five dollars a week.

At Christmas, Fisher gave Monroe a Yuletide bonus. Monroe, though technically not an employee, also was on the *Star-Telegram* Christmas bonus list. Incredibly, he received machine-printed Christmas bonus checks from at least three oil companies and one bank, becoming a kind of public entity to be maintained as one would a symphony orchestra or city park.

Monroe was such a familiar presence that on days when he was ill and did not arrive for work, people called the newspaper office to ask about him. Hotel managers came and went during the four decades without disturbing the old man with whom they shared a building. Once, a new manager looked at the pine crate and Monroe blocking the hotel entrance and ordered a desk clerk to "get rid of that old man out there." The manager was told that he would go before Monroe, and he did.

When Amon Jr. became a teenager, his father decided it was time to teach the youngster the newspaper business, and put him on the street selling at Monroe's side. "You might as well begin at the top," said the proud father. Amon Jr. became publisher after his father died and Monroe went to see his former assistant. "I just wanted you to know I plan to go on selling the *Star-Telegram*," said Monroe, assuring Amon Jr. that the empire would not crumble.

Many of his customers were celebrities passing through town. Gary Cooper came to Fort Worth in 1940 for the premiere of his latest movie, "The Westerner," and Amon introduced the cowboy star to Monroe. At the premiere hour, Cooper could not be located and press agents were frantic. They found him in the hotel coffee shop talking to Monroe. "Don't go away," said Cooper as the movie men were pulling him out of the restaurant. "I'll be right back."

During World War II, packs of Hollywood stars visited Fort Worth to sell war bonds. Barbara Stanwyck greeted Monroe with "Spencer Tracy said to tell you 'Hello.'" Will Rogers gave Monroe

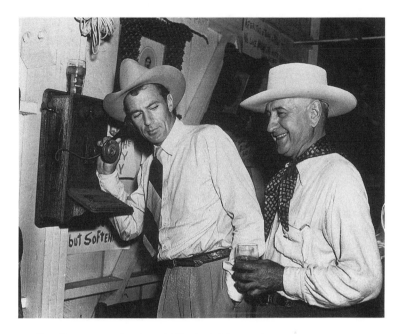

Gary Cooper samples Amon's Shady Oak hospitality, c. 1940.

twenty dollars for a newspaper, the largest single-copy price he ever received. The humorist became a favorite customer. When in town he stayed in Amon's Fort Worth Club suite, and each evening Monroe would deliver a newspaper to him. Once Rogers asked Monroe to stay for dinner and ordered filet mignon. Meal finished, Monroe thanked Rogers, adding, "Wish you'd tell 'em a little more well-done next time, Will."

"OK, Monroe," laughed Rogers.

Monroe sold newspapers to Ike and FDR and a half-dozen Texas governors. John Connally lived in Fort Worth before he became governor, and when he returned as Texas's new chief official, staying in the Worth Hotel, Monroe handed him a newspaper. "First one's free, John," smiled Monroe.

Of Monroe's encounters with celebrities, his escapade with magician Harry Blackstone has passed into legend. Monroe

Amon and FDR fishing in one of Amon's Shady Oak bass ponds.

never needed a ticket to enter the Worth Theater. He just strolled in between editions. One year Blackstone brought his magic show to the theater. The featured act was his famous escape from a wooden packing crate. At each performance, Blackstone called for volunteers on stage to nail him into the box. Show after show, Monroe watched as audience members used the magician's hammer and nails. Blackstone always escaped on cue.

Then came the closing performance. Blackstone asked for volunteers and Monroe shuffled down the aisle. He wore a carpenter's apron bulging with spike-sized nails and carried a heavy hammer. Monroe beat a steady tattoo around the box. Each nail was crossed with another, virtually welded into the wood. Orchestra members heard the perplexed Blackstone muttering, "What the hell's going on?"

Monroe ended his hammering and stepped back. The curtain closed and the band struck up Blackstone's escape music. Three times the orchestra played the music, the curtain opened and the box still was there. No escaped Blackstone. On the fourth curtain call, an assistant dressed like Blackstone stepped out and took a quick face-concealing bow. Lights dimmed quickly and the movie began.

The theater manager later revealed that the wooden box had to be destroyed to free Blackstone.

Monroe died one cool February evening shortly before midnight. A circulation supervisor found him on the sidewalk beside his stack of newspapers. At his funeral, the chapel was filled with businessmen, judges, *Star-Telegram* editors and reporters. Anonymously, Amon Jr. insisted on paying for the funeral. Other customers contributed to a fund for Monroe's widow. The *Star-Telegram* placed Monroe's obituary on its front page and as services were being conducted, the Texas legislature adopted a resolution honoring "The memory of this distinguished gentleman, Monroe Odom."

At the funeral hour, a wreath was placed on the old pinewood box and a chill wind tossed the ends of the black ribbons. People on the street wanting *Star-Telegrams* that day and forever more fed coins to a plastic machine.

7

I kinda thought I'd never see
A better host than what I be,
But H'elza Maxwell's just a starter
When it comes to Amon Carter
    —Poem by famed society hostess Elsa Maxwell, written
    in Amon's Shady Oak Farm guest book, 1938

"Dad," she asked, "What is the 'Creed of the West?'"
"To treat everybody right, then make them treat you right," I said.
    —Frank Norfleet, *Norfleet*, 1924

. . . Amon in Wonderland . . .
    —Damon Runyon, describing Amon's lifestyle, circa
    1930s

A Texan is a Texan wherever he may be.
    —One of Amon's favorite braggy statements

Amon Carter, wrote Alva Johnston in the *Saturday Evening Post*, loved crowds like a pickpocket. He glowed and gloried among mobs. Kings and presidents delighted him, washerwomen entertained him, celebrities charmed him. He never wanted to be alone. Silence made him nervous and he talked to anyone and everyone who would listen, common strangers if friends were not around.

People were Amon's fanciest doodads. His guest books at Shady Oak Farm and Suite 10G in the Fort Worth Club read like Fortune's 500 list, like society's blue-blooded roster, like a political roll call: Duponts and Mellons and Roosevelts, the Eisenhowers, Babe Ruth and the Whitneys, Amelia Earhart and Prince Bernhardt of the Netherlands, Ken Maynard and Lady Duff Cooper, Doolittle and Rickenbacker and Firestone, Durante, Nimitz and Luce.

From Charlie McCarthy to Buzz Aldrin—a young lieutenant who one day would become an astronaut and the first man to urinate on the moon—no one could escape. Shady Oak and Suite 10G became bountiful watering holes for pilgrims on transcontinental crossings.

"To visit Fort Worth without meeting Amon Carter," said an English baronet, Sir William Wiseman, "is to see 'Hamlet' without the Prince of Denmark."

In Fort Worth, the famous became Amon's guests and no arguing. "Nothin' costs nothin', either," as Jimmy Durante described the experience. Amon's hospitality, always munificent, was free, every howdy and handshake of it. He was a grand host, gracious and thoughtful and generous, or as the unbridled cowboy, wildly comic and uninhibited—whichever personality was needed.

"There's no meter on 10G," Amon was fond of saying when guests tried to force payment on him. The unofficial slogan of Shady Oak was "Light, stranger, and eat." Guests were given bed and board, booze, entertainment, and publicity, the latter a preferential lagniappe for celebrities. A man with a newspaper, radio stations, access to wire services, and a genuine brilliance for warm conviviality was a real blessing to those with large egos.

Everything was on the house. Amon's house. What must have seemed at times to Bert Honea and Jimmy North as fiscal madness had for Amon a substantive basis. He was selling Fort Worth and no price was too high. Whatever he paid, Amon believed, was money well spent.

Well, actually, the *Star-Telegram* paid, perhaps as much as $100,000 a year. Bert Honea, for whom dollars were divine, said he didn't care to add it up. Amon just partied and the newspaper paid the freight.

Though he entertained most often in Fort Worth, Amon was not above tossing a banquet for friends in Chicago or staging a boozy extravaganza in New York at places like "21" or the Stork Club or Gay Nineties, where he ordered drinks for the house, led sing-alongs in his off-key baritone, and recited ribald toasts such as:

"Here's to Eve
The mother of our race
She wore fig leaves
In the proper place
Here's to Adam
The father of us all
He was Johnny on the spot
When the leaves began to fall"

Amon liked to play and when the need struck him he played with whomever he could find. *New York World-Telegram* columnist Frank Farrell reported that Amon escorted two Ritz-Carlton room service waiters to the Stork Club, "where he partied them." Lucius Beebe, in his book *The Big Spenders*, wrote, "Carter's notion of showing good will, and one that was widely approved by its beneficiaries, was to arrive in New York's Waldorf-Astoria for the annual newspaper publishers convention, take over an entire floor and throw all the keys out the windows onto Park Avenue. He then kept open house like a maharaja for the duration."

That was Amon: festive and sociable, peddling Fort Worth, which badly needed whatever boosting he could do. His gregarious nature required an audience and his ego enjoyed the friendships. He was never without letters or telegrams from his famous friends, and without provocation would loose the messages on everyone, bragging outrageously. He bored hometown folks endlessly with accounts of his escapades among America's high and mighty.

Famous guests all were pieces of Amon's grand conspiracy to promote Fort Worth into national prominence. Anyone honored with a party, photographed and placed on page one, interviewed for the airwaves, gifted with expensive gadgets, was unlikely to forget the occasion or the city or the host. And if the celebrity owned a shred of conscience, he responded when Amon called for help.

Matthew Brush was a railroad executive. He admired aloud the Shady Oak blue crystal drinking glasses, for which Amon had paid fifteen dollars each. Instantly, Amon presented Brush with a dozen glasses. For years, the publisher had been pressing for a new Fort Worth rail terminal, and wanted Brush in his debt. Amon could have had his terminal earlier if he had not insisted that it be larger than one in Dallas; Brush had vetoed that idea.

Months after receiving the glasses, Brush telephoned Amon to announce, "We have just voted to build your goddamned Union station. We have eleven million dollars to build the station and biggest shops and freight terminal in the Southwest. And now we are all drinking to your health with your glasses.

"What," exclaimed Brush, "do you think of that?"

"Have another drink!" commanded Amon.

Flattered by his attention, charmed by his courtly western manners, celebrities responded with respect and friendship. Elsa Maxwell, the legendary hostess, wrote in *Town and Country Magazine* that she had four important men in her life: "My father, Caruso, Cole Porter and Amon Carter." Damon Runyon, the columnist and author, compared Amon with his father, calling him a "breezy swashbuckler of a man." Bob Hope authored a magazine article naming Amon the most fascinating man he had ever met. Sidney Smith, the "Gumps" cartoonist, often placed Amon in the comic strip, once having Andy Gump tell his wife, Min, of an approaching party, "Amon Carter is bringing the Emperor of China. Fred Bonfils [*Denver Post* publisher] is going to hitch up his buggy for the Prince of Wales."

As publicity-conscious as he was, Amon pretended a modesty about the whole thing, a personal shyness that he wore well and one that spawned a playful game with his *Star-Telegram* photographers. If there were famous people to be photographed, the cameraman lined up his shot as Amon stood demurely to the side. Invariably, one of the celebrities would call out, "Amon, come on and get in the picture."

His stock answer—photographers could repeat it by rote—was: "No, no. Every time I have my picture in the paper, we lose 5,000 subscribers."

That was the photographer's cue to say, "Mr. Carter, I believe we better have you in the picture."

"All right," Amon always replied, obeying reluctantly, "if you say so."

Then he stood in the middle of the group where no editor could crop him out—as if one dared.

Amon's zeal to record on film all his hosted gatherings strained the newspaper's photography department. He always furnished pictures to the guests, and the *Star-Telegram* finally hired a lab man who did nothing but print Amon's photos. A common Amon photo-order could number as many as seven hundred pictures.

Many of the photos landed on the newspaper's front page in space, editors grumbled, that could be better used for real news. The *Star-Telegram*, however, was just another cog in Amon's publicity machine. Once an airport advisory board of the Federal Aviation Administration convened in Fort Worth to discuss the city's request for a new air facility. Amon commanded that each man be photographed daily and the photos be printed on page one of both morning and evening editions. The editors howled, and Amon explained, "You may think this is silly but it's necessary to get our new airport."

Very little of importance was successful in Fort Worth without Amon Carter's imprimatur. If you sold him, you sold the project. He would hurl his communications empire, his energies, his money into the enterprise and make it happen. The story of Fort Worth in the first half of the twentieth century is the story of

Amon Carter hustling this and that event into national exposure. When Amon press-agented, he booned every doggle.

In 1941, Fort Worth golfers asked Amon to support their bid for the U.S. Open. According to columnist Bob Considine—and surely this is an exaggeration—Amon thundered, "What the tarnation is a U.S. Open?"

He agreed to help and the prestigious sporting event came to Fort Worth—the smallest city in which it had been played and its first venture into the south.

The tournament secured, Amon began promoting. Considine again: "He invited President Roosevelt, all members of his cabinet, Jim Farley, heads of U.S. and Bethlehem Steel, heads of a veritable Dun & Bradstreet bookful of big firms to attend the Open. He sent them all gold badges with their names engraved on them. He chartered floors of hotels, had the city airport cleared for the arrival of private planes and told his city to open its heart to the golfers."

Amon hosted five hundred golfers and guests at Shady Oak. Understanding that sportswriters would report all that went on around the tournament, he gave each a Shady Oak hat and feted the scribes with a special barbecue. In return, the writers presented Amon with the One-Holer Award—a garishly decorated commode lid—and named him "Texas Ace in the Hole, Prince of Hosts, Judge of Good Wines, Beautiful Women, Fine Food and Salty Song." Considine and Grantland Rice credited Amon with the tournament's unqualified success, and incidentally spread Fort Worth's name from coast-to-coast, which is all he wanted.

The One-Holer Award plaque was duly posted at Shady Oak Farm, joining the talking steer, tiger skin, cigar store Indians, and other exotic gallimaufry accumulated by Amon. He bought the 780-acre farm in 1925 from heirs of George Reynolds, a pioneer West Texas rancher. Spread along shores of Lake Worth, the farm was a landscape of blackjack and live oaks and, in season, Texas bluebonnets, Indian paintbrush, and wild daisies. There was a big farmhouse with shaded verandah and a white picket fence festooned with running roses. Nearby were a barn and corrals

and an open-fronted shed that served as a saloon for his extravaganzas, and ponds stocked with bass.

The house was a museum of Amon's curiosities: Mrs. Jarrott's
huge dining room table from his boarding house days in Bowie,
the inventory of a small hardware store in keys to cities given
Amon and in gilded spades and trowels, the spoils of groundbreakings and cornerstone layings. An array of mounted steer
horns and several animal heads, including one stuffed buffalo
head. Footballs from Texas Christian University's fighting
Horned Frog teams and a baseball autographed by the Black Sox
of 1919. A ten-gallon loving cup, post cards, Indian arrowheads,
the church bell heard by his mother as a child, and a hand-carved
desk (one drawer was stuffed with bits of string Amon saved for
emergencies). Above the fireplace was an intricately designed
wicker eagle. President Roosevelt received the bird from an artist
in the 1930s. FDR gave it to General Hugh Johnson who ordered
an aide to "send that damned old thing to Amon Carter."

The mantle was dominated by the ignoble animated head of an
enormous longhorn steer, which puffed smoke from its nostrils,
blinked with red, sixty-watt eyes, called guests by their names—
called them in fact bawdy and outrageous names—and sang off-
color songs in a voice with a slight needle-scratch. Quite often,
the steer whooped for Fort Worth and West Texas.

Outside, real longhorns grazed on the lawn, joined by a flop-
eared gray mule, the latter a gift from Harold Hough who operated the Hired Hand's Mule Ranch near Decatur—"High-grade
fancy mules but not too high-tone to pull a plow." Nearby was a
reconstructed log cabin in which Cynthia Ann Parker—mother
of the last great Indian chief, Quanah Parker—lived after her rescue by Colonel Sul Ross.

Travelair Monoplane Number 17 was retired to the farm by
the National Air Transport Authority. It had carried Fort Worth's
first bundle of airmail and bore the inscription, "To aeronautical
inspectors, United States Department of Commerce, August 1,
1931. Mr. Amon Carter has retired this ship to a peaceful existence during its declining years. Its permanent station is his own
'front yard' at Shady Oak Farm. . . . He guarantees it will never-
more take the air in pursuit of pleasure, profit or diversion of any

kind. It likewise has been 'retired' on the records of the department in Washington and its existing license number may remain in place until old age and remorse have taken their toll. [Signed] Clarence M. Young, Assistant Secretary of Commerce."

Additionally, there was the plow that broke ground when Fort Worth's first railroad reached town. And Paul Whiteman installed a forty-foot flagpole because Amon chided the orchestra leader, "You wouldn't know a flagpole from a fence post."

His parties centered on the open-fronted saloon and through the years it, too, became a repository of miscellany. There was a stuffed horse, on the tail of which Amon sometimes mounted a sign reading: "Texas Horse's Ass, You've met the New York kind." Other signs changed with the needs of a party—"Dallas Passports Must Be Validated," "Please Do Not Sit on the Cracker-barrel, It Annoys the Cat," "The Customer Is Always Right Sometimes," "Your Wife Just Phoned," and "The National Bird: Old Crow." Above the shed's opening was "Howdy, Stranger" in neon, a garish greeting sign Amon swiped from the entrance of Fort Worth's 1936 Frontier Fiesta.

In that setting Amon held a noisy, kaleidoscopic court. Disguised in his cowboy suit, astride the golden palomino, mounted in the silver-encrusted saddle, riding through shoulder-to-shoulder crowds, firing off his six-shooters, yippeeing for Fort Worth and West Texas—Amon at home, at play, an exuberant, unforgettable man.

Shady Oak, observed Alva Johnston, was a "sort of one-man Bohemian Grove . . . a millionaire and celebrity trap." It was there Johnston counted eight billion dollars bellied up to the bar one evening, and there, for one large party, that the evening's bartenders were Walter Teagle, president of Standard Oil of New Jersey; Herbert Pratt, president of Standard Oil of New York, and Charles Mitchell, president of National City Bank of New York. It was there Mayor Jimmy Walker pranced in his new high-heeled cowboy boots and posed for photographs with Lan Twohig's old steer horns, that H. L. Mencken, via WBAP radio, spoke of "Yokelry" and America's "Majority of Morons," that one later evening young Lyndon Baines Johnson lit into a fellow Democrat and was licking the man pretty good when other revelers pulled the brawlers apart, and that dignified and aristocratic Elsa Maxwell fired Amon's six-guns, whoopeeing like a soiled dove from Hell's Half Acre. It was also there that FDR, seated in the rear of an open Packard touring car, cast for and caught a five-pound bass, and that one of the world's richest men, banker Otto Kahn, insisted on paying for his grub by mowing the lawn.

Amon Carter made Shady Oak Farm an escape place where his friends could act out their western fantasies. Lord Sidney Rothermere, board chairman of the London *Daily Mail* and seventy other English newspapers and magazines, said of his two months in America that he most remembered the time spent at Shady Oak. The eminent British Lord, aides told Amon, would not under any circumstance play cowboy with him. Within a day, Amon was calling Rothermere "Sid" and had him rigged out in boots and chaps and a huge, high-crowned black hat, the kind worn only by enemies of Hopalong Cassidy. While *Star-Telegram* photographers recorded the scene for posterity, Sid Rothermere, a brand-new Texas good ol' boy, fast-drew his .45-caliber hogleg and "held up" a pair of passing cowpokes.

Amon presented the pistol to Rothermere, and the English Lord carried it to his castle in the Scottish Highlands where he mounted the gun in the smoking room as a reminder of adventuring in Amon's Wild, Wild West.

Amon's Shady Oak soirees mostly were stag affairs, where men could whoop it up without offending the womenfolk, but each New Year's Eve began an outing, often lasting forty-eight hours, for both husbands and wives. Though more restrained than usual, the party featured gambling and drinking and, invitations were sought eagerly by Fort Worth's high-society set.

Other socialities were hand-built for the honoree. Amon tossed a twelfth-birthday party for Jim Farley's son and outfitted the boy in cowboy duds while *March of Time* cameras filmed the occasion for nationwide movie audiences. For Otto Kahn, there was a special mint julep in his name, business cards reading, "For Small Loans with Good Collateral and Snappy Interest, See Otto Kahn," and above the bar a ten-foot-long sign announcing, "Bawl Eagle Saloon, Kahn, Loeb & Company/Financial Agents." Amon hosted a "shindig" for Farley and Cactus Jack Garner in 1933 with mammoth "Garner for President" banners. Conde Nast, the *Vogue* publisher, and Henry Luce of *Time* were inducted into the Longhorn Society of Fort Worth, a mythical organization founded by Amon.

When Amon stood on tables, fired his pistols in the air, and shouted "Time to eat!" the menus offered exotic dishes. An American Petroleum Institute audience was fed "Panhandle Mountain Oysters without the Fuzz [deep-fried calf testicles]," "Grilled Larded Snowbirds [white-wing doves]," and "Lubricants from the Refinery and A Bit of Tidewater." Guests received deeds to the city, gold badges naming them as honorary Fort Worth police officers, and hollow walking canes filled with bourbon (seventeen-year-old Ol' Fitzgerald bottled under the Shady Oak label). The menu for an American Airlines evening in 1945 presented more basic fare: red beans, black-eyed peas and sowbelly, sweet potato pie, chitlins, watermelon, "light bread," and "rat trap" cheese.

It was a party hosted, read a card, by "The Sanitary Receptacle Company, Amon G. Carter, Secretary & Treasurer."

Seemingly without effort, Amon could bring in real cowboys and cowgirls and host an honest rodeo, or erect a full-curtained stage for more formal entertainment. A 1940 party was highlighted by the "Shady Oak Follies" starring stripper Vanya Karanova and Kathryn Duffy's all-nude ensemble acting out "Satan's Dream" and "The Devil's Daughter." The acts were imported for the evening from Chicago's Chez Paree.

John Carl Kriendler, the "21" restaurant owner, honeymooned at Shady Oak with his new wife, the Baroness Luisa Dumont de Chassart, and Amon presented her with cowgirl clothes to match her husband's western wardrobe which, he told a *Star-Telegram* reporter, numbered "130 cowboy shirts, five dozen pairs of pants, three dozen western hats, three silver saddles, 26 pairs of boots [and] 20 rodeo suits."

The western hat Amon gave the Baroness was swapped for her chapeau, a flowery pillbox thing, duly autographed and tossed among the other famous headgear scattered around the farmhouse. Being presented with a Shady Oak hat was a rite of passage into Amon's world and most, but not all, celebrities received the famous western toppers.

It was an expensive gesture by Amon. The hats cost thirty-five dollars each and Amon bought them in such numbers that *Hat Life*, an industry publication, proclaimed him the "world's greatest retail hat customer."

Originally, the hats were western traditional—huge, wide-brimmed, high-crowned, either black or white, bought from the Barsalina Company of Italy. When Mussolini declared war on Ethiopia, Amon turned to an American manufacturer, the Stetson Company, which, after months of design research, began producing the Shady Oak model. He bought them through Washer Brothers, an old-line Fort Worth store, and later through Peters Brothers, a downtown hat shop.

Stetson's "Open Road" Shady Oak hat was of a "silver-belly shade," had a shorter crown and brim of 2²/₃ inches, looked western, but could be worn in Washington or New York without ridicule or embarrassment or having one's friends believe that you rustled cows for a living.

No one knows how many hats Amon gave away, but at least many, many thousands. The hat became his trademark, and for three decades America's best-known personalities wore nothing but Amon Carter Shady Oak hats. Patrick Hurley, FDR's first secretary of war, Will Rogers, Bernard Baruch and Cornelius Vanderbilt Whitney once met for lunch in Los Angeles and each was wearing an Amon Carter hat.

There was a kind of ceremonial ritual for the hat presentation. First, the recipient had to autograph his own hat before exchanging it for a new one. "Just another bum hat trade," and "This hat is a damn sight better than I am trading for" were Will Rogers's scribbled comments on two hats he left behind.

Inscribed on the new hatband was "Shady Oak Farm, Fort Worth, Texas, Where the West Begins. The Latch String Always Hangs Outside. Amon Carter." In bestowing the hat, Amon customarily warned, "Now, don't leave this any place you shouldn't. My name's in it." The ceremony, said reporter Mack Williams, was fashioned with a rigid pecking order. "At the bottom of the ladder were those who received a Shady Oak hat with no mention in the *Star-Telegram*." More important visitors received a hat and a small story printed inside the paper. Next level was a one-column photo. Most eminent of celebrities, remembered Williams, received their hats while standing beside the John Nance Garner bust in Amon's office. Two-column pictures of those presentations were printed on the *Star-Telegram*'s front page.

Reporters always were dragged into Amon's civic boosting schemes. Beyond the usual news duties of Bascom Timmons, the newspaper's Washington bureau chief, was the maintenance of a file on head sizes of every important Washington official. Periodically, Amon hosted a Washington dinner and distributed hats, awarding the headgear in alphabetical order to avoid bruised egos.

Williams got entangled in a hat ordeal when Douglas MacArthur came to Texas. Harry Truman had fired the general and friends urged him to seek the presidency. Testing political waters, MacArthur scheduled a series of speeches in Texas sponsored by Scripps-Howard newspapers. Williams and photographer John Mazziotta were assigned to follow MacArthur around the state. Newsmen from every important American paper, and all wire services, as well as many foreign journalists, were in the traveling press party, and the *Star-Telegram* men were delighted to be among their profession's best reporters and writers.

In Houston, his final stop before the general came to Fort Worth, Williams was preparing to take notes on the speech when he was summoned to the telephone. "Mr. Carter wants you to get the hat size of every out-of-town reporter," a *Star-Telegram* editor told him. "He wants to give them Shady Oak hats when they get to Fort Worth."

"I can get them for you in an hour," replied Williams, "the general's speaking now. . . ."

"Hold on a minute," instructed the editor. He left the line. Long minutes passed. The editor returned and said, ". . . uh . . . Mr. Carter says to hell with the speech. Get those hat sizes now."

Decades later, Williams remembered: "So while General MacArthur spoke for the ages, and the world's best reporters scribbled busily, the only notes I made were sizes copied from hats piled on a press room bench. Mr. Carter had his own priorities."

Just why and when Amon Carter began giving away western hats has been lost to history, but perhaps the tradition began as early as 1923 when he attended a London advertising conference. Delegates were invited to a morning garden party at St. James's Palace, a formal affair hosted by the Prince of Wales (later Duke of Windsor). Amon struck upon the idea of giving his cowboy hat to the prince, and spoke with several imperial minions, all of whom dismissed the idea, indicating that British royalty would never knowingly participate in such an undignified ceremony.

Eleven-thirty on the morning of July 22, Amon arrived at the palace dressed in striped morning pants and his movie-villain-black cowboy hat which, at the very least, wrote *New York Sun* publisher Gilbert Hodges, arrested everyone's immediate attention. The prince's aides attempted to head Amon off at the pass. He charged through them to the startled prince and went into his presentation spiel. The prince was delighted, reported *Printer's Ink*, and said a western hat was exactly what he always had wanted. That even may have been the truth because in August the prince passed through New York to his Canadian ranch and was photographed by the *New York World*. The royal scion smiled broadly under Amon's cowboy hat.

Harry Truman, whom Amon did not like because of Truman's anti-Texas position on offshore oil, was given only the standard Shady Oak hat, as were Presidents Coolidge and Hoover, who, being Republicans, weren't considered very important. There was another very special Stetson worn by Amon and a few of his peers, among them FDR and Churchill. It was pure beaver, embellished by ermine, and cost $150. Hornby and Freiburg, a Chicago men's store, displayed one of the fancy hats. The accompanying sign read: "This $150 Stetson is the finest hat we know of. It is a duplicate of the one worn by Amon Carter, picturesque and influential Fort Worth publisher."

Those Shady Oak hats were presented in distinctive red-satin cases while Amon's lesser hats were handed over in bunches, to whole football teams, to boards of directors, to an entire Hollywood cast attending a world premiere in Fort Worth. The record: two thousand hats given in one evening to delegates of an American Petroleum Institute convention.

Amon Carter hats became legend, and columnists often wrote of them. After the 1936 election, Damon Runyon told of a Republican who bet a Democratic friend that Roosevelt would not carry twenty states. The Republican promised to eat his hat if he lost. He was wearing a Shady Oak hat and, as Runyon explained, "The Indians in Texas collect Mr. Carter's discarded hats and use them for teepees. The hats are quite roomy."

The Republican, Runyon suggested, had bitten off more than he could chew. A French chef was located who claimed he "once cooked a buffalo, so why not a hat?" The chef pounded it thoroughly with a sledgehammer and then broiled it over charcoal, "basting it constantly in its own juices."

Delicately, the chef julienned Amon's hat "into thin slices and served [it] with a rich deviled sauce. The man said it tasted better than spinach. It had a fine nutty taste."

Involved though they were with the hat rites, and lust though they might for the expensive headgear, *Star-Telegram* newsmen were never considered eligible receivers. George Dolan admired the hats and wanted one. He was drafted to cover a hat presentation to Harvey Firestone and other tire company executives in Suite 10G. Amon asked for sizes, then selected the proper hat for each man. Finished, Amon was aware that one man—Dolan—did not have a hat.

"What about you?" the publisher asked.

Delighted, but wary, Dolan replied, ". . . uh . . . I work for you, Mr. Carter."

"Oh," muttered Amon and closed the closet door on Dolan's hat.

Only Jack Butler and photographers Al Panzera and John Mazziotta were known to have received hats. Panzera and Mazziotta photographed Amon presenting hats to a TCU football team and afterwards were told to select hats for themselves. Panzera, a misplaced New Yorker, wore his hat home to Brooklyn and presented it to his father. Later the father wrote that he had taken the famous Shady Oak Stetson to a milliner, who trimmed the brim and made "a real good hat of it."

Amon presents his famed Shady Oak hats to President Harry Truman (center) and U.S. House Speaker Sam Rayburn (right).

Butler was executive editor and recovering from open heart surgery when Amon Carter Jr. presented him with the last official Amon Carter Shady Oak hat.

Amon's hats, bestowed by the thousands, publicized by the *Star-Telegram*, wire services, and national columnists, were the most esteemed of his gifts, but his cupboard overflowed with bounty for his friends.

Alva Johnston cataloged the branches of Amon's Thanksgiving and Christmas doles, in order of importance, as "The Paper-Shelled Pecan Peerage, the Pink-Meated Grapefruit Legion, the Texas Shady Oak Hat Order, the Hundred-Pound Watermelon Cast and the Smoked Turkey Aristocracy."

Johnston overlooked some loot: diamond-studded silver buckles and hand-tooled leather belts, flowers, copies of Amon's white vicuña coat, cigars, steer horns, steaks, silver-mounted saddles, and fancy doodads he picked up here and there. Amon always was giving somebody something. Once Billy Rose presented Amon with a mammoth leather chair. Carter liked it so well he bought six more for wives of his Fort Worth friends. One wife protested that the chair did not match her other furniture. Amon replied that he didn't care, the chair was hers anyway, and it was.

If the wife was miffed by a gift she didn't want, possibly she was placated at Christmas when Amon sent her nylons and flowers. He knew the value of pillow talk and never forgot wives of hometown friends or the famous men he courted for his city. He also wooed the attention of secretaries in Washington and New York with flowers and perfumes and other feminine knickknacks to grease his entrée to their important bosses. Amon, who foisted frames for wrong-sized pictures on the unsuspecting but always left them happy, was ever vigilant of the need to keep his fences mended.

Amon's ritual of holiday-giving to America's famous names became a status symbol of having arrived, and the high and the mighty clamored for the booty flowing from Fort Worth. There indeed was a ranking to it all. The hat was conferred at Amon's whim. Other gifts were awarded according to his notion of the receiver's friendship and/or past, present, and future importance to Fort Worth and West Texas, or the condition of Amon's humors at the moment.

Katrine Deakins maintained complicated coded lists, and a name could appear on a master register for all holiday loot or merely be cataloged as worthy of one item. Lists changed from year to year with the vagaries of Amon's temper, and especially in Fort Worth many men were removed from the holiday larder for transgressions, either real or imagined. Lyndon Johnson, who made the mistake of not supporting Republican Dwight Eisenhower for president, as Amon demanded, was lopped off all gift rosters. Governor James Allred, whom Amon never liked, was demoted permanently from watermelons to the ghetto grapefruit list.

Weeks before shipping his gifts each year, Amon sent expansive letters extolling the ever-ascending virtues of Fort Worth and West Texas, noting, almost as an afterthought, that he and the Hired Hand—Harold Hough—were sending "a little something" for the holidays. The swag went out from Fort Worth packaged elaborately and bulging with more propaganda. Fruit and pecans were shipped through the Ben E. Keith Company and box labels bore the message "Longhorn Brand—Grown in Texas especially for the *Fort Worth Star-Telegram.*"

Amon practiced a small deceit, pretending that the watermelons grew at Shady Oak. Actually, they came from sandy-loam farmers in Parker County, twenty miles west of Fort Worth, and were enormous, weighing seventy pounds or more. Each was padded by straw and packed in a galvanized tub. The annual shipment filled three boxcars.

In the beginning, Amon's turkeys were shipped live in wooden crates but later he switched to smoked birds. Each belt buckle—the ultimate Amon gift—cost $350, was studded with at least sixteen diamonds, and was designed by a jeweler at the Fair, a Fort Worth department store. The steaks came after the holidays. Amon purchased the stock show grand champion steer each year, paying up to $6,000 for the prized animal. He had the steer butchered into steaks, frozen, and air-shipped via American Airlines to an elite list of men. In Washington, it became another of Bascom Timmons's journalistic duties to deliver steaks to politicians.

Amon's gift priorities were capricious, but generally presidents received the entire load, lesser men something less. Nelson Rockefeller went from grapefruit to pecans to watermelons back to grapefruit in successive years. Mayor Fiorello LaGuardia of New York and Minnie Hutchinson of Bowie, Texas, a widow, were paired on the grapefruit roll. Oilman Harry Sinclair, convicted for his part in the Teapot Dome scandal, received pecans while in prison. Paul Whiteman, columnists Bugs Baer and Damon Runyon, W. R. Hearst, and golfer Bobby Jones were among the select diamond-buckle crowd. Sherman Billingsley, the Stork Club owner, Otto Kahn, Rube Goldberg, and a DuPont or two received steaks. Watermelons—as many as five hundred in a shipment—were directed to a large catalog of celebrities, including Tris

Speaker, Tex Rickard, J. C. Penney, Sam Goldwyn, and Edgar A. Guest. The latter responded with a perfectly awful poem titled "A Friend in Texas"; it began: "For once every year out of Texas, a Friend/A red-headed melon remembers to send. . . ."

Hough's letters, gems of Texas humor, were written under the aegis of "The Truth Society." He described the rigors of harvesting the foodstuff: "Your melon, originating from fancy seeds and growing in the dark, had to be killed. It grew so fast it pulled the vines all over the patch and wore out the little melons, so we killed it with an ax to protect the rest."

Once Amon declared he wanted to grow personalized watermelons and experimented with scratching initials on the young fruit. At maturity, however, the letters were lumpy and illegible.

"No, no," advised Paul Whiteman, "the way to do it is to paste gummed letters on the melons. Get the kind they paste on hatbands. The letters will be stenciled in white under the letters."

Amon thought the idea splendid and the next year names were glued on five hundred melons. A week before harvest time, a farmer called to say field mice had eaten every famous name. Amon tried again with adhesive tape but results were not satisfactory. The few successful melons were sent and Hough called them "self-pronouncing." Amon abandoned his dream of monogrammed watermelons.

Each shipment of gifts contained drawings of Hough tending turkeys or struggling with oversized melons. One year there was a photograph of Hough dressed in overalls standing beside a tractor. Otto Kahn was seated on the machine pretending that he, one of the world's richest men, was a Shady Oak stoop laborer. Another year, Amon sent pictures of every Fort Worth structure bearing his name, a conceit that would have shamed a lesser man.

Of all edible gifts, Amon's turkeys were most coveted, and friends with only grapefruit or pecan standing were envious of those receiving the smoked birds, which Hough described as "so large you only need eight to make a dozen."

Amon's turkeys graced White House holiday tables for three decades, even before he was forced to give up the live-bird program. "Have expressed to you a 31-pound Texas Tom Turkey strong enough to carry a good-sized saddle and which you may

Amon prepares to ship one of his traditional Christmas turkeys.

ride before eating," Hough wrote to President Calvin Coolidge. Silent Cal had no problem with his live Christmas dinner. He merely turned it over to the White House chef.

Those lacking presidential prerogatives were as bewildered as if they had been presented with a Tibetan yak. Living, gobbling, Texas turkeys were alien to eastern offices and city apartments.

Amon personally delivered two live toms on leashes to Mayor Jimmy Walker, who graciously, if uncomfortably, posed for photos. After Amon left, Walker, distressed by the loud gobbling and mounting piles of turkey droppings, ordered the beasts shipped to Central Park Zoo.

What to do with live turkeys in the city? "The modern New York apartment is not designed with an eye to the accommodation of live turkeys," explained the *New York Sun*, describing the experience of Gilbert Hodges, its publisher. A twenty-five-pound turkey, reported the *Sun*, arrived by van. The driver confronted the doorman, asking for Hodges.

"I got a toikey for him," said the driver.

"You have a what, my good man?" questioned the ritzy doorman.

"Toikey, toikey! I said it plain. Don't you know English?"

"If I am supposed to understand that you are delivering a turkey to this house for Mr. Hodges, you should know enough to take it to the service entrance."

"Aw, go chase yourself 'round the block. It ain't that kind of toikey."

The crate was muscled to the sidewalk and lugged into the Hodges's apartment. "Mr. and Mrs. Hodges . . . were thoroughly puzzled as to what could be done for the housing and entertainment of their startling visitor," reported the *Sun*. Hodges's solution was to rent an apartment across the hall while the couple sought a butcher brave enough to tackle the job of converting the tom into dinner.

Geoffrey Konta, a New York attorney, had to hide his turkey in his building's basement. Bob Small, a Washington newspaperman, said his tom arrived when only his children were at home. The kids released the bird and it attacked them. Later, Small chased it upstairs and down before subduing the turkey with a baseball bat. Herbert Jones, a New York advertising executive, wired that "The Texas Tom arrived in good shape with enough fertilizer to supply requirements of my farm." *Chicago Tribune* Publisher Robert McCormick wrote, "The ostrich arrived in good order. The first thing it did was to lay an egg." Henry Milholland, vice president of the *Pittsburgh Press*, related that his uncrated turkey "immediately hopped up on my desk and backfired all over me and the office." O. R. Boyd, an executive with the American Petroleum Institute, said he was home sick when the turkey was delivered to his office, so a secretary sent the bird to his house by taxi, the cabdriver leading it on a leash like a fox terrier.

Not all recipients were overwhelmed by their live gifts. Bud Fisher shipped his to a farm near Lake Mahopac, New York, and became friends with it. From time to time the bird appeared in his "Mutt and Jeff" comic strip. The bird died of old age at the farm. And Harry Sinclair wrote of his, "I have taken him for a walk along Fifth Avenue, tea at the Ritz and the theater at night."

Underwood Nazro, a Houston oilman, noted, "He was so beautiful and aristocratic that we would have liked to allow him to strut in his royal splendor but he, like so many aristocrats and royalty, strutted too much and the mob turned on him, cut off his head and devoured him. *Sic Transit Gloria[Mundi]*."

Anguished wails flowing from the Northeast forced Amon to quit his live-dinner program. He switched to smoked birds, which necessarily limited the number of turkeys and made them all the more valuable.

Amon's gifts were manna for his friends but, too, they were shamefully blatant bribes to keep Fort Worth in the minds of men who could shape the city's destiny. Amon never denied that but, being a neurotically generous man, he delighted in the orgy of giving. Only once did a gift embarrass him. After World War II, General Jonathan Wainwright—the Pacific hero and Japanese prisoner—visited Fort Worth. Amon threw him a dinner. The general, an outdoors enthusiast, was given a distinctive gift—a blooded Texas hunting dog. Amon proudly presented the hound to Wainwright and passed over its leash.

As Wainwright spoke a grateful thanks to the crowd, the dog stood beside the general, raised its leg, and peed all over the foot that had survived the Bataan Death March.

8

[Texas Governor] Jim Ferguson mailed out pardons like Xmas cards. He once pardoned a man, and the man wrote him that he hadn't been caught yet.
—Will Rogers, 1928

He [Amon] was a vain fellow, and eager to be respected as an exponent of Texan truculence. Indeed, he always spoke of himself, not as a simple Texan, but as a *West* Texan, which connoted a familiarity with firearms and a willingness to use them.
—H. L. Mencken, *Thirty Five Years of Newspaper Work,* 1994

Don't be misled by the low-down, dirty, stinking lies being printed in the *Star-Telegram.* . . .
—Jim 'Pa' Ferguson, 1932

You have only three friends in the world: God Almighty, Sears-Roebuck, and Jim Ferguson.
—Political rally speaker, Austin, 1932

Two governors for the price of one. . . .
—Ma Ferguson's 1923 campaign slogan

He [Amon] was as drunk as a boiled owl.
—Governor Miriam Ferguson, 1925

$\mathbf{P}$rohibition in Texas was little more than a textbook theory, and bootlegging—the state's third oldest profession—became a trade as uplifting as the ministry, as honorable as undertaking, and more public service than either. Every town of any pride and ambition had its "Fruit Jar City," an area of camouflaged saloons from which was sold good homemade corn liquor or the real stuff smuggled across the Rio Grande from Mexico. Understanding doctors prescribed medicinal alcohol to be collected from the nearest friendly druggist. If nothing else was available, the public could fall back on the enormous stock of patent medicines, like Lydia Pinkham's soothing toddy, which were almost as intoxicating as a good cocktail.

Star-Telegram reporters had their favorite speakeasy, a carefully disguised old house several blocks west of downtown. Jimmy North maintained a charge account there throughout Prohibition. James Record, whose dignity would not allow him to drink with the boys, enlisted Ned, his brother, and sportswriter Flem Hall to buy bootleg whiskey and deliver it to the newspaper office.

As most drinking Texans, Amon felt Prohibition was an insanity to be humored but not seriously practiced. He did not often resort to bootlegging products, though late in the game he was forced to contract for several loads of liquor regularly flown into Fort Worth from Mexico.

Practical as always, Amon tried to stock up for the duration.

Shortly before the Eighteenth Amendment shuttered saloons and breweries, he purchased the entire stock of the Casey-Swasey Wholesale Liquors warehouse. He also buried ten barrels of good whiskey for unforeseen crises. (The emergency cache was never to be drunk; the barrels leaked and were empty when exhumed.)

Most of his warehouse booze was stored in the underground vault at his home, the door of which was so heavy that Amon needed two helpers to open it. The vault was guarded by a siren alarm system. Amon alone had the combination but, as Nenetta remembered, "He hid it behind every picture in the house."

Amon was settled in for a long dry spell.

By 1928, Prohibition was a generally detested, and largely unenforceable, law. Harold Hough explained the moral situation

Left to right: Will Rogers, writer H. L. Mencken, and Amon pose in the extra-large version of the publisher's cowboy hat, c. 1928.

to WBAP listeners, "The Antis have all the laws they want and the Wets have all the liquor they can drink, so everybody's happy." Not everyone. In the South, in Texas, where drinking was a religious dispute, Prohibition remained an emotional proposition: the Lord was dead set against liquor.

Why, then, did the Democratic Party allow itself to be lured into a southern convention? It was a self-destructive decision, out of which came Al Smith, a Catholic drinker, to be paired against Herbert Hoover, the Eagle Scout Republican candidate. But in 1928, the Democrats marched into the South, into Houston, for the first major political party convention below the Mason-Dixon line since the Civil War.

Partially, the Democrats were drawn south by a $200,000 cash gift from Houston capitalist Jesse Jones, for whom the convention was a very good deal. A reporter wrote: "He [Jones] owned the overcrowded hotels the delegates slept in, the theaters where they sought escape from a fierce summer heat, the banks where they cashed their checks, the newspapers they read, and his lumber company built the hall where Alfred E. Smith was nominated. The politicians lost their shirts in the laundry, and they lost their tempers when they learned that this man, Jones, owned the laundry, too. They eventually recovered their tempers, but not their shirts."

So Democrats came to Houston as Jesse Jones's well-paying guests, headquartered in the Rice Hotel. Amon arrived with cases of his warehouse liquor, Will Rogers, Paul Patterson, the *Baltimore Sun* publisher, the astringent columnist H. L. Mencken, and Carl Smith, Tarrant County's sheriff. Amon took a third-floor suite, from which he committed what Jimmy North forevermore called "The Houston Incident."

It was a circus convention. As meetings began, Houston night riders lynched an accused black rapist; the poor man was dangled from a bridge. Heavily bankrolled by Republican money, Fort Worth Baptist minister J. Frank Norris was there, preaching against the double-dose wickedness of Catholicism and liquor. There were slogans, "Smith or Suicide" and "Al for All and All for Al," countered by picket placards, "Alcohol Is All for Al" and "Democratic Drinking Devils." Women prayed in one nearby church, wrote a newsman, ". . . lifting their sad tired voices in despair, invoking the power of God against Al Smith." During heated debates on the convention floor, a half-dozen fistfights had to be quelled by police with nightsticks. The 1928 Democratic Convention was not a very pleasant meeting.

Amon was mad. He came to campaign for John Nance Garner, who as a Texan and convention dark horse candidate, steadfastly maintained he did not want the nomination. Amon grumped around fringes of the convention, angry because an outsider surely would be nominated, angry at the Drys' emotional attack, but especially angry with elevators.

Too small for a national political convention headquarters, the Rice Hotel was mobbed with people. "The lobby is so packed," wrote Will Rogers, "I have reached up and mopped three brows before I could find my own." He told of an early morning meeting of Republican ladies: "The breakfast was billed for 9 o'clock on the roof of the hotel and on account of the elevators we all arrived for a lovely luncheon."

Amon's suite, shared with Rogers, Patterson, and Mencken, was headquarters for the *Star-Telegram*'s convention coverage. Silliman Evans, the newspaper's political reporter, manned a desk in the center of the living room. Usually, he sat in his underwear, typing stories from notes delivered by runners from the convention floor. The bathtub was filled with ice and beer. Windows were open wide to coax in the small breezes astir in the humid summer heat.

On the convention's third day, Amon and Sheriff Smith left the suite to attend a meeting on the hotel's eleventh floor. As usual, the elevators were delegate-crowded and slow and Amon fumed at the contraptions. That day, three upward-bound elevators passed the men despite Amon's impatient thumbing of the call buzzer.

Moments after the fourth elevator slipped by, Amon had a mad spell. He snatched Smith's pistol from its holster and fired six bullets—or perhaps four; there were differing reports— through the glass doors. Next time, the elevator stopped for Amon.

That, briefly, is North's "Houston Incident," and how witnesses and Houston newspapers reported the episode. (No account of the shooting ever appeared in the *Star-Telegram*.) Amon's version was different. He told Alva Johnston of the *Saturday Evening Post*: "No shots were fired into the door of the elevator shaft."

Jimmy North wrote a more detailed explanation to Johnston: "What happened was . . . some friends phoned Carter and asked him to bring his friends up to the 11th floor for a visit. Carter was on the third floor, and accompanied by . . . Carl Smith, they started out. It was in the summer and the sheriff was in his shirtsleeves and wearing a .45 Colt revolver. They pushed the elevator button time and time again. The hotel was so crowded the elevators did not stop. Carter, becoming disturbed over [the elevators] not stopping, took the Sheriff's six-shooter out of the holster and hammered on the glass door of the elevator shaft with the barrel of the revolver. The door was glassed with heavy meshed wire which when hit with the . . . revolver shattered but did not fall out—thus created a shatter on the glass that looked like a cobweb. The glass was not broken but gave the impression to anyone looking at it that it had been shot through. Meanwhile, the elevator stopped. . . ."

That rendition was never believed, particularly by Flem Hall, who saw the holes. Hall was in Houston to cover a baseball game—the Fort Worth Cats—and visited the *Star-Telegram* suite. To Hall, the bullet holes in the glass elevator doors looked like bullet holes.

There is no dispute, however, over Amon's other Rice Hotel pistol-shooting exhibition. He fired shots though an open hotel window with Mencken as a startled witness. Mencken wrote of his encounter with Amon in *Thirty Five Years of Newspaper Work,* a book manuscript he completed in 1943 and sealed from public view until 1994.

The columnist was unimpressed with Amon's hospitality in Fort Worth, and wrote that it was "more of a nuisance than a joy." Texans, in fact, "were simply not my kind of people." Mencken remembered that in Houston Amon visited his room too often, usually accompanied by his "retainer, the Sheriff of Fort Worth . . . a gigantic fellow, always drunk, and carrying in a holster a huge pistol studded with rubies—a present from his admirers among the Fort Worth bootleggers."

Mencken confirmed that Amon indeed fired shots through the elevator doors, and was seized by "city cops" who "let him go on the ground that no one had been hurt, and that firing a pistol was a natural sign of discontent in Texas."

Earlier in the day, Mencken wrote, Amon had come alone to his suite and "refused to be got rid of."

"Finally," Mencken remembered, "I had to turn my back on him, and resumed my work. Suddenly he pulled a pistol and fired three shots out of the window. The aim of his volley, as I learned, was simply to entertain me pleasantly in the Texas fashion, but what ensued was an uproar that kept me busy for two hours. . . ."

Three bullets hit a hotel across the street, close to the window of a room in which the Ku Kluxers were holding a caucus."

Texas Rangers came to Mencken's suite, searching for the shooter, who by now had drifted on to visit with other conventioneers. Mencken had to deal with the rangers alone.

"After we got back to Baltimore [publisher Paul] Patterson wrote to the manager of the Rice Hotel asking him to send on the fly-screen with the three bullet-holes in it. This was done, and a segment of it showing the holes was framed. For some years thereafter it hung in Patterson's office," Mencken wrote in an exasperating tone.

"The Houston Incident" trailed Amon for the remainder of his life, recounted by writers and storytellers any time they wanted to regale an audience with the publisher's outrageous antics. It even became a side issue of a 1932 gubernatorial campaign by James E. "Farmer Jim" Ferguson, who was stumping for his wife, Miriam, running against incumbent Ross Sterling.

Speaking in Arlington, Farmer Jim warmed up on Sterling, describing the governor as "the big fathead" and "big fat boy." He then turned to Amon, calling him "the old cuss" and "consummate ass." Ferguson rehashed the Houston elevator episode, adding new elements. Amon, charged Ferguson, was drunk and the "elevator [was] occupied only by a little girl." He said the publisher almost shot the innocent child. Ferguson also claimed that Amon, in 1928, had voted for Herbert Hoover, which, in yellow-dog Democrat Texas, was an indictment as vile as being accused of child molestation.

One path into the *Star-Telegram* news columns was an attack on Amon. Ferguson's comments landed on page one, introduced by an editor's note calling Farmer Jim's slurs "a smokescreen" because the newspaper had uncovered "favoritism" and "riotous extravagance" in Miriam's previous administration. Ferguson's charges, although libelous to Amon, were being printed, the note continued, "because the public has a sense of humor. A cash discount can be taken on most of Mr. Ferguson's statement."

Amon and the *Star-Telegram* once again were campaigning against the Fergusons, though privately the publisher knew she would be elected governor. He had written to Sterling, whom he did not like, "the times support her kind of politicking."

Ma and Pa. Only in Texas. For three decades they espoused a demagogic populist brand of earthy politics, depending on the "Ferguson vest-pocket vote," which were the 150,000 poor, largely rural, Texans for whom Ma and Pa could do no wrong. For everyone else, they could do wrong, and did.

Each served two terms as governor. Son of a central Texas minister and a wanderer, Jim panned for California gold, was a bellhop in Colorado, a railroad pick-and-shovel laborer near Fort Worth. Finally, he settled down, married Miriam, farmed a little, read law books at night, and was admitted to the bar. He also founded Temple State Bank and, in 1912, began dabbling in politics. Two years later, he was in the governor's mansion.

Pa campaigned in rural areas, boondoggling tenant farmers with harangues against Texas's wealthy, educated class. Dressed in a claw hammer frock coat, fists clinched and raised to Heaven, Pa was a portentous demagogue promising eternal riches to work-weary sharecroppers. By 1917, in his second term, Pa was a man marked for impeachment.

Charges were brought, and, as the subsequent Senate trial proved, Pa was something of a scoundrel. He had loaned himself $5,000 from public school funds; accepted $156,000—in small bills—from brewery lobbyists anxious to stave off Prohibition legislation; deposited $500,000 of state money in his Temple bank—a clear conflict of interest violation—then spent portions of the money to pay his own overdrafts; and used taxpayer funds to buy his groceries, cattle feed, automobile tires, gasoline, and even the fat chickens Ma fried in the mansion kitchen. Pa Ferguson, testimony revealed, bought a ukulele with state money.

Impeached and outraged, Pa set about to restore his good name. In open violation of law pertaining to impeachment, Pa again ran for governor, but lost. He was a losing candidate for the U.S. Senate. At the top of the Know-Nothing ticket, he campaigned, hopelessly, for president.

In 1923, Pa settled on a simple solution to his problem by having Miriam become a candidate for governor. Seemingly a nice, uncomplicated woman devoted to her husband, Ma stumped for the state's vest-pocket votes. In the *Ferguson Forum*, a weekly statewide newspaper founded by Pa, she was pictured in a poke-style bonnet, baking pies and feeding chickens. One headline announced: "Ma Drops Campaign Worry to Preserve Three Gallons of Figs." On the campaign trail, Ma rarely spoke but pronounced a few words of welcome then turned the platform over to Pa, who blistered his enemies and promised to take care of those little farmers who had supported him during all his years of persecution.

Ma became the first woman elected governor of a state, and the second to take office; Nellie Ross of Wyoming was inaugurated a few days earlier. Ma's first official act was to pardon Pa for his impeachment crimes. Pa was back in business.

He took over the affairs of Texas while Ma, knitting like Madame Lafarge, performed ceremonial duties and fried chicken in the mansion. Pa became legal counsel for a group of railroads. The *Ferguson Forum* was bloated with ads bought by companies doing business with the state. A daughter managed a bonding firm whose clientele solely was utility companies and highway contractors depending on the State of Texas. Pa sat with official commissions, boards, and state agencies, illegally issuing orders and instructions. It was the best of times; it was the worst of times.

When Ma/Pa began pardoning criminals, Amon and the *Star-Telegram* stepped into the Ferguson mess.

No governor had ever emptied prisons faster than Ma. Her predecessor, Pat Neff, signed 92 full pardons and 107 conditional pardons during his entire four years in office. Ma pardoned two thousand criminals during her first twenty months as governor, releasing up to three hundred prisoners in a single day. Her final month as governor, noted the *Star-Telegram*, Ma granted "full unconditional pardons" to 33 rapists, 133 murderers, 12 robbers, and 127 liquor law violators.

Texas's "open-door policy" seemed satisfactory to convicts but was disturbing to the general public. There were cynical jokes—"Pardon me, Ma did" was scribbled in the dust of a Model T chassis—and scurrilous asides about Ma's "cash and carry clemency administration."

The *Star-Telegram* kept score on Ma, daily publishing on its front page a prominent box marked "Pardon Record" in which the cumulative executive clemency totals were spread for all of Texas to see. One read: "Governor Ferguson's pardon record, compiled Monday in Austin, shows that the woman governor has since her induction in office, issued up to date 2,328 clemency proclamations. Of this number 614 have been issued since April 6, this year [1925]. The classified list of proclamations follow: Conditional pardons, 771; Full pardons, 378 . . . paroles, 168 . . . reduced bonded forfeitures, 17 . . . jail and bond forfeitures remitted, 1. . . ." And so on.

Ma and Pa were indignant over the *Star-Telegram*'s publicity about their pardon and parole business. Except among the vest-pocket *lumpenproletariat*, who still cherished the demagoguery of Fergusonism, Texans were irate with the wholesale release policy. More trouble for Ma and Pa was coming.

Silliman Evans uncovered the sticky asphalt topping scandal within Ma's Texas Highway Department, the three-man ruling commission which had been joined by a fourth, unofficial, member—Pa. "The commission cordially invited me to sit with them," Pa told the *Star-Telegram*. "I thought I ought to accept their kind invitation."

Evans reported that the highway commission issued suspicious contracts, without bid or public notice, to the American Road Company—a Delaware-incorporated firm with total assets of a secondhand asphalt plant and five old automobiles. A month after American Road's incorporation and with its new Texas highway contract, the company declared a $200,000 dividend. Sixteen days later, another dividend of $319,000 was handed to stockholders. Within six months, American had paid $709,111.35 to fortunate stockholders.

American Road never spread asphalt on any state highway. It subcontracted the job. A similar deal for topping was given Hoffman Construction Company. It was to be paid thirty cents per square yard but, as American Road, Hoffman sublet its contract at nine cents a square yard. In six months, Hoffman was paid by Texas $908,443.24 for work costing $296,805.50.

Tempers were short in Austin. A highway commissioner attacked and beat Evans in the Driskill Hotel lobby. Threats against Amon filtered into Fort Worth, and he hired guards for his home and family. Dan Moody, Texas's young, red-haired attorney general (and a declared gubernatorial candidate) took the *Star-Telegram*'s research and went to trial, during which one witness, W. T. Montgomery, told of his conversation with Frank Latham, the highway commission chairman.

"Montgomery," said Latham, "I had nothing more to do with letting the American Road Company contract than you did."

"Who did?"

"Jim Ferguson."

American Road was ordered to refund $600,000 to the state treasury, and the Fergusons were furious with Amon and his newspaper.

Ma and Pa fumed well into autumn when, as always, Amon's attention turned to another passion—football.

One weekend, he dressed in his cowboy costume and with Nenetta drove to College Station for the annual Thanksgiving football game between Texas A & M and the University of Texas. In the Aggie stadium, Kyle Field, Amon was startled to find himself seated directly behind the Fergusons.

Predictably, the game enthused Amon. The Aggies, his favorite, were winning, and Amon was up, pacing and cheering, loudly urging A & M to pour it on. Then Amon, unexpectedly, and probably spontaneously, yelled: "HOORAY FOR DAN MOODY AND THE TEXAS AGGIES!"

Ma and Pa squirmed. The crowd applauded.

Pa whispered to an aide, who told Amon he must stop yelling. Amon eyed the man.

"HOORAY FOR DAN MOODY AND THE TEXAS AGGIES!"

Ma and Pa summoned a Texas Ranger. Amon was escorted out of the stadium. Within twenty-four hours, Amon's expulsion was on newspaper front pages everywhere—except Fort Worth. Jimmy North sighed and pretended nothing was happening.

The *New York Times* devoted four columns to the football episode and ensuing uproar. O. O. McIntire wired from Paris, "You certainly busted all the front pages over here. Atta boy!" "Sic 'em," messaged Frank Phillips from Oklahoma. John Willis, the automobile manufacturer, offered, "If you need bail, call me."

Back in Austin, Ma and Pa held a press conference.

Ma declared: "He [Amon] was drunk and waving a cane, and I know it was filled with liquor."

She claimed he gave away the liquor-filled canes in wholesale lots and, she added, he also gave friends liquor flasks shaped like family Bibles. Ma announced a five hundred-dollar reward for the arrest and conviction of persons "worth more than $5,000" who violated Prohibition laws. She referred to a "North Texas publisher" who "dispenses pints of liquor by the dozens in public places . . . and goes scott-free [sic], when poor and underfed men in the same city are being sent to the penitentiary yearly for carrying a thin pint."

Amon told the *Houston Post* that the A & M tableau was more evidence of Ma and Pa's public chicanery. The game had excited him. He paced the grandstand, cheering the Aggies' first and second touchdowns. By the sheerest of coincidences, Amon contended, he was beside the governor's box when he just happened to insert Dan Moody's name into the cheer. The aide asked Amon to be quiet. Who was that man to tell him what to do? He yelled again and the Texas Ranger escorted him outside where, according to the publisher, the following conversation occurred:

Amon: "Is it against the law to cheer for Texas A & M?"

Ranger: "No, Mr. Carter."

Amon: "Is it against the law to cheer for Dan Moody?"

Ranger: "No, Mr. Carter."

Amon: "Then what's all the shootin' about, anyway?"

Ranger: "Aw, forget it and let's go back inside."

Amon also denied to the *Post* that he had been drinking. (Nenetta agreed that he was not drunk.)

Three days later Ma released to state newspapers a letter she had written Amon. Editors deemed it libelous and refused to print it, and Amon immediately issued a statement to the *Associated Press* waiving the libel law. The letter went onto front pages across Texas—even the *Star-Telegram*'s—where it was preceded by an editor's note in which Amon stated that Ma's correspondence was being printed "as a means of getting the matter before the public and in a sense of fair play. . . ."

An answer was promised the following day. Amon meant to have the last word. It is generally believed that Ma's letter was written by Pa, but whoever was responsible, it was a wonderfully sardonic piece of political literature. The letter began by recounting the Aggie episode, noting that there were 25,000 people at the game, including "thousands of young boys and girls, students and friends."

"[When] you gave vent to your vociferous exclamation you were only a few feet from me," the letter continues. "Your friends who know you best assure me (and I believe them) that when you are in a normal condition you are a courteous gentleman to the manner [sic] born and I attribute your seeming affront to your unusual condition and the influence under which you were laboring at the time. . . . I gladly forget the apparent discourtesy to me as from my own observation I know you were not responsible at the time."

Ma turned to other matters, scolding Amon, "I am told that last year you fitted up a building owned or controlled by you (perhaps a garage building) in the old fashioned bar room way, providing a bar with the footrail, and the sawdust on the floor, and behind the bar you had a man dressed in the old fashioned bar tender, white apron style. I am also informed that at said reception given by you many became stimulated and others under the influence of an invigorating concoction and that you in company with your guests participated in the consumption of the beverage."

Ma claimed that Amon served drinks that were "to say the least, stimulating, and that [you] caused to be given souvenir canes in which there was a hidden phial some thirty inches in length that contained approximately one pint of beverage."

In all ways, concluded the governor, Amon had displayed "vices that are repugnant to the ideal of strict morality and sobriety." She alleged that he was not fit to serve in a public position and demanded his resignation as board chairman of Texas Technological College at Lubbock, a newly opened, state-supported college that Amon and the *Star-Telegram* had lobbied into existence.

A day later, Amon printed his reply, beginning with the classical quotation, "Whom the gods would destroy, they first make mad." He refused to resign from the Texas Tech board, charging that Ma's statements were "malicious and without justification" and a "smokescreen to divert the real issues from the public." The governor was mad, said Amon, because the *Star-Telegram* had exposed corruption in her highway department. He spoke of Pa, "the real actor who like a ventriloquist behind the scenes puts his voice and his words to figures on stage."

Amon revealed that emissaries from Pa came to Fort Worth, to the publisher's office, to threaten him and attempt to stop the newspaper's highway scandal stories.

As for the garage barroom, the accusation was "a farce comedy" representing "an effort to make fiction out of fact and is ancient history . . . there was no violation of the law and there could have been none. Present were city and county law enforcement officials." He denied giving away whiskey-filled walking canes.

Turning to the Aggie incident, Amon declared his "right as one who paid his way in . . . to yell for the team of my choice, and Dan Moody for saving taxpayers' money.

"The story that I was under the influence of liquor when I cried out on the one hand for A & M and on the other for Dan Moody, is not only false in every particular but could only support the conclusion in the mind of 'Gov. Jim' that anyone who declared for Dan Moody was either drunk or crazy."

And there the matter simmered.

Most immediate result of the public exchange of letters was a demand for those whiskey-filled walking canes that Amon denied giving away. "I have established a great trade on the Dan Moody walking canes," he wrote a New York friend. "I have just had to place an order for 50 more."

Ma, it seems, was correct in almost all her accusations of Amon and his "bar room" liquor party. The room was Amon's garage, and the crowd mostly executive board members of the American Petroleum Institute, who were meeting in Fort Worth. Each guest received a walking stick filled with Amon's pre-Prohibition whiskey. A good time was had by all, particularly local law enforcement officials, all of whom received a cane, and especially an assistant district attorney who, witnesses reported, was carried out feet first.

Amon received more than four hundred letters from Texans supporting his public argument with the Fergusons. And the newspaper continued gathering evidence against Ma and Pa. None was printed, probably because public sentiment had turned against the pair, and Moody—campaigning with the slogan "Hooray for Dan Moody"—appeared to have enough votes to win. The evidence, mostly collected by private detectives, was stored in Amon's files. There was a notarized deposition, stating, "That on Jan. 23, 1926, the governor called for a quart of whiskey delivered to the capitol at 2:25 P.M. The governor paid $6 in the presence of Carlos Brents, U.S. Prohibition Agent." Another placed Pa in the "craps game on the 12th floor of the Texas Hotel, raided the night of March 10, 1926. . . ." And there was a picture of a still operating on Pa's ranch near Meridian in central Texas.

After Ma was defeated, Pa wrote Amon, "If in the heat of the campaign I have in the past said anything I ought not to have said, I regret it." He asked Amon to reply. Amon stuffed the letter into his files and dismissed such a silly appeal from his mind.

But he and Texas were not yet free of the Fergusons. Ma ran again in 1930 and was beaten by Ross Sterling. By 1932 the Depression was on Texas, and demagoguery again was fashionable. The vest-pocket vote returned her to office. A year later, when Eleanor Roosevelt made the trip to Fort Worth to meet Ruth Googins, the first lady asked Amon to set up a private breakfast meeting at Meacham Field. As everyone sat to eat that morning, the Fergusons arrived, unannounced and uninvited.

They stood around, waiting to be asked in. Amon ignored them. Angry, Ma and Pa left.

"Why didn't you stay for breakfast?" a reporter later asked.

"Ask Amon Carter!" snapped Pa.

"I arranged for the breakfast," Amon answered. "I paid for it. I ordered it. I could ask who I pleased. Jim Ferguson has never given me anything."

Ma and Pa were in the area, first, to attend a charity horse race at Arlington Downs, between Fort Worth and Dallas, and second, to be platform guests in Dallas's Hotel Adolphus for a political banquet honoring John Nance Garner, the new vice president, and James Farley, postmaster general and chairman of the Democratic National Committee. Both men were touring Texas. Dallas snubbed Amon and didn't invite him to the banquet. At the time, Will Rogers and aviator Frank Hawks were visiting Amon. The trio decided to crash the dinner and flew from Fort Worth to Dallas in Hawks's plane.

Rogers entered the banquet hall. Applause broke out as he was recognized. He ambled to the front table to speak.

"I come here only on one condition," said Rogers. "I brought a friend. If he's welcome, I'll stay. Neither of us was invited. We just butted into this party. I reckon I'd better go on back to Fort Worth with him."

Boyd Gatewood wrote in the *Houston Post*, "A thousand voices roared 'Bring him in!' In came Amon Carter."

"Amon harbors no ill will toward you," cracked Rogers. "And I don't either. Amon came here with the distinct understanding that he was not to take this hotel back to Fort Worth with him. I know, Mrs. Governor and . . . er . . . er . . . well, both of you. . . . I know Amon has no ill will toward you."

The audience roared.

A week later, *Time* devoted a page to the Garner/Farley political blitz of Texas. The reporter wrote little of the politicians but concentrated on Amon Carter's cowboy persona.

Amon gawddammed *Time*, a fledgling publication doing all it could to attract attention. He authored a scathing reply to the article. Amon's letter remains the longest ever published by the magazine, and has, within the heat of its words, the merest suspicion of a possible lawsuit. Point by point, Amon—sometime fudging on the truth—disputed *Time*. His letter read:

> It is to be regretted that ideals once formed should be shattered
> and fine conceptions overturned. In the past *Time* has won its way
> in public favor through its accuracy in presenting current events
> in a crisp, snappy and concise form, and thus vitalizing its news,

Will Rogers and Amon.

rather than fictitious stories, interesting because they are scurrilous.

Why you should have turned aside to make me the target for rancid legends is quite mystifying, inasmuch as I am a private citizen, holding no office and caring for none. I am not thin-skinned but even the most callused individual would resent untruths and false insinuations that drip from page 13 of your October 30th issue.

Let us take up your attack in the order in which is made:

FIRST—You say that "Publisher Carter was reputed to have financed the Garner-Farley junket over American Airlines of which he is a heavy stockholder." Permit me to say that I own no stock in the American Airlines, though at one time I was possessor of 50 shares which I disposed of.

SECOND—You also assert that I bought the *Star-Telegram* eight years ago with money made in cattle, oil and advertising. This assertion is a piece with the rest of your article. The *Star-Telegram* had its origin Feb. 1, 1906, nearly 20 years in advance of

141

the time recorded in your story. The paper began as the *Fort Worth Star* and embraces, though successive purchases, in two competitors of that time, the *Evening Telegram* and the morning *Record*. My connection with it dates from the first issue of the Star of which I was the advertising manager—in fact, the entire advertising department—and has continued uninterrupted, throughout its development. It has always been a legitimate newspaper and its progress had nothing to do with investment on my part in cattle or oil, but its circulation of 140,000, the largest in the Southwest, was evolved from the patronage and support of the people of Texas, particularly of the West.

THIRD—You state that "Carter marshaled the Farley-Garner party out to his box at Arlington Downs to witness the rebirth of horse race betting in Texas. There an unforeseen unpleasantness occurred. While Host Carter was out making a bet, Governor Miriam (Ma) Ferguson and her husband, James, popped in uninvited to chat with Postmaster General Farley." That statement is entirely erroneous and is also an injustice to the Governor and her husband. The Farley-Garner party were guests, together with Governor Ferguson and her husband, at a luncheon given in the Club House by Mr. and Mrs. W. T. Waggoner and their sons, Paul and Guy, owners of Arlington Downs. I did not attend the luncheon as I presided at another given by the combined civic clubs at the Fort Worth Club in honor of Joseph T. O'Mahoney, first assistant Postmaster General. Following this luncheon, I accompanied Mr. O'Mahoney to the races at Arlington Downs and did not in any way come in contact with Governor Ferguson and her husband, made no bets on the races, nor did there occur any unpleasant event during the entire afternoon.

FOURTH—You state that "Amon Carter in 1925, full of high spirits, paraded back and forth behind the Fergusons" seats crowing in behalf of the man who succeeded Mrs. Ferguson after her first term as governor: "Hooray for Dan Moody." In answer to this accusation, the writer was not "full of high spirits" and was doing no crowing. Dan Moody had not succeeded Mrs. Ferguson as she was still in office. However, having been a long time admirer and rooter for A & M College, I did exclaim, "Hooray for A & M College and Dan Moody" following the touchdown by A & M against Texas. I was not concerned about the Fergusons in any way and said nothing in disparagement of them. I merely exercised my personal privilege to lift my voice for Dan Moody, the Attorney General. I thought he was entitled to recognition at the time because as Attorney General, he had sued the road contractors to recover moneys they had procured through juicy contracts with the Highway Department during the Ferguson Administration. That I was justified in this is borne out by the fact that later Moody was instrumental in recovering from those contractors for the State of Texas something like one million dollars and was elected Governor. The story that James E. Ferguson, as you stated, offered a reward of $500,000 to any police officer that would arrest Amon Carter is as real as Cinderella and the glass slipper, and quite as untrue as the innuendoes in your article abound. It is doubtless true that had such a reward been offered, the rush of police officers would have been far greater than that of the A & M line.

FIFTH—You further state that "When I found that the Fergusons had horned in on a party of mine last week that I stomped away and did not return to the box until they had gone." This is entirely erroneous, has not a semblance of truth and is another injustice to the Governor.

SIXTH—You made the further statement to the effect that 'The lights of Shady Oak, the comfortable country place on Lake Worth where publisher Carter and his wife do so much of their entertaining, generally burn far into the night and that he never serves beer because he dislikes it, but there is always an abundance of Texas corn and Scotch, his favorite drinks, which he usually takes neat.' The statement is not only slanderous and false, but that you should introduce Mrs. Carter's name into such an atmosphere is proof enough that a gentlemen is needed to edit your copy.

SEVENTH—You state "Mr. Carter's generosity as a contributing Democrat is only equaled by his enthusiasm for the cause and, perhaps by his ambition to hold office." It is the first time the writer has ever been aware that either a man's generosity or his loyalty to his party should be subject to criticism or slander. As for my ambition to hold office, this in itself is ridiculous. I have never held office and have repeatedly stated in the publication with which I am associated that I never expect to hold one. Therefore, it would seem that you take malicious delight in endeavoring to embarrass me with the fact that I am doing these things merely for a selfish reason—trying to acquire a public office, which I would not accept if it were tendered me. It may be that in your environment you are so accustomed to things being done for a purely selfish motive, that it is difficult for you to comprehend that there are people who do not belong to the "Axe Grinder's Club" and that in Texas things are done on a broader scale. Perhaps on this account, allowance should be made for your insinuation.

It is true that I have patronized baseball, football, and polo games and prize fights; however, I do not own an airplane that will fly—merely a retired one as a souvenir at Shady Oak.

EIGHTH—You further state that "At Houston in 1928 Carter threatened to beat up Rev. J. Frank Norris, a Protestant preacher, who opposed the Presidential Nomination of Catholic Al Smith. When Smith was nominated, Amon Carter's exuberance knew no bounds. In his exhilaration he shot his sixgun through the door of an elevator in the Rice Hotel." This entire statement is pure fabrication, false, slanderous, libelous and vicious.

NINTH—You state that "last year Carter was an early passenger on the Roosevelt bandwagon, now supervises Texas patronage distribution." I have never climbed aboard anyone's bandwagon. As Chairman of the Garner Finance Committee, I supported Mr. Garner for President until the time Governor Roosevelt was nominated and Mr. Garner was nominated for Vice President. From that time, I naturally supported Governor Roosevelt and Speaker Garner vigorously, for which support I have no apology to make. As for controlling patronage in Texas, I have absolutely nothing to do with it. The patronage in this state is controlled by our two Senators, Vice President and our Congressman.

TENTH—You further make a statement that the writer sends the President, at least twice a week, long telegrams and occasionally a sleepy operator is waked up or aroused with a message "from the White House to Publisher Carter." This is not only false and ridiculous but it is unfair to the President, as I have never received a wire of any kind from him or sent other than congratulatory messages. It is my observation that he keeps his own counsel and is perfectly able to do a wonderful job without consulting me or even you.

ELEVENTH—You state the political bickering at "Shady Oak lasted long after Vice President Garner had retired at 10:00 P.M." In the first place there was no political bickering in connection with the party. It was purely a social gathering. Vice President Garner left the farm at 10:00 P.M. in keeping with our promise on his acceptance of the invitation. Postmaster General Farley remained until 11:30 and the writer accompanied him to the city. It may be that some of our guests stayed later, a fact which I fail to see should be of any concern to you or even a matter of public interest.

TWELFTH—You state "The Fergusons were placed on Postmaster General Farley's right at the Dallas banquet next night, so Amon Carter sat at the press table." The insinuation is entirely unwarranted. The committee in Dallas invited both Will Rogers and myself to the dinner. We flew over by plane from Fort Worth in company with Col. Frank Hawks, about 8:00 P.M. Rogers was called to the front by the toastmaster and asked to address the crowd. He insisted on my joining him. During the time he was talking, I occupied a vacant seat which happened to be at the Press Table. My attending the party in no way conflicted with the attendance or entertainment of Governor Ferguson and her husband or the seating arrangement for the honored guests.

THIRTEENTH—In your wise crack, which is false, slanderous and vicious, you state that "The Farley party headed back to Washington, which, thought some of Amon Carter's friends, was where Amon Carter wishes he was going on official business." At any time I have a desire to go to Washington on official business, I usually go.

All the foregoing statements are not only false, but like half-truths are infinitely more harmful than if they were bare-faced shameless falsehoods. They are beneath the level and dignity of any high-class journal or publication. Your gullibility in swallowing these accusations, hook, line and sinker, is unthinkable. I cannot understand how any self-respecting reporter, however careless or incompetent, could fail to ascertain the facts before putting such a story to print. It appears this article must have been inspired from other sources, as it would be difficult to impute to your publication such a total absence of the elementary principles of decency and fair treatment.

Of the thirteen or fourteen statements supposedly setting forth facts, I find but three correct:

I was born in Crafton, Texas. I am 53 years old and as a boy I sold chicken sandwiches at the railroad station platform at Bowie. I might also add that I waited on tables at a hotel, sold soda-pop at the ball games and races on Saturday, sold newspapers, worked for a doctor for two years taking care of his horse and buggy, sweeping out his office, and in addition milked a cow—all for my board to enable me to go to school. I am not sensitive as to my age or ashamed of my early efforts to earn a living. While I have given Crafton no claim of distinction by reason of my birth, I know of no cause for reproach on that score. I might add that if the editor of *Time* had been fortunate enough to have enjoyed some of my earlier experiences and hardships, the chances are he would not have been so gullible as to have swallowed a story of this nature or so lacking in the instincts of good sportsmanship.

Another statement in your article preceding your barrage of inaccuracy and fiction concerning the writer is your reference to Honorable John N. Garner, wherein you mentioned "the Farley expedition was for the purpose to rediscover little old hawk-beaked Vice President Garner." This statement in itself to fair-minded people stamps you as thoroughly lacking in the proper attitude of mind or even the respect a wayfaring man pays to the Vice President of the United States. Mr. Garner is a highly respectable, patriotic gentleman, having served his country for 30 years, brilliantly, successfully and courageously, at Washington. A good old fashioned "elm club" should be the proper rebuke for a contemptible remark of this kind.

In conclusion, come to Fort Worth, where the West begins, and we will extend to you the same cordial hospitality we accord to any and all gentlemen. It is proper to add that we always give our visitors the benefit of the doubt.

If you are interested in facts or possess as much intestinal fortitude as you show gullibility, you will publish this reply in full without garbling or editing it, giving it equal prominence with the original story. . . .

Amon Carter is returning by airplane from South America. Annexation of that continent to Fort Worth has not been announced yet.
—*Dallas Journal*, 1934

They remind me of the Davis Mountains in West Texas.
—Amon's description of the Andes, 1934

I spied a dear cow boy, wrapped up in white linen,
Wrapped up in white linen as cold as the day.
—Verse 1, "Streets of Laredo"

Amon always may be depended upon to give a leather-lunged whoop for West Texas.
—Will Rogers, about 1932

In 1911, Daredevil Cal Rodgers flew from the Atlantic to the Pacific and crashed only sixteen times, something of a miraculous feat. No one believed a transcontinental flight possible, not even the Wright Brothers, who sold Rodgers an airplane for the insane journey. Sponsored by Vin Fiz, a new soft drink, Rodgers's historic flight left from a New York racetrack and flew only a few hundred miles before crashing into a Pennsylvania chicken coop. Undeterred, Rodgers paid for the dead chickens, repaired his biplane, and continued west along the shores of the Great Lakes to Chicago, then turned southwest to Saint Louis and Oklahoma.

In mid-October, Rodgers flew into Texas, racing (he later wrote) an eagle to a pasture on Fort Worth's north side. Ten thousand people cheered as Rodgers climbed out of the plane, and there was Amon Carter, first in line to shake the daredevil's hand.

From the moment he saw one (possibly as early as 1909 in New York City), Amon worshipped airplanes, the rattling gimmickry of them, their adventure, the sheer thrill of being up there in those metaphorical canvas-and-bailing wire butterflies. He first flew about 1915 and forever after, said a friend, "Amon liked to be on a plane, going somewhere."

Months before Rodgers crash-landed his way across America, Amon promoted the first airplanes into Fort Worth. The *Star-Telegram* raised ten thousand dollars by public subscription to sponsor the International Aviators, a group of Frenchmen touring the United States. The Frenchmen brought their airplanes— by train—to Fort Worth and demonstrated their skill at staying aloft, often for as long as five minutes. It was a heady experience for Amon, and he predicted that airplanes one day would circle the earth.

He was so taken with airplanes that he and a *Star-Telegram* artist concocted a full-page futuristic drawing depicting the newspaper being delivered to homes by air. This vision came true. Not only did an American Airlines plane regularly drop the newspaper over a far West Texas ranch headquarters, but in the 1920s, when the Trinity River flooded and blocked automobile traffic over bridges, the newspaper was flown over the river and dropped in large bundles, collected by Bert Honea, and delivered to west side homes.

By 1917, Amon had secured three World War I flying fields for Fort Worth as training sites for army aviators. His political connections brought the first airmail service to Texas in 1925, and he begged early Public Works Administration funds from his Washington friends to expand Fort Worth's municipal airport for early passenger planes.

He stole from Dallas the southern division headquarters of Southern Air Transport (later American Airlines), and moved it to Fort Worth, but the deal was successful only because of a harrowing flight to New York with pioneering aviator Frank Hawks. Amon had to reach New York to sign agreement papers for the airline headquarters' move. Hawks was in Fort Worth to visit relatives. Weather was too rough for commercial airliners, but Hawks agreed to fly Amon in his Lockheed. The men left Fort Worth on a stormy March afternoon, bouncing through thunderstorms so violent that winds tore fabric from the plane's right wing.

Over Alabama, as Hawks later told reporters, "There was a big clap of thunder and lightning, and I ducked my head down. I heard the motor missing and felt the ship losing altitude."

Hawks made an emergency landing in Birmingham where he tinkered with the engine while Amon ate ham sandwiches. They swept again into the rain clouds. The flight of eleven hours and thirty-five minutes unnerved Amon, who claimed, "Those were the worst storms I ever saw." He signed the papers and took a train back to Texas.

At that time Southern Air Transport was the largest commercial system of the young industry. It started life as Texas Air Transport, founded by the eccentric, snuff-dipping Alva Pearl Barrett. One of Barrett's peculiarities was to line up his employees each morning and have them sing: "My old fiddle, she's tuned up good/Best old fiddle in the neighborhood/ting-aling-aling, ting-aling-aling, tee-dee."

TAT carried passengers and mail but made most of its money from selling five-dollar thrill rides in Fort Worth. Amon helped Barrett secure financing for his small airline, and he was one of six men who invested $57,000 each. Barrett merged with other commercial passenger firms to become Southern Air Transport, which had landing rights at all important airfields from Atlanta to Los Angeles, including a convict camp near Monroe, Louisiana. A syndicate later bought Southern Air Transport and renamed it American Airlines. Amon was the airline's largest stockholder and a board member.

It was Amon's influence that brought Carswell Air Force Base—it would become a Strategic Air Command facility—to Fort Worth, and through the years he hosted aviation's most celebrated fliers, from Lindbergh to Earhart to Rickenbacker. On one cherished occasion, the entire U.S. Air Force, numbering four planes and four pilots, arrived in his city to be wined and dined by Amon.

Amon and airplanes were inseparable, and in the 1930s, when American aviation was pioneering world commercial routes, Amon was there, a cowboy Magellan exploring a new age. First was the Pan American World Airways Miami-to-South America inaugural flight in August 1934, when the huge flying boat hopped from river to river, taking its fuel from fifty-five-gallon metal drums shipped ahead and stored.

Back home, Amon wrote an introduction for the diary of fellow passenger Ed Swasey, vice president of Hearst's *American Weekly*, titled "The Thrill of Progress." The *Star-Telegram* published the diary with a route map and photo of Amon standing beside the clipper ship floating on a Brazilian river while almost-naked Indians muscled heavy fuel drums to the plane.

In 1936, Pan Am staged its inaugural flight across the Pacific to Hawaii and the Philippines. Amon was aboard with Roy Howard, the Scripps-Howard president; Juan Trippe, Pan Am's president; Paul Patterson, publisher of the *Baltimore Sun*; California Senator William McAdoo; and Cornelius Vanderbilt Whitney. Amon's name had been second on the historic flight's six-passenger waiting list, put there by his friend Will Rogers four years earlier when the airline began planning the route.

Rogers asked that his name be placed on the roster, then added, "Better add Amon Carter, too. He wouldn't miss a chance like this." [After Rogers was killed in the Alaskan plane crash, Amon was moved up to the first-seat position.] Eleven hundred persons had applied for one of the passenger spots (a movie actress, told she was number 319 on the list, offered to charter the inaugural flight to ensure a seat).

In late September, Amon joined the other five in Alameda, on San Francisco Bay, for what was to be the world's longest non-stop commercial flight—2,410 air miles to Honolulu. As befitting the important occasion, the men wore tuxedos. The flight was delayed momentarily when the launch ferrying passengers to the seaplane had to return to shore so Senator McAdoo could kiss his wife goodbye.

The plane landed safely in Honolulu, and the men spent several days resting. A photograph showed Amon standing on the white sand beach at Waikiki in front of the Ala Moana Hotel. He was dressed in his ice cream-white suit and the semi-cowboy rig of big hat and boots, his face almost obscured by rings of orchid leis.

The Clipper flight continued to Midway, where Amon, in a mock ceremony, organized the first chamber of commerce for that isolated Pacific island. Trippe named Amon mayor of Midway. Then on to Guam where, reported the *Los Angeles Times*, Amon tasted a tree oyster—a kind of fungus—and pronounced it almost edible. In Manila, Manuel Quezon, the Philippines' president, exchanged one of his tropical hats for an Amon Carter Shady Oak Stetson.

Amon flew on to Hong Kong, where, in addition to the thousands of dollars worth of Oriental doodads and gifts for his family, he sampled boiled shark fin for the first and last times in his life. Returning, everyone except Amon bragged that they had read *Gone With the Wind* during the long flights. Amon asked the pilot to radio an emergency call for the TCU-Texas A & M football score.

In 1939, Amon was aboard as Pan American inaugurated the last of its major routes from New York across the North Atlantic to England. During the flight of nineteen hours and thirty-four minutes, passengers passed their time playing penny-ante poker and Chinese checkers and missed a drama as they slept. Midway over the Atlantic, one motor quit and the flight engineer crawled out on a catwalk to the wing and repaired the engine.

In London, the *Times* inspected "the tall, bronzed Texas newspaper king" and pronounced him 'picturesque'" in "his cowboy hat, trousers tucked into ornamental, blue, white and brown

151

boots." He was, added the *Associated Press,* the "cynosure of all eyes. . . ."

Interviewed by the *London Evening News,* Amon bragged "Yes, flying's a bad habit for us. When I came up from Southampton last night, it was the first time I'd been on a train in five years. Altogether, I've been 300,000 miles by plane."

On its return flight to America, the Clipper paused in Ireland, splashing down on the River Shannon near the village of Foynes in County Limerick. A long motor-launch sped to the plane. A group of "Foynes Cowboys" unfurled a banner proclaiming: "We Want Carter!"

Amon waved and called out, "Top of the morning, you Irish folk."

He was handed a scroll. It read: "I, Cornelius Aloysius Georgius Fitzgerald, of the clan, Fitzgerald, horsemen of renown, direct descendant of Fitzgerald, first king of Ireland, whose ancestral home was in Foynes, do hereby extend greetings to the mighty Carter of Texas, son of the Lone Star State. I also, on behalf of the Foynes Cowboy Association, challenge said Mighty Carter to ride an Irish Bronco. The bet—freedom of Foynes against his ten gallon hat. Greetings, son of Texas. I am finished."

In the village, Amon was led to his bronco—a twenty-year-old bored donkey named "Manna."

Delighted, Amon rode the donkey through Foynes as villagers cheered. His bet—and town--won, Amon magnanimously returned Foynes to its owners and left behind his white Stetson.

Any man who loved airplanes and flying as much as Amon had to have his own airport. By 1937, Fort Worth's municipal air facility, Meacham Field, was surrounded with industrial development and could not be enlarged for international flights, as Amon felt his city deserved. His first idea was that Dallas and Fort Worth could build a joint-use airport, and the larger city, which felt about Amon the way Ahab felt about the white whale, almost went along with the plan for "the biggest and best airport in the world."

The cities studied the situation in the early 1940s and planned an airport halfway between their boundaries. An engineering firm suggested the terminal building be built on a site that necessitated facing it toward Fort Worth. In an interview, Dallas Mayor Woodall Rodgers complained that the positioning was highly insulting—the terminal rear would point toward his city. Amon answered Rodgers with a two thousand-word telegram, reprinted, of course, in the *Star-Telegram*. He chastised the mayor for his narrow vision, noting that the rear-door feature "may not be as important as you think." He pointed out that the proposed airport site was one mile nearer Dallas than Fort Worth and his city was not objecting.

Amon added: "Some of us in Fort Worth are just plain country folks and while we may still eat with our knife we have felt somewhat encouraged because we have learned to do it with skill . . . while you were willing always for a 50-50 deal we had found that to mean one horse and one rabbit and unfortunately we in Fort Worth had always gotten the rabbit and of late you had even been skinning the rabbit for us."

Actually, Dallas dissolved the mutual airport agreement because of Amon Carter. Dallas leaders feared he would do with the shared airport as he did with Fort Worth—as he damn well pleased. Dallas had no intention of building Amon an airport.

Airplanes grew larger and faster and jet-powered, and it was obvious that Meacham Field's limited facilities could never accommodate passenger planes of the future. Meanwhile, Love Field in Dallas became busier and bigger and, to Amon's consternation, Fort Worthians had to go there for many flights. Amon was determined to build his city—and himself—an airport.

First he sold the city a 2,155-acre tract of land south of Fort Worth for $628,699. The FAA, however, determined the site was not suitable for an airport. Then Midway Airport—a tiny private strip near Arlington, the hyphen between Fort Worth and Dallas—became available. Fort Worth optioned the land and expanded its city limits to include the site. Amon repurchased the 2,155 acres for a cash price of $685,000, providing taxpayers with a profit and badly needed funds with which to begin planning the new airport.

Amon set about to sell the idea—never popular—to Fort Worth's citizens. Editors of the period remember that the *Star-Telegram's* airport coverage "was totally one-sided."

"Opposition simply was not reported," said one. Amon insisted he be consulted on every word written about the new air center.

A few months before the airport opened in 1953, Amon, attorney Raymond Buck, and Red Mosier, an American Airlines vice president, met in Suite 10G. They had drinks. Mosier told of his recent conversation with a pilot about Fort Worth's new airport. According to Mosier, the pilot proclaimed the new field would be the safest in the United States. The men continued drinking. Mulling over the anonymous pilot's opinion, Amon decided that *Star-Telegram* readers should know such a startling thing. He summoned a reporter, who arrived in the suite "finding Carter, Mosier and Buck partaking of liquid refreshments, of which there was an abundant quantity on a large serving table on wheels."

Carter and Mosier waxed enthusiastic about how wonderful the airport would be. Mosier related that the pilot with whom he had spoken said Fort Worth's airport would be the world's safest and fliers everywhere were falling over one another to begin using it. Carter was overjoyed by the ever-growing accolades and prodded Mosier to provide more details about the new airport's grandeur. With voluminous notes, the reporter rushed to his desk and wrote a seven-page story, then returned to the Fort Worth Club for Amon's approval.

Amon—his glasses had fallen halfway down his nose—read the story aloud very slowly. He and Mosier dictated changes and additions, making the airport more magnificent with each pencil mark.

The reporter wrote his story again. Back to the suite, where "the refreshments on the serving table were disappearing with jet-like speed." Amon proposed more alterations, each of which portrayed the new airport in ever-more-glowing and extravagant terms. Amon insisted that the story contain the fact that in the very near future, Fort Worth's air facility would be bigger and better than the airports of Los Angeles and Chicago combined.

The final version was a remarkable tale, and the reporter recalled that Amon was "extra proud of the almost-fictitious story."

The airport opened in April 1953, without Amon because he had suffered two heart attacks the previous February and was confined to a hospital bed. In his father's absence, Amon Jr. stepped forward and read a statement in which the hospitalized publisher predicted the airport would serve two million passengers annually.

Irv Farman, a fine feature writer, was overly enthusiastic about the airport program and infused his story with pages of flowery phrases and editorialized praise for Amon Carter. Before publication, Farman took the story to Amon for approval. Amon read it silently, then tossed it back to Farman, grumbling, "I hope you wore a bow tie when you wrote this. I'd hate for all this stuff to splatter off the keys and stain a good tie."

The Greater Southwest International Airport was Amon's largest failure, though he died believing it was an unqualified success. The airport never made a profit, and slowly airline service was moved to Love Field in Dallas. Finally, the facility—also known as Amon Carter Field—closed, and the mammoth terminal building, which faced neither Fort Worth nor Dallas but in a northerly, neutral direction, became a ghostly and empty building.

In the 1970s, the federal government coerced Fort Worth and Dallas into building a joint-use airport a few miles north of Greater Southwest. When it opened, it was the largest airport in the world.

Amon and airplanes were colorful pioneers. The cowboy loved aviation; it respected him. In 1950, he received the Air Force Exceptional Service Award—the highest honor that can be bestowed on a civilian. That same year he was given the Frank M. Hawks Memorial Award for his contributions to U.S. aviation history and praised as "one of the true pioneers of American Aviation." Accepting the award, Amon recalled the stormy night he flew with Hawks, of the hail and wind, thunder and lightning, of his terror in the skies over Alabama.

"My greatest fear," he said, "sprang from the fact that I didn't know anybody in Birmingham."

On a hot day in August 1935, in Matanuska, Alaska, Will Rogers had a similar problem. The Oklahoma humorist looked into the upraised, expressionless Eskimo faces and asked, "Anybody here from Claremore?"

He grinned his famous grin, unknown there in the shadow of Mount McKinley. The impassive faces stared at the smiling white man in the western-cut Shady Oak hat. His pilot—patch-eyed, crusty Wiley Post, a one-time Texas farmer who had soloed around the world—laughed at the remark and continued tinkering with his airplane, a Lockheed Orion.

Will tried again: "You see, Wiley does the flyin' and I do the talkin'. It's about a fifty-fifty job."

The Eskimos stared. Rogers and Post were there near the Eskimo village at the top of the world, waiting for the fog to dissipate, waiting to fly off to Siberia, for reasons unclear today. In June Post had explained to Bascom Timmons that he and Rogers wanted to inspect a possible Alaskan-Russian airmail route. A month later, in Texas, Rogers told Amon that the Alaskan trip was only to "get in a little huntin'." Perhaps they were there just for the adventure of it.

Rogers would have liked that—the adventure of flying into the unknown. He was an eager traveler, a million-miler in the air, a man, like Amon, always going somewhere. In the mid-1930s, William Penn Adair Rogers, of the laconic, drawling wisecrack, of the hesitant, pungent wit, was an American institution and Amon Carter's great friend.

Of all Amon's celebrity friends, only Will Rogers had Amon's complete admiration and love. Each was naturally attracted to the other. Each had risen from rural, folksy origins to a wealthy fame. If Amon's celebrity was less than Rogers's, that was acceptable to the publisher; he was willing to stand in Will Rogers's spotlight, or even far in the background. They meshed: Amon talked, Will listened. Rogers's leisurely mannerisms balanced perfectly against Amon's energized exhibitionism. "Amon never runs short on talk," Will would say when Carter's long-winded speeches seemed endless.

Rogers wrote often of Amon in his syndicated column, poking fun at Carter's windy ways, at his constant threats to "make a speech."

In return, Amon laughed loudly at Will's jokes and urged him to perform in Fort Worth free of charge. Fort Worth was Will Rogers's second home, and he was in and out of town—and Suite 10G—so often that he kept extra clothes in the apartment. He liked the Fort Worth Club, especially the food. Chefs kept a pot of chili bubbling for him and made cornbread and fried chicken. Dr. Webb Walker's "conglomerate salad" was a favorite of Rogers, and he wrote of the dish: "I had dinner with him [Amon] . . . and there was an amateur doctor Walker that mixed up a batch that layed [sic] me low. The doctors called it catarral jaundice. . . . I never have heard who else died from this Carter dinner. The dish was: Open all the cans of tomatoes you have, all the cans of cove oysters, lots of sliced onions, mix 'em in a big bowl. It's sort of soup salad. It's called 'We have scraped the bottom salad.'"

Rogers first came to Fort Worth in 1913 but did not meet the publisher then. Will performed his rope act—no talking—at an Elks Club smoker and afterward he and Jimmy North had chili in a downtown cafe. Probably Amon and Will met in 1922 during a party at John McGraw's house in New York. From then until the humorist's death, the men were close friends. If Rogers wasn't in Fort Worth—he called it "the Cowman's Paradise"—Amon was visiting at Will's California ranch.

They also met often in Washington, usually in their favorite capital hotel, the Mayflower, which had a grand style, quiet countenance, and imperturbable atmosphere. Many wealthy, elderly Washingtonians lived there, using the tranquil marble lobby for afternoon naps. Once when Rogers entered the Mayflower, he surveyed the nodding elderly faces and solemn silence. He stood in the lobby's center, cupped his hands, and yelled: "HOORAY FOR AMON CARTER, FORT WORTH, AND WEST TEXAS!"

Amon's great unfulfilled dream was canalization of the Trinity River from the Texas Gulf Coast to Fort Worth. He foresaw the day when ocean liners would dock at the city's doorstep. Amon wanted Will to understand and believe in this grand vision. He drove the humorist to a spot where the Trinity bent around Fort

Worth and the men walked the river bank, Amon explaining the canal idea in exacting detail, Will listening without comment. Finally, Amon could stand the silence no longer.

"Well, what do you think?" he blurted.

Rogers looked at his friend, looked at the river, then turned his eyes to the sky.

"I can see the sea gulls now," he declared.

Will carried the canal joke to his column, writing," Fort Worth is several hundred miles from the nearest seagull but Amon wants to give Fort Worth the benefit of a tidal wave. They have had droughts, floods, boll weevils, cattle fever, ticks and were struck by two visits of Jim Ferguson, but they have never tasted seawater. It's the only thing they haven't tasted in a bottle."

Rogers was a problem for *Star-Telegram* reporters. Each time he visited, Amon wanted a story published. Newsmen expected funny quips from Will, but he would say little for publication. "I get paid for being funny. I can't waste my talents," he once snapped to a reporter.

When Will Rogers Jr. was eighteen, the humorist asked Amon to "put my son to work on the *Star-Telegram*." As O. O. McIntire later wrote in The *Saturday Evening Post*, Amon agreed immediately, adding, "I'll put the boy up at the Fort Worth Club until he can get located."

Rogers warned: "Don't you do any fool thing like that! Let him hunt up a good five-dollar-a-week boarding house. Also you better ask the fire department to wake him up for awhile. That kid is a powerful sleeper."

Will Jr., who later in his life would be owner/ publisher of the *Hollywood Press*, moved into Fort Worth's YMCA and worked in the *Star-Telegram*'s advertising department. Soon Will wired Amon: "I have a distant son that used to be in Texas somewhere. He can't write so we figured he must be on the *Star-Telegram*." Amon promised to have the son write more often.

Amon put aside his other business whenever Will was in town and the men would sit all night in Suite 10G, Amon drinking his scotch, Will sipping an occasional beer, talking about money. ("Both were trying to get all the money they could," remembered Bascom Timmons.) Or Amon would hire a dozen cowboys and stage a rodeo for Will at Shady Oak. Rogers always involved himself in the show, doing his lariat tricks, which including roping a lighted cigar from Amon's mouth.

When Fort Worth and West Texas suffered from drought and Depression, and with the *Star-Telegram* vigorously denying either was present, Amon spoke of the double blight to Rogers. Back in California, Rogers thought about the situation and wired Amon: "Keep this to yourself and wire me at once how it sounds. I will come to Texas towns, pay all my expenses, and donate all proceeds to unemployed. . . ." Amon was delighted, immediately offering a plane and pilot, the *Star-Telegram*, his radio station, and "anything else in my power."

Rogers canceled his scheduled appearances and toured Texas, stumping for relief money—Fort Worth's contribution, $18,000, was largest. Amon pulled most of the money from his wealthy friends, including W. T. Waggoner, which caused Rogers to write, "Why don't you do this, Mr. Waggoner? Turn over what little of your fortune Fort Worth and Amon has left you, and just let them have it and put you on an allowance, then they wouldn't have to go through all this rigmarole."

In his Fort Worth show, Will introduced Amon with: "Just say 'Hello,' and shut up, I want to talk about the Trinity.

"I been telling Amon we oughta pave it," cracked Will. "It doesn't flow, it oozes. Pappy's [Waggoner] cows would drink it up."

In July 1935, Will Rogers visited Fort Worth. He and Amon flew to West Texas, to Stamford for the Cowboy Reunion—an annual rodeo and chuck wagon gathering for ranchers and cowhands. Then Will stayed and rested a few more days in Suite 10G. He bought a new shirt and blue suit at Washer Brothers and left his old suit in the apartment's closet. He described for Amon the planned flight to Alaska and "maybe on to Siberia."

Amon drove Rogers to the airport. The plane was late, delayed in Chicago for sacks of mail to be loaded. Will fidgeted, anxious for the plane to arrive.

"You have to remember," explained Amon. "You're in the third-greatest airmail center of America. They have to work all the airmail here."

"Work it or write it?" asked Will, and soon he flew away.

That August morning in Alaska, Rogers and Post waited for the fog to lift, and finally the pilot said, "I think we can make it." "If it's good enough for you, it's good enough for me," agreed Rogers, and the Lockheed lifted into the fog to fly over coastal mountains toward Point Barrow, 510 miles north. Probably Post lost his way. The plane landed at Walakpa Lagoon, sixteen miles south of Point Barrow, stayed briefly, and began to move again. It rose from the water and then nosed over.

Eskimos came to the wreckage and collected the broken bodies of Post and Rogers. In their village, the Eskimos dressed each body in long nightgowns and wrapped the men in white sheets. Almost a day passed before the outside world knew Will Rogers was dead. Amon was in Washington when news came to the White House. He wept for "dear sweet Will," and immediately set off toward Alaska.

Bush pilot Joe Crosson flew the bodies of Rogers and Post from Point Barrow to Fairbanks where they were placed aboard a Pan American World Airways plane. The plane flew to Seattle and a grieving Amon Carter. Amon sat beside the sheet-shrouded body of his friend throughout the long, night flight to Los Angeles.

The death of Will Rogers was a national tragedy. All America mourned, and afterward there was a clamor for suitable memorials to America's most beloved man. Eddie Rickenbacker became chairman of the Will Rogers Memorial Commission, which was to raise funds benefiting, in the humorist's name, crippled and underprivileged children. Amon was the fund chairman in Texas.

It was an intense matter—in Fort Worth more than any other city—and especially within the Star-Telegram, where an aggrieved Amon Carter dictated an editorial urging his city and state to "lead the nation in per capita contributions." The editorial asked for "pennies, nickels and dimes" from everyone, a literal request because Amon's fund-raisers collected a five-cent coin from every school child in Fort Worth. Daily, the Star-Telegram published county-by-county totals and inaugurated a front-page box to honor "100% Companies" in which every employee gave to the campaign ("Marvin D. Evans Printing Co., 11 employees, $4.45").

Between Rogers's death and January 1936, the *Star-Telegram* published more than two thousand stories about the fund drive. It printed an eighteen-part biography of Will and featured old, favorite columns of his. Virtually all donors had their names published in the newspaper, even a convict who donated twenty-five cents, and 240 newsboys who collected twenty-four dollars.

To raise money, the newspaper sponsored a football game between Breckenridge, Texas, and Pauls Valley, Oklahoma, high schools. Boyce House, reporting the game, exhibited the pressure on him and others, writing, "A spectacle that will form an ineffaceable picture in the minds of all who were there. . . ."

Clearly, it was more than just a football game.

In the end, Texas and Amon indeed raised more than any other state—$256,489 of the total $1.7 million.

Still sorrowing over Will's death, Amon had the humorist's portrait painted and placed in his office. It was lighted day and night. He was not finished. Amon caused a coliseum and auditorium complex built by the Public Works Administration in Fort Worth to be named for Will Rogers. He wanted more, and commissioned Electra Waggoner Biggs, Pappy's granddaughter, to sculpt Will seated on his favorite horse, Soapsuds. (She used a New York police horse as a model. The statue cost Amon $20,000, and he placed one copy on the campus of Texas Tech University in Lubbock because Will once worked on a ranch in the Panhandle, and another at the entrance of the Will Rogers Memorial in Claremore, Oklahoma.)

The statue was completed in 1939, but Amon was not ready to dedicate his memorial to Will. For the next seven years, he stored the sculpture, waiting first for Amon Jr. to return from war, then for the correct dignitary needed to solemnize this important ceremony.

In 1946, the statue—three thousand pounds, ten feet tall— finally was mounted on a grassy lawn, ready for unveiling. But the sculpture could not be seen. Amon had boxed it up, which made Fort Worthians curious and many sneaked out to "look at old Will." What that meant was ripping the boards from the statue late at night. Amon was infuriated by what he considered base vandalism and defilement of Will's memory.

One week in mid-1947, Will was unboarded twice. The first midnight raid was by Amon's friends at the Fort Worth Club. They had been drinking heavily and became curious. Next was a group of teenagers. Not very artfully, they ripped away Will's fresh planks and gawked at the towering memorial.

Before nine o'clock in the morning, Amon offered a $5,000 reward for arrest and prosecution of the vandals. In those days, police could receive citizen awards and officers dropped everything to pursue the statue caper.

Almost immediately, one teenager told his girlfriend, who told her mother, who told police and asked for the $5,000. The teenagers were rounded up and brought before a ranting Amon Carter. He lectured the boys, told them their names would be printed in the *Star-Telegram*—a reversal of a long-standing policy of publishing no names of juvenile offenders—and barred them from the Will Rogers buildings for life.

His mad spell over, Amon softened and decided not to prefer charges against the boys, one of whom was Elston Brooks, who was to become the newspaper's entertainment editor and columnist for more than four decades. Amon also decided to donate the $5,000 to the Fort Worth Police Benevolence Society.

Finally, the statue of Will Rogers was officially—and legally— unveiled in late 1947 as Dwight Eisenhower spoke and Margaret Truman sang and Amon Carter wept a last time for his friend.

Amon rides stuffed alligator in this early souvenir Florida postcard.

Amon joins Postmaster General James Farley (right) for FDR's 1933 inauguration ceremonies.

Amon Carter driving a stagecoach down Wall Street.

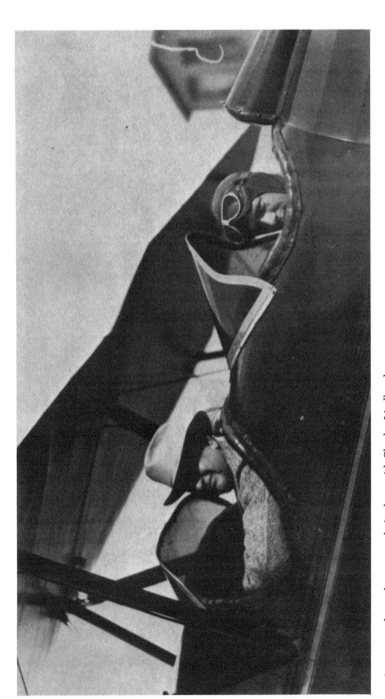

Amon samples early open-cockpit plane with Charles Lindbergh.

President Harry Truman speaks with Amon during White House ceremony to mark opening of Big Bend National Park, April 20, 1950.

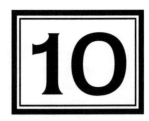

To me "No" is just a word in the dictionary. I don't often consult the dictionary.
  —Amon, *Saturday Evening Post,* 1936

It's a long way from cornbread to caviar but just a short way back.
  —A favorite homily used by Amon in speeches

You can't live off your community, you must live with it.
  —Amon, explaining the *Star-Telegram*'s public service policy, about 1950

The Depression was late to Texas and later still to Fort Worth, which was flush with good times from a mid-1920s oil boomlet at nearby Ranger. Amon bragged to his Northern friends that his town would escape the Depression, that it was bedrock solid, financially. Then what was that strange 1930 incident Pappy Waggoner called a "money stampede" that caused Amon to rage in a front-page editorial about "the ridiculous spectacle brought on by idle gossip, unfounded rumors and a state of hysterior [sic]?" Could it have been a classic Depression-era bank run?

February 18, a Wednesday. Three o'clock. First National, one of Fort Worth's larger banks with stated deposits of $24,139,069.37 and cash on hand of a million bucks and change. Minutes before doors were locked for the day, a thousand people arrived shouting for their money. Other depositors, and still more, rushed downtown until they filled the bank lobby and clogged the streets.

Panicked bank officials called in Sheriff Red Wright and a posse of deputies. A single Texas Ranger—Captain Tom Hickman— arrived, with city police, at least a dozen of whom suggested that they be given their deposited cash before the civilians became unruly. The crowd's anxiety doubtless was intensified by the failure two weeks earlier of Fort Worth's Texas National Bank, which collapsed under a load of bad loans. So First National depositors refused to move outside and just clamored louder for their money. Reluctantly, the bank began paying out.

Amon knew none of this. He was home in bed, ill with the flu, ordered there by his friend and physician, Dr. Webb Walker. Now Walker, a bank director, telephoned Amon and begged him to come to First National. The publisher arrived at five o'clock with Pappy Waggoner in tow. They joined Councilman William Monnig and bank officials in conference, after which a First National officer announced that the bank would remain open all night, if necessary, to serve depositors. *Cheers of relief.*

Amon stepped onto a lobby table and began talking. In print, the *Star-Telegram* softened its publisher's role, but the *Press* issued an extra detailing Amon's part in the extravagant five hours. Shouting for attention, Amon began calming the depositors.

"I was in a sick bed," he declared, sniffing, "and I couldn't believe this thing when I first heard it. . . . This is the safest bank in the world and you'll soon find that out. It is paying off every dollar as fast as you are passing in your checks, and for every dollar it is paying you it is taking in six more. Why, right now $2,500,000 is coming from the Federal Reserve Bank in Dallas."

As though hailed from the wings—*OK, cue the money*—a convoy of heavily armed men swept into the lobby and forced an aisle through the crowd. The guards carried large U.S. paper currency pouches and smaller coin bags.

"See there!" shouted Amon. "What did I tell you? You can't take your money out as fast as they can bring it in. Let's boost for our city. Let's not go mad like this. Let's go home, and in the morning your money will be right here for you. The organization I represent has a hundred thousand dollars here and I expect to leave it here."

Amon called on the laconic Waggoner to deliver his first public speech. The rancher/oilman explained his views in terms he could understand:

> I have been a cowman and have swung onto many a cow's tail in a stampede, but this is the first stampede like this I ever saw. . . . [Amon urged him to speak louder] . . . I am here to tell you this stampede is worse than cattle stampeding, and I want you to stop it and go on home. This bank has been in business for fifty years and will be in business long after we are gone.

With raised hand, Pappy vowed, "I hereby pledge to you every cent I own and possess in this world that you will not lose a single dollar in this bank. I will sell every cow and every oil well if necessary to pay for any money you lose. Go home, I tell you, go on home!"

Hesitant applause.

Pappy, whose assets were ten times those of First National, repeated his promise. *Light cheering.* The *Press* reported that Waggoner's talk began "to turn the tide." He personally escorted an elderly widow back to a cashier, and redeposited her $5,000.

Bank officers spoke, and city officials. Amon remounted the high table, over and over urging reasoned thought and action. He lectured on Fort Worth's economic stability, its limitless financial future, how one day it would be a rich behemoth city of consequence. Just think, he shouted, Fort Worth already was the nation's third-ranking airmail center!

Many depositors who earlier collected their cash had rushed to place it with the U.S. Savings Department of the Post Office. Postmaster Billy Moore arrived at First National with all that money—$21,000—and redeposited it. That demonstrated, he announced, that the United States of America had confidence in the bank's stability. Withdrawals slowed. At 6:30 P.M. Amon sent out for cheese sandwiches and hot dogs. He fed the multitudes. Two orchestras arrived from nearby Hotel Texas and set up at each end of the lobby. They began playing "Singing in the Rain" and "Hail, Hail, the Gang's All Here." A few couples danced. Others sang along. Flasks of bootleg whiskey were passed around and lawmen nipped from them along with the crowd. Amon announced that depositors could use their bank passbooks for free admission into the Majestic Theater, and two hundred people rushed off to see William ["Stage"] Boyd in Pathe's all-talking picture show, "Officer O'Brien." The *Star-Telegram* reported that the bank run abated and turned into a kind of block party. At eight o'clock, Amon returned himself to bed, the bands played "Home, Sweet Home," and it was over. Next morning, bank officials announced that more cash was on deposit than the day before. A grand jury investigated the panic but reached no firm decision, although many people were convinced that Red anarchists masterminded the bank run. Amon messaged his famous and influential friends that the aborted bank run proved Fort Worth was "financially able to take care of itself."

Within two years, the Depression had sidled into Fort Worth for what appeared to be a lengthy siege of bad times. The *Star-Telegram* held on. No jobs were lost, but everyone earning more than twenty dollars weekly accepted a 10-percent salary reduction.

Amon was concerned. At home he called Nenetta and the children together and announced that the family would reduce its lifestyle. They would discontinue all luxuries except the servants and new cars each year. Actually, bad financial times affected

Amon very little. As usual he was broke and in debt, even several months behind on his grocery bills, just as he was during the 1920s money boom. During the summer of 1934, he decided his home needed new window screens. Amon asked Bert Honea for a salary advance. The penurious treasurer advised Amon to repair the screens. Amon griped to Nenetta that "Bert Honea is the stingiest ol' sonovabitch in the world," but he patched the screens.

The Depression burrowed deeply into Fort Worth's economy for the next four years, until 1936. That was Texas's centennial, and the state was obliged to commemorate its one hundred years of greatness. A commission was appointed to determine how the state would solemnize the occasion. The answer was an exposition—a statewide extravaganza of everything good in Texas, a spectacular show well larded by educational displays and cultural events.

Amon was appointed to the elite body but did not participate in its debates, except to ask for funds with which to expose West Texas's role in the state's development. A board of historians rejected the claim on grounds that West Texas "contains no history to commemorate."

No history! shrieked the indignant *Star-Telegram*, ticking off the region's contributions to Texana: fourteen major Spanish explorations . . . Ysleta, oldest town in the state. . .oil, ranches, railroads, cowboys, cattle, Indians. The editorial even exhumed the skeleton of a giant bison found in Pleistocene gravel of the Panhandle to demonstrate prehistoric importance. James Record dispatched a fleet of reporters into West Texas to begin a weekly series of stories on history out there. The series continued for more than a year.

Being ignored historically was insulting enough for Amon, but slight beside the commission's next announcement: Dallas would be the site of the exposition.

Amon had not pushed Fort Worth for the honor. As did most everyone, he believed San Antonio or Houston, each directly involved with Texas's independence battles of 1836, were logical locations for the centennial celebration. Dallas didn't even exist in 1836 and had no more claim on the birthday party than Fort Worth. Dallas, however, had cash—a deciding catalyst in

Depression-weak Texas. Told of Dallas's centennial coup, Amon gawddammed the inequity of it all.

June 1935, Amon gathered his close friends to decide what must be done with Dallas. They agreed on a scheme in which Fort Worth would show its neighbor city "how the cow ate the cabbage"—Fort Worth would produce its own separate, competing, unofficial centennial exposition! Amon always credited William Monnig with the original idea, but the impetus creating the Fort Worth exposition, and its final form, clearly was the publisher's. No one else would have dared try it. Besides, Amon found Billy Rose.

Earlier, Fort Worth had solicited federal funds for its Depression, but more were needed. The planned bogus centennial created a new demand, and Will Rogers's death in the summer of 1935 provided an acceptable approach. Fort Worth asked for a Public Works Administration grant to construct a combination coliseum/auditorium/tower, which would become a centerpiece for the centennial show, and named for Rogers.

The proposal caused terrible-tongued Harold Ickes, FDR's interior secretary and PWA director, to snap, "I can't understand why a memorial to Will Rogers should be built in Fort Worth just because he was Carter's friend." Ickes denied the grant.

Site of the anticipated complex was a 135-acre tract west of downtown, across the Trinity River on a mild hill. It had been a horse ranch, and failed residential development, and World War I military training area. In 1935, the hill was bare of everything but scrub oaks and ebony-eyed sunflowers. The complex, if built, would have a life after the centennial as headquarters for the annual Southwest Exposition, Fat Stock Show, and Rodeo—a statewide event that grew out of the city's north side cattle industry.

Thus, in Washington, Fort Worth's PWA request became known as "Amon's cowsheds."

Ickes wrote Amon of the denial, pointing out that he had approved a school building and tuberculosis sanatorium for Fort Worth, each of which "clearly outranked a livestock pavilion as socially desirable projects." Amon fired a telegram at Ickes: "You have knocked us in the creek for good." Naturally, he went over

Ickes's head to the White House. In Washington, the publisher outlined Fort Worth's program to Postmaster General James Farley. Farley presented Amon's plan to FDR. He asked Amon to wait, and purposely left the door ajar.

Farley spoke loudly to the president, "Amon wants to build a cowshed."

"Cowshed!" exclaimed Roosevelt.

The eavesdropping Amon rushed in, shouting, "Now, gawddammit, it's not a cowshed, it's . . ."

Roosevelt and Farley collapsed with laughter.

Fort Worth officially resubmitted the project, and Farley wired Amon, "Your proposal received. Was always in favor of large cowsheds." Early November 1935, Jesse Jones, director of the Reconstruction Finance Corporation, wrote Amon, "Your cowshed has been approved by the administration."

Amon telegraphed his appreciation to FDR: "The cowshed has arrived."

11

He who would do some great thing in this short life must apply himself to the work with such a concentration of his forces, as to idle spectators who like only to amuse themselves, looks like insanity.
—A scribbled Amon axiom, found in his private file

This surpasses anything I have been in Paris, Havana, New York and Buenos Aires.
—Jorge Sanchez, Cuban sugar baron, 1936

Good Heavens, Billy! It's better than your publicity. It's a goose's dream.
—Fannie Brice, Broadway musical star, to her husband, Billy Rose, after seeing *Casa Mañana*, 1936

Casa Mañana had its name within two minutes after the thought flashed through the mind of Billy Rose that here was something at least a decade beyond the dreams of any other showman in the world. The largest cafe-theater in the universe. The most fabulous outdoor entertainment arena in existence. A structure of . . . sweeping magnitude. . . . What else could it be but the House of Tomorrow?
—Notes from *Casa Mañana* program, 1936

T-T-Texas is G-G-God's c-c-country.
—Mary Louise "Stutterin' Sam" Dowell, Broadway showgirl, bragging about her state to Walter Winchell, about 1939

Fort Worth's outlaw exposition moved along, planned for a thirty-eight-acre section adjacent to the PWA complex and mostly in the well-meaning but inexperienced control of the town's women, who set out to create an enlightened production heavy with religion and *haute* cowboy traditions, a show with all the excited theatrics of an elementary school pageant.

In the women's defense, they knew no better, being amateurs at revenge on Dallas and having very little with which to work. Dallas planned to immortalize Texas with an $15,000,000 exposition of empyrean refinement, of artsy, even fustian, culture. With a few thousand dollars, Fort Worth's women began to fashion a ragamuffin replica of Dallas's show, a religio-historic pageant replete with homemade parts: Boy Scouts painted as fierce Indians, a reproduction of frontier Fort Worth, jelly and baking competitions, food booths and a museum, the city symphony for uplifting musicales, and an amphitheater in which to present a dramatic gala featuring church choirs.

Amon gawddammed the dullness of it all and set out to find a remedy.

About the time the women mailed valentines promoting their centennial ("Prairie schooner to limousine, Sunbonnets to crepe de chine; Texas history, watch it grow, at Fort Worth's Centennial show"), Amon contacted Rufus LeMaire, MGM's casting director and a former Fort Worth resident. By coincidence, LeMaire knew of a producer in need of a project. Billy Rose.

William Samuel Rosenberg was thirty-seven—but claimed to be thirty-five—when he went to work for Fort Worth. He would become an extraordinary figure in American theater life, ranking beneath the Barnums and Ziegfelds he emulated, but affecting the style of the stage as no other showman between the middle 1930s and postwar years. Quality was not Rose's genius; bigness was. As DeMille of the movies, Rose created glossy, oversized pageantry, as eye-stunning as it was mediocre.

Billy Rose had a brilliance for overwhelming the senses of a popcorn-and-lemonade audience, and the shows he devised for Fort Worth in 1936 were perfect for their time and place. In that year, Rose was not yet a theater immortal, was, in fact, little known beyond a few blocks of Broadway where bystanders snickeringly called him "Mr. Brice," referring to his famous wife,

Fannie, the Ziegfeld musical-comedy star. He had been a world shorthand champion and Bernard Baruch's secretary and was a songwriter of minor acclaim (very minor; his opus was *Barney Google*— "with the goo-goo-googly eyes"). He was producer of the entertaining *Jumbo*, a circus show on Broadway. His New York cabarets, *Casino de Paree* and *Music Hall*, briefly were popular. As the year began, Rose was desperate—even neurotic—to shed his "Mr. Brice" title.

In retrospect, the unauthorized centennial was the consequence of timing and personalities: Amon, in a classic snit at Dallas; Rose, anxious to be something other than Fannie Brice's husband; John Murray Anderson, peaking in his abilities as a stage director; Albert Johnson and Raoul Pene Du Bois, still in their twenties, reaching for perfection in stage design and costuming; Dana Suesse, only twenty-one, rising to become one of the few successful female songwriters of her era; Paul Whiteman, establishing himself as a legendary symphonic jazz musician; and shrewd, petite, and naked Sally Rand, who would make feather fans and rubber bubbles the standard for staged nudism. Thirty years after the centennial, Rose wrote, "I don't know what would have happened to my ragtag career if Amon Carter hadn't offered me a job. . . ."

Casa Mañana, the centennial's largest show, believed Rose, was "by all odds the best I've ever had my name on." A *Star-Telegram* editorial described *Casa Mañana:* "No attraction of its size and lavishness has been produced in the history of American theater." For once, the newspaper's chauvinistic rhetoric perhaps was not exaggerated. *Casa Mañana* seems to have been a benchmark of musical spectacle. For the first time, there was dramatic grandeur beyond Broadway. With only thinly disguised differences, Billy restaged his Fort Worth show for the remainder of his theatrical life.

As Rose and Amon began plotting the centennial, James Reston, then an *Associated Press* columnist, reported, "Never has Broadway been so interested in a project outside New York."

In the beginning, Rose was unimpressed. He came to Fort Worth. He listened. He inspected the grounds, learned of the Boy

Scout Indians and religious undercurrent and the minuscule budget. Shaking his head, as much in disbelief as in refusal, Billy reboarded an American Airlines plane to New York. Still talking, Amon came aboard and sat beside him. When the airplane landed in New York, Billy was sold into becoming director general of Fort Worth's Frontier Centennial, though there was a question of who sold whom. His salary was $1,000 a day for one hundred days.

The show's finance committee gulped.

Amon made his next announcement. Fort Worth must assemble a million-dollar war chest, and quickly. The publisher chaired the fund drive. First, he emptied his and his friends' pockets. Then he raided the *Star-Telegram* for $65,000, which infuriated Bert Honea. Selling bonds at fifty dollars each, the chamber of commerce collected another $250,000. Amon begged funds from the Texas Centennial Commission, and somehow wrangled still another $250,000 from the United States Centennial Commission. He put the PWA, and Ickes, under siege. And Amon dogged American industry—the companies run by men he had gifted with hats and smoked turkeys and diamond-studded belt buckles. The corporations already were committed heavily to Dallas's official centennial; few responded to Amon's first call. General Motors denied Amon six times, each refusal being less and less polite. He refused its refusal, and his files reveal a full range of appeals, from threats to wheedling to outright groveling. Ultimately, GM handed over twenty-five thousand bitter dollars as sponsor of the showground's public address system. Most companies eventually contributed hush money to halt Amon's telephone calls and telegrams.

March 7. Ground was broken. Rose announced his plans, remarkable because he had none, a situation that would have burdened a less impertinent man. His first press conference, conducted as he perched atop a gargantuan white stallion and posed for newsreel pictures, was pure stream of consciousness.

"You people," he shouted at the crowd, "stick with me and I'll make a big state out of Texas."

Q. "Do you miss Broadway?"

A. "Hell, I am Broadway!"

Once tapped, the Rosian wellspring flooded: "I'm going to put on a show the like of which has never been seen by the human eye. This Fort Worth show will bring 5,000,000 visitors down here. It should gross $2,000,000 ... no, no ... It'll be a $5,000,000 show. We'll give them a bold ball-of-fire. Let Dallas, at the central centennial, educate the people. We'll entertain them in Fort Worth. We'll have a 'Lonely Hearts Ball' weekly, where all lonesome women can come and find a partner in a drawing. In years to come there'll be kids telling one another that their grandma and grandpa were thrown together by fate and fell in love at the Fort Worth Frontier Centennial. I'll get Shirley Temple, Mae West, Guy Lombardo, Jack Benny. I'll get 1,000 beautiful girls for the Frontier Follies. I'll have a Texas Pageant to be called 'The Fall of the Frontier' ... 'The Battle of San Jacinto' ... or some other Texas name. I'll have 2,000 Indians and 1,000 cowboys, and guess who wins? I'll have a chorus line of 500 pretty girls. I'll have an open-air dance floor for 3,000 dancers, and singing waiters. Dallas has all that historical stuff so we don't have to worry about that. We can just show the people a good time. I plan to drive Dallas nuts. Every time Dallas says something about its exposition, I'll give 'em Shirley Temple. This is the biggest thing I've ever done. This'll make 'Jumbo' look like a peep show."

Rose promised to import *Jumbo*, utilizing "900 extras and truckloads of circus animals." He announced a theater-restaurant seating 4,500 persons and a faithful re-creation of an old-time saloon with a dozen 200-pound beauties dancing atop a splendorous bar.

Reporters decided what they had on their hands was a fat little raving madman.

Standing a pot-bellied five feet, two inches, Rose looked like a tall, overweight urchin (John Nance Garner, the vice president, called Billy a "pursley-gutted little feller"). He had sudden, excited movements, with a hopscotching kind of walk and flinging hands, smoked endlessly—though he never bought cigarettes; merely reached into the nearest pocket and filched his tobacco needs. Within days of arriving in Fort Worth, he was addicted to Dr Pepper, then a Texas-only soft drink with a reputation for curing constipation because everyone believed its secret formula began with prune juice. Rose's nighttime lifestyle had given him the complexion of a fungus. He looked sickly, reporters thought, until they tried to match his twenty-hour days and field ideas popping from his eight-story mind.

Billy scrapped the women's centennial program (their museum, he said, would have looked like "hell and a bunch of spinach"), and relegated them to positions as tree planters, greeters, and scrapbook keepers. A week after his thunderbolt introduction to Fort Worth, Rose was back in New York assembling a production staff, hiring chorus girls and entertainers, closing *Jumbo,* and mostly trying to figure out what kind of centennial he would produce. He arrived almost hidden under an Amon Carter cowboy hat and flashing a gold-plated sheriff's badge. Billy swaggered into the Hippodrome and said "Hidy" to everyone. Standing on Rosie the elephant's footstool, he declared, "My friends, I am now a Texan. I commute between this great city and Texas, a state they have given me as a plaything."

Mid-April. Two thousand men toiled at the centennial site, rushing to meet an impossible June opening date. Flitting among the workers was the quixotic Rose, shouting, bumming cigarettes, swigging Dr Pepper, directing construction from pencil sketches drawn by Albert Johnson back in New York. Rose still had only the slightest of notions what his million-dollar show would be. Billy established headquarters in the downtown Sinclair Building, where he held court and auditions in a suite. He installed a wide desk and behind it, an elevated chair that sat him high above everyone. Katrine Deakins thought Billy on his lofty throne "looked like a knot on a dead stump."

Newsmen were intrigued by the array of characters flowing through Rose's office: four-foot-three-inch John Fox—once Buster Brown for a shoe company; seven-foot-three-inch Dave Ballard—a schoolboy from Commerce, Texas; seventy-five-year-old Josie DeMott Robinson—a bareback rider who had worked for P. T. Barnum; a strong woman who bent nails between her fingers; Gozo the mind-reading dog; Tiny Kline, once arrested in New York for sliding down a slack wire from a hotel roof to a theater; Joe Peanuts and his Simian Gigolos—a sixteen-piece all-monkey band; a man who looked and dressed like Abe Lincoln; a real Russian count who spoke no English; an aviatrix who flew planes upside down; a parachutist who leaped from balloons; a rancher with a four thousand-pound, six-foot-two-inch-tall longhorn steer; a promoter with a frog circus: and a frontiersman carrying a human spine spiked with Indian arrows.

Through *Star-Telegram* pages, Rose issued a call for "whittlers, snuff-dippers, crackerbox philosophers, old couples, ox-drivers, town half-wits, village drunks, etc." to populate Sunset Trail, main street of the frontier section.

A Fort Worth man arrived clutching a leather briefcase. He opened the case and dumped a live, wriggling snake onto Rose's desk. Billy hopped up on his high chair, chittering, "Get that thing the hell out of here!" The snake had two, perfectly formed heads, each of which could be fed separately. It was trained to eat from the man's hand and follow him like a loving pet. Rose, despite his terror, recognized a sterling exhibit. He hired the snake.

What had Amon wrought?

Rose was asked to complete in less than two months what Dallas, ten thousand workers, and $15,000,000 were doing in a year. The June 6 deadline could not be met; Dallas's centennial opened on schedule. Amon fumed. Rose, at last, knew what he would stage, but the absence of final plans had not blunted publicity. Rose went ahead with propaganda and stunts that had Fort Worthians gape-mouthed. He telegraphed Mrs. Wallis Simpson, who was called by polite society columnists, "friend of King Edward of England": "Would consider it a privilege to present you in person at the Fort Worth Frontier Centennial here in Texas Stop Am prepared to offer you $25,000 a week for four weeks' engagement Stop If interested, please cable." No reply, but the offer made headlines. Billy wired Germany to request the airship Hindenburg for transportation of one hundred showgirls from Broadway to Fort Worth. No answer. He offered Ethiopian Emperor Haile Selassie, then fleeing a short-lived palace coup, $100,000 to appear "with your lions." Silence. He messaged Gypsy Rose Lee, promising her "3 G's to perform." The premier stripper wired back, "Strings or Grands?"

Billy—shouting irritably, "I don't need a forty-hour week, I need a forty-hour day"—hired real Indians: Comanche, Apache, Navajo, Hopi, and Sioux, and contracted for a Monkey Mountain. He wrote billboard copy that said nothing, but said it very well: "BIGGEST ENTERPRISE DEVOTED EXCLUSIVELY TO AMUSEMENT IN THE HISTORY OF THE WORLD . . . Monkey Mountain . . . 92 other attractions of Magnitude and Merit . . . Not Cheap Catch Penny Peep-Shows . . . Take your Entertainment Sitting Down."

Eleven thousand billboards were erected across nine surrounding states. They showed near-nude girls gamboling in a Western motif, and the slogan: "GO ELSEWHERE FOR EDUCATION, COME TO FORT WORTH FOR ENTERTAINMENT." That anti-Dallas *ipse dixit*, appearing in various renditions, became Fort Worth's battle cry.

Preachy as ever, the *Star-Telegram* urged Fort Worth citizens to "get into the Fiesta spirit," and lectured women on proper dress for shows—"Do not wear freakish costumes like slacks, overalls or beach pajamas." The newspaper, "as a public service for our non-Texas visitors," printed a lexicon of western terms ("Chouse: to stir up cattle more than is good for them"). It reported on reactions beyond its borders: "Fort Worth stole the show last night when WLW, the world's most popular radio station, saluted Texas from Cincinnati. It was the first Texas city mentioned and received four mentions to Dallas's two."

Into his final plans, Billy was building a mountain for *The Last Frontier*—his western epic. He said it would incorporate a full rodeo because "rodeo is grand opera on horseback." Billy had never seen a rodeo. Amon suggested Rose add square dancing. He agreed, then asked *Star-Telegram* reporter Bess Stephenson, "What's square dancing?" She drove him to Fort Worth's north side, to Peacock's Tavern, where Goober Dixon called a double-L swing while the Rabbit Twisters, a string band, played "Sally Goodin'." Billy sat in silence through the performance, then whispered in Bess's ear, "Where's the sex in it?" When they were leaving, Rose announced, "I'll have 200 dancers." He had one hundred and thirty-six, with Goober chanting:

"Hurry, girls, and don't get lazy,
Big fat hogs and lots of gravy,
Star-Telegram, full of news,
Grab that gal with the high-top shoes."
The Rose-conceived square dance was choreographed by Alexander Oumansky, late of the Diaghilev Russian Ballet Company. Billy often was intemperate but he was never common.

Mid-June. Casts assembled, rehearsals began. The showgirls arrived from New York and immediately asked to see cowboys. One strolled to a nearby drugstore and inquired of a clerk, "Which way's the village?" Indians poured in by the tribefuls. Within days, Navajos were feuding with Sioux, Hopis with Apaches, and Comanches with everybody. Reporters caught Navajo braves doing the family wash. Local archers beat the Indians in a bow-and-arrow contest. The Indians struck *The Last Frontier* because they were ordered to enter single file. They could not, they protested, because there were six chiefs among them and each chief had to lead. Rose handed down a Solomonic decision: "Make them all chiefs, irrespectable *[sic]* whether they are or not." All Indians became chiefs. Rehearsals continued.

John Murray Anderson arrived to direct the *Casa Mañana* show. At fifty, Anderson had straight, combed-back hair, a long unsmiling face, and a tongue that blistered. He was a widower, a polished gentleman, a Canadian educated in Europe. No two men could have been more ill matched than the sophisticated Anderson and the Bronx-made Rose, but their stage marriage was perfect. Rose dreamed, Anderson made dreams real. Neither especially liked the other. Once Billy bragged of his wealth to Anderson, shouting, "I have a fistful of money. What do you have?"

"I," replied Anderson quietly, "have one friend."

Erudite and cosmopolitan, as proven by his Ziegfeld extravaganzas on Broadway, Anderson nevertheless had a tinseled, beery eye for pomp and pageantry. He knew what sold on stage. His directing style was one of sarcasm and nettled wit and as rehearsals progressed, fascinated reporters spent leisure hours "watching Anderson yell."

183

"You half-wit with the cigar," he lashed at one actor. "Project what little voice you have out here, not into the wings." He commented to an out-of-step chorus girl, "God only knows where that small mind of yours wanders."

Anderson invented whimsical nicknames for everyone. Among his Fort Worth chorus girls were Dry Ice and Child Frightener, Goo-Goo, Fuzzy, The Cobra, Birthday Cake, Eyebrows, Chigger, Cigar, and Spaghetti. Anderson called Rose The Mad Emperor, and Amon, simply and unimaginatively, The Big Chief (surely he sensed Amon's dislike of familiarity from the hired hands).

No nickname's source was more obvious than for the girl he called Stuttering Sam—Mary Louise Dowell, the nineteen-year-old daughter of Fort Worth's police chief. She was six feet tall, possessed of perfect legs, a pert face, and bright-red hair. She had unaffected stage presence, and carriage and smile that projected even into the nickel seats. Except for the stutter, she was the model showgirl. Stuttering Sam became the focal point of the *Casa Mañana* chorus line, both in 1936 and 1937, then Rose transported her to Broadway as centerpiece for his "Diamond Horseshoe." Mary Louise Dowell immediately became New York's most celebrated showgirl. James Montgomery Flagg painted her. She dated show business's leading male stars. Columnists Ed Sullivan and Walter Winchell publicized her stuttering quips ("Where did you get that mink coat?" a Stork Club diner asked Mary Louise. "I found it on the s-s-s-s-subway," replied Stuttering Sam). She captivated everyone with her tales of Texas, explaining the processes of milking cows, feeding chickens, frying steak, and picking pecans. She complained because Toots Shor didn't serve cornbread and buttermilk in his famed restaurant. Shor affectionately called Sam his "crum-bum doll."

Her career was secondary, though, because what Mary Louise really wanted was to become a writer, and she did produce a column irregularly for the *Star-Telegram*, bylined "Stuttering Sam." The columns pattered on about Broadway and its characters, about her adventures in the big city, about other Texans displaced in New York. Abruptly, in 1942, Stuttering Sam quit show business and took her typewriter to Hollywood, to Warner

Brothers, where she was hired as a scenarist. There was talk of a film on her life but nothing came of the idea. Two years later, Sam left Hollywood without writing success.

Not everyone was enchanted by the centennial. Albert Johnson went for breakfast one morning, and the waitress, hearing his accent, asked, "You one of them New York actor folks?" He admitted he was. She frowned. His meal served, Johnson called after the woman, "Say, I asked for buttered toast."

"Butter it yourself," she snapped. "Yore arm ain't broke."

It was not only Texans' natural suspicion of outsiders but also Rose's abrupt manner and his ideas, which had little to do with real Texas history, that created problems. A veteran's group complained Rose refused to give them space for their war weapons display. Pushed into the background, the women weren't content with their trash cleanup campaign, sponsorship of school centennial clubs, and restoration of a log cabin. They publicly condemned the scantily clad cowgirl symbol on billboards and lamented the absence of a church in the reconstructed frontier town. A Miss Shelton suggested doing away with the saloons and adding Fort Worth's symphony orchestra and an opera "each fortnight."

Preachers went after Billy Rose's sinful hide, mostly over advertising for *Casa Mañana* that depicted bare-breasted—albeit nippleless—girls splashing in the theater's lagoon. A committee of incensed Baptists investigated the centennial's immorality and reported that all ingredients for public corruption certainly were there—nude advertising with suggestive words and phrases, half-naked showgirls, booze, and slot machines. One Baptist minister, S. H. Frazier, told city council members of the "nude women above the water" and asked the tantalizing question, "Are we going to show visitors the old days only as drinking, gambling and carousing?"

Fort Worth's General Ministers Association voted a resolution condemning the advertising and general lack of religious orientation. A delegation was dispatched to confront Rose. Billy later commented, "They were all nice, except one, and he looked like he had sixty yards of rope under his hat to hang me." The meeting changed nothing. Privately, Rose was elated with the preachers' attack. It was better publicity than he could contrive, and the ministers' catalog of centennial wickedness showed customers exactly where to look for what they wanted.

There was nudity, unadorned breasts in Sally Rand's *Nude Ranch*. Sally performed in *Casa Mañana* but owned and produced the nudie show. *Variety* reported Sally netted $1,000 weekly from her nudes. That sin should pay so well provoked Baptist preachers to even more bombastic outrage. The Reverend Joe Scheumack commanded that city councilmen "see to it that those girls put on clothes or that the show is closed."

Had he seen the show? "I have not," he replied indignantly. "I just saw the statues out front. They are an open violation of the law in themselves." Hitting his stride, Reverend Scheumack said the *Nude Ranch* "is a contamination of the centennial and flagrant violation of this state's penal code. I think they're about as low as they can get. Such things have a tendency to corrupt the morals of people."

Folks rushed to see the objects of Scheumack's harangue. The nude business got better.

Sally Rand was one of the most successful strippers in history, though she disliked the term and, in fact, never undressed on stage—she danced naked but hidden behind fans or balloons and bathed in a baby-blue light. Nobody ever saw anything she didn't want seen, thus her coined wisecrack, "The Rand is quicker than the eye." She was hired at Amon's suggestion. During that first horseback press conference, Rose promised his productions would have "neither nudity nor smut. Only once has the public responded to smut. We don't need any fans or bubble dances at the Texas Frontier Centennial and we won't have them."

Curious, Amon asked about the popular smut.

"At the Century of Progress in Chicago," said Billy. "Sally Rand had a nude act."

"Pulled 'em in, did she?"

"By the thousands."

"Let's get her."

The *Nude Ranch* was billed as the "only educational exhibit on the grounds," and tickets were a quarter each. Out front were

Sally Rand and girls.

replicas of classic Greek and Roman female statuary with those
bared plaster breasts irking the Reverend Scheumack. Patrons
entered through a re-created ranch house front porch, on which
sat Adolph, King of the Nudists. He was seventy-four, with a long
black beard that fell across his Roman tunic. His toes were badly
afflicted with corns and bunions, reporters noted.

Inside were the eighteen girls and thirty-six breasts. Each girl
wore boots and hat, a green bandanna, skirtlet, tights, and the
brand "SR" rubber-stamped on each fleshy thigh. The "show"
consisted of the girls lounging on swings and beach chairs. Some
played with a beach ball. Others shot bows and arrows. One or
two sat on horses. A screened floor-to-ceiling wall separated
viewers from breasts. Jack Gordon, the *Press* entertainment columnist, described the girls as "goona-goona." There was a "kick-
off" room to extract another two bits from spectators. Inside was
Florence dressed in an organdy gown. A maid helped Florence
undress, removing even the black step-ins, and get into a milk
bath. Florence bathed in milk twenty-five times a day. The sinful
Nude Ranch was as chaste as those old nudist-colony films, but
the male spectators seemed not mind the innocence of it all.

June passed. Enter July. Still no Fort Worth Frontier Centennial. Amon fidgeted. Dallas's centennial was doing big business. Critics praised the Dallas show, lauding its edifying theme. Visitors said they enjoyed most the General Motors building in which Jan Garber's orchestra played beside a crankshaft spinning 1,700 revolutions a minute, and the Chrysler exhibit with its organ and harp concerts. Eddie Barr, a Dallas columnist, sneaked a look at Fort Worth's showgrounds and decided the centennial there "probably will be mediocre and cheap."

Fort Worth made its move. Opposite the main entrance of Dallas's exposition, Rose and Amon erected the world's second largest sign (only a chewing gum billboard overlooking Times Square was larger). The green and red neon sign was 130 feet long, sixty feet high, and its message blinked day and night: "FORTY-FIVE MINUTES WEST TO WHOOPEE." Fort Worth was spelled out in neon letters 17½ feet tall. Dallas began scurrying around for non-educational exhibits.

In late June, in preparation for its centennial celebration, Fort Worth ended its statewide beauty contest to select Texas Sweetheart Number One. She was Faye Cotton, a Borger waitress—five-feet-six-inches tall, 120 pounds, gray eyes, and a 35-24½-35 figure. The new sweetheart told reporters she read the Bible daily and had hobbies of dancing and shooting. The *Star-Telegram* commented that the beauty queen had "less personal vanity than a Salvation Army settlement worker." She immediately entered the hospital for a tonsillectomy.

The *Dallas Morning News* chided Fort Worth for not choosing a sweetheart with a higher social standing than that of a waitress. The *Star-Telegram* angrily defended the selection with an editorial praising motherhood in West Texas.

Rose still was hiring acts. He brought in the Foster Girls—seventeen teenage bareback riders shepherded by Allen K. Foster, who did not allow his cast to date, smoke or drink, enforced a midnight curfew, and made the girls go everywhere, even to meals, as a group. Billy announced that he had hired for *Jumbo* the lovely Barbette—"Most breathtaking aerialist in Europe." Daily, Rose issued reports of Barbette's progress toward Fort Worth, of how Barbette was the toast of Paris, of Barbette being wined and dined by crowned heads of Europe. Barbette, newsmen decided, was something special. She was. Or rather *he* was. Barbette was Clyde Vander of Round Rock, Texas, a female impersonator and circus aerial star in Europe.

July 18. Finally, the Fort Worth Frontier Centennial opened with 25,000 spectators crowding the entrance to Sunset Trail. FDR was in his yacht, the *Sewanna*, fishing in the Bay of Fundy off Cape Sable, Nova Scotia. At 3:30 P.M. he punched a button, sending an electrical impulse to a Maine relay station, which beamed the wave across the United States to Texas, to Fort Worth, where it electronically snipped a lasso. Then Amon entered the grounds driving a Wells Fargo stagecoach, dressed in his cowboy costume, whooping and yippeeing and firing his pistols for *March of Time* newsreel cameras. That day Dallas newspapers announced that two million people already had visited the Texas Centennial. Dallas presented a bizarre ceremony, perhaps to upstage Fort Worth. At mid-afternoon, Violet Hilton was married to James Moore, a slide trombone player, on the fifty-yard line of the Cotton Bowl. Five thousand people paid twenty-five cents each to attend the wedding. It was a simple dignified service. The bride wore white, as did her Siamese twin sister, Daisy.

But there was little Dallas could do to lessen Amon's opening. One thousand newspapermen, including New York's best-known columnists and critics, were in Fort Worth, invited there by Amon, who provided transportation, food, and booze. The New Yorkers came by American Airlines plane. Billy Rose met the group, outfitted in one of Amon's cowboy rigs, with spurs, oversized hat, and boots. Two guns hung on his hips. Billy quick-drew a pistol, aimed at the newsmen, and shouted, "Bang, bang. You're dead." Columnist Lucius Beebe wrote that Rose looked like "an east side kid playing cowboy."

That evening Amon primed the writers with champagne and chili at his Shady Oak Farm, then sent them to *Casa Mañana* for a special press preview. An hour-long, eighty-five station, nationwide radio broadcast on NBC's network preceded the show with Amon's WBAP announcers handling microphones. Harold

Hough was anchorman. He lamented that Sally Rand's *Nude Ranch* would not be presented adequately, adding, "But after all, we do not have television." Predictably, the press preview was a huge success. Stories about Amon's centennial blanketed America. Burns Mantle wrote, "For valor, valor touched with profligacy, I give you Fort Worth, even if it suspects all scotch drinkers are sissys *[sic]*." Robert Garland of the *New York World-Telegram,* gushed, "So gargantuan . . . so fantastic . . . so incredible. They have merged the dreams of Buffalo Bill with Broadway Billy. I like the imagination of it, the what-the-hell-do-we-care of its 2 million-dollar whoopee." Ward Morehouse, the *New York Sun's* drama critic, suggested that a Casa Mañana theater be built in Central Park. (Rose later opened a cafe/theater by that name at Seventh Avenue and Fiftieth Street in New York, but it was never popular.) Beebe thought the show was "thrilling . . . a dream come true," but went on to call Texans "scammy" because a drunken cowboy had tried to sell him a 2,200-acre ranch.

Damon Runyon, writing for the Hearst syndicate, was most effusive: "Broadway and the wild west are jointly producing what probably is the biggest and most original show ever seen in the United States. If you took the Polo Grounds and converted it into a cafe and then added the best Ziegfeld scenic effects, you might get something approximating *Casa Mañana.*"

In post-show interviews, Rose claimed his one thousand-dollar daily fee was too low. "I'm worth much more than that," he bragged.

"What will you do when you're through here?" he was asked.

"I'll get one of those little Balkan wars and go on tour with it."

Then he sat down and wrote unsubtle advertising for his smash-hit, *Casa Mañana:* ". . . Not only a day but Decade in Advance of its Time . . . The Largest Theater-Cafe ever Constructed . . . Tables and Chairs for 4,500 Amusement Lovers . . . A Gargantuan-Revolving-Reciprocating Stage . . . Three and a Half Times Larger than that of Radio City Music Hall . . . Two 450 h.p. Motors Required to Operate this Liviathan *[sic]* of Rostrums, with its 4,264,000 Pounds of Actual Deadweight plus its Lovely Freight of 250 Eye-Bedeviling Coryphees Over a Pool of Limpid Crystal containing 617,000 Gallons of Real Water . . . SPECTACLE

and SONG, DANCE, AND COMEDY . . . Past Peradventure, the BIGGEST
SHOW EVER PRODUCED!"

Every summer and fall evening, at least four thousand people
filled Casa Mañana. The crowd often was mixed with tuxedos
and overalls, ball gowns and print dresses, but nobody cared.
They came, ate the $1.75 dinner, and sighed as Everett Marshall
sang, "The Night Is Young and You're So Beautiful," to Faye Cotton, who dazzled spectators with her $5,000, forty-pound gold
lamé gown designed by New York jewelers Whiting and Davis.
(The song, which became the centennial's unofficial anthem,
was written by Rose and Dana Suesse in Billy's Worth Hotel
suite, and by early 1937 rode high on hit parade lists.) Marshall
and Cotton portrayed newlyweds who honeymooned at the Saint
Louis World's Fair and liked it so much they went on to fairs in
Paris, Chicago, and, of course, Fort Worth, wandering among the
chorus girls and stars, singing to the baton direction of Paul
Whiteman.

Ann Pennington danced as Little Egypt. (She "cootchied" so
violently on opening night, wrote Jack Gordon, that her beads
broke and bounced into front-row soup bowls.) Sally Rand was
featured as a "Ballet Divertissement" in the Chicago scenes, alter-
nating her fans and balloons. The latter were five feet in diameter,
colored light-blue, cost twenty-five dollars each, and were made
by Goodyear. She lost a couple of them to sudden night breezes
and thereafter used the balloons only on perfectly calm evenings.

The Marshall/Cotton spectacle, Paris's Eiffel Tower outlined
with five thousand blinking lights, Ann Pennington emerging
from a papier-mâché "100-gallon hat"—all brought applause, but
nothing compared with the final scene when the mammoth stage
rolled back. One hundred and thirty-six feet in diameter, and
actually only three times the size of that at Radio City, the stage
seemed to balance on a blue lagoon. Each of its revolutions
required a minute and forty-five seconds, and front-row customers would set their beers on the edge and watch the steins go
around. In that final tableau, the entire cast assembled as eighty-
five fountains exploded with colored water, the six flags under
which Texas served were paraded and waved, and Marshall sang
"Lone Star" while gondoliers poled gondolas across the lagoon.

The spectacle was so visually numbing that nobody ever wondered why Venetian boatmen appeared in a western scene.

Amon boasted that he saw *Casa Mañana* sixty times.

Other productions were less popular. *Pioneer Palace* was a honky-tonk with ten-cent beer, slot machines, and pig races on a forty-foot-long bar. Whiskey-voiced Lulu Bates starred, singing "I'm In Love With The Man With A Handlebar Mustache," a song written by Rose and later appropriated by Amon Carter, who sang it for anyone who would listen and many who did not care to. The *Palace* chorus line was filled by the Rosebuds—a sextet of super-sized women dressed in ruffled frocks and scarlet hair ribbons. The smallest weighed 215 pounds, the largest, 340. Rose later transferred the *Palace* concept and acts to New York for his most successful dinner theater, *The Diamond Horseshoe.*

The Last Frontier was Rose's bogus western pageant staged in an outdoor amphitheater and advertised as "The Vivid, Visual Saga of the March of Civilization . . . THE OLD WEST LIVES AGAIN . . . See Attack of the Hostiles . . . Womanhood in Jeopardy . . . Thank God the Rangers! Battle of Arroyo Grande . . . and The Mail Goes Through."

"Many, many moons ago, the smile of the Great Spirit beamed upon the land of the Red Man. Great herds of shaggy buffalo thundered westward . . ." began the narration, summoning Indians, buffalo, the cowboys, Texas longhorns, and cavalry. There were Indian attacks and stage holdups by bandits, a rodeo, trick riders and ropers, those sixty-eight teams of square dancers—all performing to incongruous Broadway music. The *New York Times* reported that on opening night "A berserk bronco catapulted himself and his rider into a 15-foot pool and a Texan, inflamed by the heady goings-on, reached for his .45 and shot out an amber floodlight."

Jumbo was a bust. It was the only inside big show, housed in a bright-red building with white castle towers and serrated roofline. Rose didn't know about Texas summer heat and the building was stifling. Temperatures reached 112 degrees on the bandstand. Chorus girls fainted. Three of six pythons died. After opening week, Anderson cut *Jumbo* from two hours and twenty-three minutes to one fast hour.

Dallas, meanwhile, got the message. It opened *Streets of Paris,* a semi-nude show. Gordon reported that the half-naked girls were "built like stevedores."

Fort Worth was wide-open during its centennial. Illegal liquor openly was poured everywhere. Curfews were removed. Clubs stayed open all night. People danced at Casa Mañana until 3:00 A.M., then swarmed into such dine, dance, and drink emporiums as the Crown, the State, and the Buccaneer. Musicians from the Whiteman and Joe Venuti bands jammed until dawn. A craps game at the Ringside Club, from which Whiteman broadcast nationwide we⁻kly, went on for three months without interruption. Two million people came to the centennial party, playing through the grounds, eating ten-cent banana splits and fifteen-cent ham sandwiches, touring the re-created living room of Will Rogers's Santa Monica home. They entered the grounds beneath a neon "Howdy Stranger" sign and through a log stockade gate, finding immediately the few educational displays, placed there, said Rose, "so the people can see them and then go have fun." At night, the grounds were bathed in an eerie pink neon light. The peculiar color anguished Rose, who nevertheless announced that it had been created purposely to give women a "peaches-and-cream complexion."

It was a wonderful, memorable time in Fort Worth. There were multitudes of famous visitors: George White of *Scandals* fame, Jack Schubert, and Earl Carroll, the *Vanities* producer, came from New York. William Knudsen, president of General Motors, played "Let Me Call You Sweetheart" on a xylophone. Cactus Jack Garner led an endless piffle of politicians. J. Edgar Hoover visited in September, talking about his plans to fingerprint "the whole country." Amon outscored Hoover with rifles at the shooting gallery. Ernest Hemingway, driving from Wyoming to Memphis, became intrigued by the billboards and detoured through Fort Worth. Maximilian Adelbert Baer—Max Baer, the heavyweight boxer—sparred for photographers with Barney Oldfield, the pioneer auto racer hired by Amon to act as official centennial greeter.

Amon haunted the shows, often narrating *The Last Frontier,* strutting in an Indian headdress. He sang in the *Pioneer Palace* and played drink-mixer at what Rose called "the world's longest bar" in Casa Mañana. Aubrey Kennedy, explained in the *Star-Telegram* as "an early silent-film producer," announced the pending production of an eight-reel movie with the centennial as background. Hoot Gibson, he said, would star. The movie was never made. *Billboard* announced that other Casa Mañana theaters would be built in Miami, Cleveland, Atlanta, and Havana.

The eclectic pace of the centennial went on. Chorus girls judged a knock-knock joke contest for the *Press*. John Search-The-Enemy, a seventy-three-year-old Sioux medicine man, died, death being attributed to a gastrointestinal malfunction brought on by eating raw beef kidneys. A businessman ordered three beers in the Palace, poured them into his upturned straw hat, and drank. Three coeds working in the *Nude Ranch* were recognized and notified by their colleges that they could not return in the fall. The two-headed snake died August 14, presumably done in by the heat.

The opening of *"Beauty and the Beasts*, featuring Mademoiselle Laurene NeVell, intrepid Eve daring the ferocious onslaught of seven blood lusting Nubian Lions" diluted the *Nude Ranch* business. Three monkeys escaped and pounced on the lions, scaring the toothless old cats into several days of non-onslaught with Laurene. The monkeys also rang the bell in the school tower, drank beer in *Pioneer Palace*, and dived into Florence's milk bath.

The *Star-Telegram* gorged itself on centennial stories. E. Clyde Whitlock, the newspaper's eminent and prim critic, dutifully reviewed every piece of music on the grounds. The Pioneer Palace's melodies were, he wrote, "cabaret style, for those who like that kind of thing. It sounds fast and loud, which are the two requisites for the type." Whitlock examined *Casa Mañana* and devoted fewer lines to Sally Rand than to her stripping music—a melange of Beethoven, Brahms, and Debussy. For the critic's slight of Sally's bare charms, his reporter colleagues demoted Whitlock to E-flat Clyde.

Slowly, preachers lessened their attacks on Sally Rand, mostly because the public had decided Sally was not what everyone thought she was. Done up in a sunbonnet and calico granny dress, she arrived driving a chocolate-colored Lincoln touring sedan, and for the next three months she was the best publicity of the centennial. She threw out the first ball opening softball season, removing only her sunbonnet and promising the crowd, "You'll see more of me." She spoke to every service club in town. "I am an exponent of truth in advertising and consequently I stick to the bare facts when selling my merchandise," she told Kiwanians.

Sally explained to an advertising club: "I'm in the same business as you. Selling white space."

She spoke to PTA groups, traveled to Dallas and Waco and Wichita Falls on centennial promotion trips, bought fifty memberships for the civic music season, donated time and money to underprivileged kids. In tight shorts, hair braided, Sally gave a pep talk to TCU's Horned Frogs football team. She was photographed in the kitchen of her rented home, baking a cake. She directed traffic at high noon in downtown Fort Worth. Her grandmother, Molly Grove, came to visit, and Sally threw a tea party. Reporters sat around with show business's best nude act talking of crochet patterns and lemon chiffon pie recipes.

C. L. Richhart—also known as Rich—was assigned by Jim Record to write an in-depth story on Sally. Rich went to her dressing room, knocked, and was summoned inside where he found Sally, naked, lying on her stomach reading the Bible. She stretched, rolled over, and covered her mons venus with what Rich later said was Proverbs 3:18.

Of the seventeen thousand stories appearing around the country on Fort Worth's centennial, half featured Sally Rand. Her pictures appeared 947 times in Texas newspapers alone in a ninety-day period. November 6 was declared Sally Rand Day in Tarrant County. The stripper who dared inflict bare breasts on Fort Worth was cited for her "graciousness and consummate artistry," and publicly thanked for bringing "culture and progress."

Chilly weather forced a closing on November 15. Billy Rose spent the entire million dollars and more. Investors lost everything, but no one seemed to care. Fort Worth prospered. Beer sales were up 75 percent, soft drinks up 30 percent. Barbers cut

40 percent more hair and grocery stores sold 30 percent more food. The Depression had been blunted.

For what it was and where it was, Fort Worth's Frontier Centennial, especially *Casa Mañana*, perhaps was the most successful exposition of its type in history. When Damon Runyon reviewed the 1939 New York World's Fair, his appraisal was: "No hits, no runs, no Carters."

Billy Rose went on to produce *Aquacade* in 1937 at Cleveland, then moved the show to New York World's Fair where a highlight was the lavish parade of America's forty-nine flags—one for each state, and Fort Worth's city banner.

Casa Mañana returned in 1937 with Rose presenting a musical revue of famous books. Dallas, too, reopened, but surrendered after that summer because of poor business. As the *Frontier Fiesta*, Fort Worth's show continued in 1938 and 1939 with vaudeville acts in *Casa Mañana*, featuring such stars as Eddie Cantor, Edgar Bergen, and Ray Bolger. Morton Downey was the last entertainer to play on the revolving stage.

By 1940, it was clear that war was coming. Casa Mañana—the House of Tomorrow—was shuttered forever.

The Dallas/Fort Worth rivalry has been overstated. They're both good towns. Fort Worth is progressive and modern. It has outstanding leadership and fine people. Of course, I never go over to the goddamned place.
　　　—Dallas businessman to Postmaster General James
　　　Farley, early 1940s

Amon Carter is a damn fool on many things. . . .
　　　—*Amarillo Globe*, May 11, 1936

Dallas is softer, shady, an edge of East Texas. Fort Worth has a bigger sky, is a little hotter in the summer, colder in the winter, drier . . . the West. We are city; they country. Visitors like them better. We try too hard.
　　　—Bill Porterfield, Dallas author, about 1975

Fort Worth is regarded by Dallasites as a dinghy trailed behind a yacht.
　　　—Stephen Brook, *Honkytonk Gelato*, 1985

I have not been accused of being partisan to Northeast Texas and Dallas, and I don't believe you have to live in Fort Worth and West Texas to get to Heaven, although it won't be detrimental in case you get an invite.
　　　—Amon, to Hearst Columnist Inez Robb, late 1930s

Yes, Dallas does have something Fort Worth doesn't have—a real city thirty miles away.
　　　—Amon, at opening of the Frontier Centennial, 1936

Dallas. Fort Worth. Presently, Dallas/Fort Worth, or as it is written on the argument's western half: Fort Worth/Dallas. Note the subtle difference. That awry grammatical device is no mere virgule but a true slash mark of the two towns' obstreperous feuding history.

Now mellowed with age, the cities no longer openly backbite and bloody one another, but once they were America's best, most contentious, municipal opponents.

Amon Carter, ever the immoderate trench-fighter, loved nothing better than beating Dallas at something, anything, and old Cactus Jack Garner grumbled, "Amon wants the government of the United States to run for the exclusive benefit of Fort Worth and, if possible, to the detriment of Dallas." Yes, that's precisely what he wanted.

Amon didn't invent the intercity scrimmage, but he made it famous. For any cocked ear he slandered Dallas, joked about it, verbally lashed it. He stole from the larger city, ignored it, vented his wrath against its wealthy prominence, schemed against its perpetuity, gawddammed, doomed, and condemned it to hell— all without very great harm to Dallas's civic tide and fortune. Mostly, Dallas feasted, Fort Worth got indigestion.

They were never twin cities on the North Texas prairie but rather a pair of disparate communities thirty miles and poles apart, rent by the ninety-seventh parallel and all logic. That small piece of range could not support two big, rich cities, and Fort Worth early was cast in the lesser role because it played on a barren stage to a destitute West Texas audience while Dallas wooed northern monies and practiced mercantile shrewdness.

For its part, Dallas viewed Fort Worth as Conrad Hilton looked on the Bide-A-Wee Motel, slightly bemused and indulgently condescending. Dallas grew into a city of contrived *haute* culture. Fort Worth became a comfortably ambitious town with a high society always one generation removed from flour-sack underwear. Dallas was skyscraper banks and Neiman-Marcus, Fort Worth, stockyards and Leonard Brothers Department Store, where one spat tobacco juice on the floor and shopped for day-old bread and Big Mack overalls. Dallas was eastern, Fort Worth, western. In Dallas, quipped Damon Runyon, "the women wear high heels, in Fort Worth, the men do."

Each city's character was established from the beginning. Dallas opened as a single trading post on the Trinity River, Fort Worth as a wilderness army post. As the towns grew, so did the rivalry. Dallas built a thriving business section, laughing that Fort Worth was unable to muster one decent saloon. Even Belle Starr, whose genealogy was less than blue blood, preferred Dallas's criminal life to Fort Worth's.

The feud began early. Buckley B. Paddock, the *Democrat* editor and ardent Fort Worth chauvinist, stole a flock of eastern capitalists bound for Dallas. He met the men in Texarkana and talked up his town. He was persuasive. When the financiers arrived in Dallas, Paddock chartered a fleet of buggies and led them on to Fort Worth. Dallas fumed.

In 1906, a Dallas newspaper noted: "Word has reached here from Fort Worth that two men have drowned in bathtubs in the last six months. It proves that Fort Worth at least has two bathtubs."

The *Uncle Jake Sports News*, a short-lived Texas horse-racing paper, recorded in the early 1920s what probably was the first printed Amon/Dallas jibe: "This boy Amon Carter . . . lays awake all night thinkin' up things t' help his town. I figger if th' world wus cumin' t' a end Amon wud hav' it cum t' a end in Fort Worth 'fore it reached Dallas."

Will Rogers later used the crack on his radio program and, as Amon's close friend, perpetuated the intercity dispute as often as possible. Rogers and H. L. Mencken, the Baltimore iconoclast, flew into Fort Worth and Rogers quipped, "Had a wonderful trip down here, but I looked for Dallas on the way in. Couldn't find it. It still around here?" A wire to the *Star-Telegram* from Rogers read, "Hello, Amon, I was in Fort Worth this morning. Got gas, a silver cup, and a *Dallas News*." When the humorist's radio program was broadcast by CBS, he once originated it from KRLD studios in Dallas. Next day, the elated *Star-Telegram* whooped that Rogers mentioned Fort Worth six times on the air and "never once said 'Dallas.'"

The *Star-Telegram* rarely taunted Dallas—gentleman Jimmy North allowed pettiness only when pressed by Amon—but in 1928 a story told of the arrival of the dirigible Los Angeles at Fort

Worth's helium plant, pointing out that the airship "overflew Dallas." A mid-1930s editorial observed: "[In the past] we have commented on the special sort of fog which hangs over a certain area situated thirty miles down the Trinity. It produces a peculiar mental effect upon those who are constantly exposed to it."

Al Altwegg of the *Dallas Morning News* probably assessed the bickering correctly, writing, "If Dallas and Fort Worth have a problem, it's primarily Fort Worth that has the problem." It did. No matter what Amon and Fort Worth tried, Dallas continued to prosper and grow, which irritated Amon all the more, and he raged in a letter that Dallas "is run by a bunch of tin-horned bankers and jews *[sic]*."

One of those Jewish leaders was Stanley Marcus, whose family founded Neiman-Marcus—Fort Worth wags called it Needless-Markups. Neiman's had many customers among Fort Worth's society crowd but the *Star-Telegram* would accept no advertising from the elegant specialty store. Amon bragged that he bought everything he needed in Fort Worth and others should, too. That was not quite true. Nenetta kept a Neiman's charge account secret from Amon and even he sent an occasional envoy to buy special gifts not found anywhere else. It was joked, and may even have been true, that his lady friends removed Neiman-Marcus labels from their clothing and replaced them with tags from Fort Worth stores. Stanley Marcus knew of Nenetta's private account and Amon's clandestine shopping but being a businessman, kept the intelligence to himself. Carter and Marcus finally met at a cocktail party, and Amon complained that ad lineage was down.

"Why not let us help you by advertising in the *Star-Telegram?*" suggested Marcus.

Amon fixed him with a steely glare and replied, "The minute you open a store in Fort Worth."

Amon v. Dallas stories are legion, though many are pure fiction. He, everyone said, always carried a sack lunch to Dallas rather than buy a meal there. Amon did that a few times, for a joke. Once, he attended a society ball in the Adolphus Hotel. He made himself the center of attention by leading Freddie Martin's Orchestra and delivering a longish, humorous speech about

Dallas. When waiters began serving dinner, he dismissed them and opened a large basket. It was filled with Shady Oak fried chicken. Another tale has him forced to remain overnight in Dallas and going unshaven rather than patronize a barbershop there. People said he carried a full tote can of Fort Worth gas in his car trunk and refused to use Dallas's service stations. His peach orchard outside Arlington, midway between the cities, spread over the Tarrant County line into Dallas County. He showed his trees to a visitor and they gathered a basket of peaches in the Dallas County section. He insisted they walk back across the line to eat. Once he told a guest that peaches in the Dallas County zone simply didn't grow as well "in all that hot air."

It is true that he won a bet of two suits from a Dallas friend but refused to collect because the loser stipulated a Dallas tailor must stitch up the clothes. Will Stripling was president of Fort Worth's Civic Music Association one year and asked Amon to purchase a season subscription. Amon replied sarcastically, "If there is anything in the world I am crazy about, it is music, and I was especially tickled to think that my membership entitled me to attend, without further penalty, all the concerts to be presented by the Dallas association. It will be a red-letter day in my life and a rare privilege to be able to contribute something to Dallas. I will probably go wild over the Spanish dancers November 29. Those Dallas boys have been feeding us so much bull for the past twenty-five years, that I just cannot keep from having a hankering after Spanish dancers."

Printed cards once appeared in Fort Worth urging, "Please flush twice when you use the washroom! Dallas needs the water." Amon was blamed for the cards. He denied it, but in a letter to Will Rogers noted the benefit of Lake Worth, "which supplies Dallas with water when we pull the string."

Much of the rivalry was contrived because Amon had fun with it. He was friendly with most nationally known columnists and endlessly fed them items, both true and fanciful, about the inter-city quarrel. He told Inez Robb, "It seems we have been in Dallas's hair all our lives. Dallas has the nicest people individually, but collectively, we look upon them with a degree of suspicion as to what they would do if we turned around to spit. Fort Worth is Where The West Begins and Dallas is where the East peters out."

Amon explained to Damon Runyon that Dallas and Fort Worth "have tried to bury the hatchet many times . . . but somebody always leaves the handle sticking out." Walter Winchell reported on a dinner given Amon by Jim Farley in New York's Ritz Tower. The menu inscription told of Amon's "college yell": "Bring in the liquor/On with the mirth/To Hell with Dallas/Boost Fort Worth."

Now and then, Amon made peace overtones. Once he hosted Dallas leaders at a Shady Oak party. At first, all was friendly. Then Amon stood to speak on the new cooperative spirit of the cities, but the longer he spoke, the more he edged into the past, recalling old slights and affronts. He concluded with a strong denouncement of Dallas. His guests were more amused than offended, and when Dallas Mayor R. L. Thornton rose to respond, he held up a paper sack. "This is my dinner," said Thornton. "I brought me a ham sandwich out here from Dallas. I'm not eating anything you got."

Later in the evening, Amon explained to Thornton another side of the Dallas/Fort Worth rivalry. "It's really a constructive thing. If I want to get something done in Fort Worth, if I want to get some of these people off their asses, all I do is remind them that 'You don't want those Dallas bastards to get ahead of you, do you?'" Many never recognized that piece of the quarrel, and every slander of Dallas by Amon brought denunciatory letters from Big D citizens. John Ford, an attorney, chided Amon and his town: "When we get all tense and tired out from the noise and strife of city life, we like to go out in the country for a few hours and relax. And for this purpose we find that Fort Worth is fine—unless the wind is blowing from the north [the stockyards]."

After the publisher stole a company from Dallas and boasted loudly of the theft, a woman wrote, "You showed more ignorance than I ever thought any one man could possess. I have heard of some of the dumb things you have done, but I never imagined any one man could be so crude and ignorant. . . . Stay in that hick-town you belong in as you have acted like a real country boy."

Stealing from Dallas was Amon's great raging fever. He coveted every brick and smokestack of its industries and ached to remove everything to Fort Worth. As a one-man chamber of commerce he endlessly searched out new businesses, especially courting those already in the Dallas ledger. "The great Magnolia skyscraper reaches its steel claws down into bedrock and holds on like grim death when Amon passes by," wrote Tom Gooch, *Times Herald* editor in 1935. Amon persuaded Phillips Petroleum to move its southwest headquarters from Dallas to Fort Worth in 1925, and Frank Phillips wired the publisher, "It pleases us to do this largely because you want us to." In 1933, Amon visited W. E. Sinclair in the oilman's New York headquarters. He inspected a wall map showing Sinclair offices across America. One red pin indicated Pierce Oil Company in Dallas.

"That pin mean you bought Pierce?" asked Amon. Sinclair nodded. Amon smiled, extracted the pin from Dallas and punched it into Fort Worth. Soon Pierce Oil moved its headquarters to Amon's town.

The corporate theft that provided Amon with greatest satisfaction and rankled Dallas most was South West Air Craft Corporation's move into Fort Worth. The company would become American Airlines, with Amon as a founder, board member, and, eventually, largest stockholder. Losing South West enraged the Dallas establishment. "Once more," shrieked a *Dallas Journal* editorial, "we have been Amon Cartered. We boast that Dallas isn't a one-man town. But in this connection, it is pretty weak boasting."

The *Dallas Morning News* wrote of "Mahatma Carter . . . who keeps Dallas sitting on everything that isn't nailed down for fear he will move it to Fort Worth."

Those were rare victories. Amon lost more than he won, though he never stopped trying. He wrote Nelson Moody, president of Prairie Oil and Gas, when that company was considering a move to Dallas, "We are still anxious to locate the Prairie's Texas office at the most logical point, Fort Worth. We understand that your representative cannot even get a tire fixed on Sunday in your present Texas headquarters [Amarillo]. If you move to Fort Worth, I will have the mayor fix your punctures." Standard Oil of California bypassed Fort Worth for regional offices in Dallas and Amon sent the company's president, K. R. Kingsbury, a black-bordered sympathy letter. He later complained to Walter Teagle,

Standard of New Jersey's chief operating officer, that the move was "a slap in our face."

Losing was always personal to Amon. In fact, everything about Dallas was personal. Attorney Berl Godfrey, in the late 1940s, was president of the Fort Worth Chamber of Commerce. He spoke at a Dallas Chamber membership banquet. The *Star-Telegram* assigned reporter Irv Farman to cover the speech. He joined John Rutledge, a *Dallas Morning News* writer, at the press table.

Godfrey spoke of cooperation between the two cities and, heady with the message's reception, ad-libbed, "After this wonderful hospitality and wonderful meal, I think it would be ridiculous for anyone to bring his sack lunch to Dallas." The audience howled. Only one man supposedly brought sack lunches to Dallas.

Farman, knowing his boss, ignored the remark. Rutledge led his story with the quote, and implied Godfrey's remark was a direct slap at Amon. Farman was summoned to Carter's office. Amon had the *Morning News* spread on his desk.

"Did Godfrey say this?" Carter asked.

"Yes, sir," answered Farman. "But I didn't think it was news-worthy."

"Next time somebody says something bad about me, you write it and let somebody higher up kill it out."

Godfrey, Amon said, had already called to apologize.

"I told him I neither want nor accept his apology. What hurts me most," said Amon, "is that one thousand of Dallas's leading citizens think someone else is speaking for Fort Worth."

Amon stopped abruptly, stared out the window for long moments, then turned again to Farman. With a reddened face, he shouted, "By God! I speak for Fort Worth!"

Fighting Dallas was a lifelong crusade for the publisher, and he needed only the slightest provocation to go for the city's jugular. He interrupted an American Airlines board meeting to complain that the airline's 1938 brochures did not feature "a picture of Fort Worth air terminal or Fort Worth itself. Dallas has more mentions although our southern headquarters is in Fort Worth." He railed to a *Saturday Evening Post* editor, "I wonder how in hell you gave the story a Dallas dateline when Dallas had practically nothing to do with it." In 1934, the Warm Springs Foundation sponsored fund-raising galas around America, and afterward, Dallas was praised for its participation. Amon complained to President Roosevelt: "Dallas only raised $6,500 before expenses. Fort Worth raised $25,000 and no expenses, one-fortieth of all the money raised."

During World War II, a roguish salesman bought thousands of candles and dyed them black. In Dallas, he sold as many as ten thousand as "real blackout candles that the enemy can't see." Amon whooped and hoorayed over Dallasites' gullibility and spread the story among friends and columnists everywhere.

Despite Amon's assaults on Big D (which he often wrote as "Big d"), the city remained generally cordial, and in 1939 the *Morning News* devoted two pages of pictures and praise to the publisher—"Builder of a whole region." He was named an honorary Dallas citizen and the newspaper remarked that he "punches Dallas like cowboys are wont to do slow steers in a shipping chute." That tribute, strangely, appeared while Dallas remained in a furious snit with Amon over football and TCU and the Cotton Bowl, all because he wanted to show his eastern friends "how the cow ate the cabbage."

Amon was never an athlete but he was, wrote columnist Bob Considine, "America's Number One Sports Fan." Grantland Rice, too, conceded the title to Carter, and Damon Runyon. An All-American spectator. His ego required the uproar and hubbub of sporting crowds, and for most of fifty years he was a World Series fixture, a colorful ringside rooter at heavyweight boxing championship bouts, a hundred-dollar window addict and mint julep veteran of the Kentucky Derby. He would don his cowboy costume to strut, holler, jeer, cheer, and jabber on happily, making a spectacle and, many believed, complete fool of himself. For the second Dempsey/Tunney fight, Amon invited eighty friends, including Will Rogers. Each wore one of Amon's Shady Oak western hats and carried his patented bourbon-filled walking canes. They marched lockstep to ringside, Amon leading, joshing with the crowd, whoopeeing for Fort Worth and West Texas. Westbrook Pegler viewed the pageant and reported, "Mr. Amon

G. Carter . . . lent a strong intellectual force to the assembly and played a brief solo on a fish horn. The customers decided the fight was not as loud as the solo. He sat down with the unanimous consent of all present." Pegler's "fish horn" likely was a cow's horn, which Amon loved to toot.

Before it became socially indecorous, Amon would fire off his six-shooters to punctuate the excitement. Promoters loved to have him center stage. Charles Comiskey furnished season passes to all Chicago White Sox games, as did John McGraw for the New York Giants. Tex Rickard, the sports promotion entrepreneur, signed a permanent pass to Madison Square Garden, decreeing, "This is Amon Carter. Let him through any door, any gate, any time. And don't argue."

Amon's athletics were limited to a few innings of softball in an early newspaper league and at *Star-Telegram* picnics. Briefly, he golfed, but confessed "they have improved the courses to the extent that it is difficult to find old balls and I eliminated golf as a matter of economy." His Shady Oak Farm pond boiled with hungry bass, but he lacked the patience for fishing. He went hunting fewer than a half-dozen times in his life and mostly for the companionship, never the wild game. He was not a camper or hiker or outdoorsman because nature, he decided early, was excessively uncomfortable.

Amon had been a batboy for the Bowie baseball team when it played against Henrietta's town team. Neither side could afford new baseballs, and it was young Amon's duty to retrieve batted fouls. He went into the crowd to recover a ball one afternoon and immediately got into a fight with two larger boys. The fracas turned into a general brawl halted only when Henrietta's town marshal charged in with drawn pistol. That was George L. Rickard, then called "Dink," and he and Amon became close friends. "Tex" Rickard later rode his horse to the Yukon, where he gathered enough gold for a ranching stake and parlayed that into a position as America's leading boxing promoter. Amon visited often with Rickard, who regularly had the publisher fire his pistols to start six-day bicycle races. In 1926, heavyweight champion Jack Dempsey was prodding Rickard to find him a suitable opponent. Dempsey, who had not defended his title in three

Amon and Jack Dempsey in Amon's office after signing for the Tunney fight.

years, agreed to meet Gene Tunney. The matter was settled by telegram, and Dempsey, in California, wanted Rickard to come there for the contract signing. Rickard suggested they meet halfway and, said the promoter, that was Amon Carter's office in Fort Worth.

April 21, Rickard and Dempsey sat at Amon's desk as the publisher hovered in the background directing his reporters and photographers. Dempsey, who would lose to Tunney, was euphoric over the anticipated $1,000,000 gate and unusually chatty with sportswriters, though possibly his banter was more prompted by the water glass of straight gin he drank for breakfast. Amon boasted that the publicity would increase his city's growing fame and urged Rickard to stage the bout in Fort Worth. Prizefighting was illegal in Texas, but Amon promised to have the law changed. Rickard selected Philadelphia.

Despite the law, there were local fights, and Amon was a ringside fixture. Because the matches had no legal status, official decisions could not be rendered. Newspapers determined the winners, and Flem Hall was the *Star-Telegram* boxing judge. For one Saturday-night match, an out-of-town boxer showed Hall a clipping-filled scrapbook. The stories glowed with praise, and Hall wrote a column touting the boxer as a sure winner. At fight time, Amon was front row center, directly across the ring from Hall. From first bell to last, Hall's fighter was whipped soundly by a local boxer. Hall could hear his publisher loudly booing the out-of-towner. Amon glared across the ring at Hall. Moments after the fight, almost before the boxers cleared the ring, Carter slid under the ropes—and crawled on hands and knees across the apron to Hall. He yelled, "I thought you said that bird could fight!"

"He had a scrapbook full of clippings," protested Hall.

"Hell," retorted Amon, "all his gawddammed scrap was in his book."

Amon crawled back across the ring, slipped between the ropes, and reseated himself, oblivious to the laughter around him.

That was Amon the Spectator, never a disinterested bystander. He paced football field sidelines, exhorting his team to more inspired play, jeering opponents, whooping crowds like a cheerleader. At games of the Fort Worth Cats baseball team, of which he briefly was part-owner, Amon often came onto the field to dispute calls with umpires, or he would roam the stands collecting bonus money for players who made winning plays. The 1920s Cats perhaps were baseball's finest minor league team, so popular in Fort Worth that the twelve thousand-seat Panther Field overflowed with fans, and often as many as one thousand people stood behind the outfield. Managed by John Jacob "Jakie" Atz, the Cats won six consecutive Texas League championships and five of six Dixie Series pennants. Amon doted on his winning Cats, and in 1924 even showed off Clarence Kraft, whose fifty-five home runs led all minor league hitters, and Joe Pate, a thirty-game winning pitcher, to Calvin Coolidge. The players and Amon, Harold Hough, and Silent Cal posed for pictures on the White House lawn.

Amon made the president an honorary Fort Worth citizen. The publisher also handed the president a gold key to his liquor-filled vault, but teetotaler Cal's response to that Prohibition-era generosity has been lost to history. He called Amon, "Cowboy." Leaving, Hough said, "Sure am glad you got to meet me, Mr. Coolidge." The president grimaced politely.

The group traveled on to New York for the World Series then returned to Fort Worth, where Pate and Kraft entertained cronies with tales of the White House and girls on Broadway. Kraft noted that "they sure got some swell post office up there."

Amon warms up his pitching arm before a Fort Worth Cats baseball game.

Flanked by Fort Worth Cats baseball stars Joe Pate (far left) and Clarence Kraft (far right), Amon presents a ceremonial key to President Calvin Coolidge, 1924.

Amon blustered loudly and long about the Cats, and cartoonist Bud Fisher placed his "Mutt and Jeff" in Fort Worth for a visit. In one comic strip, Jeff told Postmaster Billy Moore that they were the only Republicans in town, while Mutt begged Amon for a tryout with the Cats, claiming he was better than "Rogers Hornsby ever was." Fisher was so fond of Amon that he named one of his race horses "Star-Telegram." The horse, a filly by Shortgrass out of Adele, won few races.

The Dixie Series settled the question of the South's minor league champion and was the most important sporting event in the region. For an early series, Amon and the newspaper chartered trains to transport fans to Memphis. The idea proved so wildly popular that Amon continued it for twenty years. The trains took fans to TCU football games and delegates to Democratic political conventions. The *Star-Telegram* even sponsored booster trains into West Texas for Fort Worth businessmen. Amon's trains were rolling carnivals, and he was resident overseer, host, musical director, poker dealer, and bartender, always resplendently western as the bogus cowboy.

Star-Telegram reporters wrote mile-by-mile accounts of the shenanigans and photographers recorded high-jinks for posterity. There were bands and pep squads, troops of motorcycle cops, occasionally even horses and riders. Whenever the trains paused for water and fuel, Amon unloaded his carnival and staged impromptu parades for startled citizens of stray villages. Not surprisingly, there was hard drinking, and baggage cars served as rolling gambling dens where Amon played for dimes or hundred-dollar bills and crap games lasted from first chug to last. Flem Hall remembered watching Paul Waggoner, son of old W. T., crap out for a $1,500 pot. When TCU's band was aboard, there were jam sessions and dancing in the aisles and sing-alongs, most often led by the *Star-Telegram*'s Bess Stephenson, who was considered to have had musical training because she once interviewed a man who played washboard in a country band.

From three to six hundred fans packed into the special trains each trip, but those remaining behind were not forgotten. Amon related in a Christmas letter of how the *Star-Telegram* broadcast [via WBAP] that year's Dixie Series. Thirty-two direct telephone lines were installed in the newspaper office, and sixteen operators responded to as many as ten thousand calls a day. Special trains and telephones and baseball teams merely were part of the Amon Carter/*Star-Telegram* public service package for readers.

All baseball trains—to Memphis, to New Orleans, to Atlanta, and occasionally a TCU railroad expedition—had to move east through Dallas, a hard fact of geography that even Amon could not change. But he extracted a certain amount of amusement out of the Dallas crossings. Bill Corum, the Hearst sports columnist, quoted Amon: "Let me tell you, young man, that there's no such place as Dallas. Dallas is a mirage on the Texas plain. When I ride past the wide place in the tracks called Dallas on the train, I get up in the cab with the engineer and ring the bell and blow the whistle, and refuse to let him stop even for water. Which is all you'd get in Dallas, anyway."

He did that—commandeered the engine cab and rang the bell, blasted the whistle, hooting at Dallasites. Once he even rode the cowcatcher and another time, mounted the top of the engine, straddling it as though it were a real iron horse, yippeeing and waving his hat to startled onlookers.

Amon's well-publicized trans-Dallas excursions caused this puzzler in the *Dispatch-Journal:*

Q. What is the fastest thing on two wheels?

A. Amon Carter passing through Dallas on a bicycle.

That satirical question was asked as the bitterest Amon v. Dallas confrontation was stalemated. It was a vicious little sniping war waged over the post-season bowl decision of TCU's Fightin' Horned Frogs—the 1938 national collegiate football champions, undefeated and untied and hardly tested, and completely under the influence of Amon Carter, who at last had a proper weapon with which to bloody Dallas.

Always busy, Amon only had time for winners. Before the Cats reached for their first Texas League pennant, he was a lukewarm baseball patron. TCU had been playing football for decades, but until it was taken into the Southwest Conference and began winning consistently, Amon was uninterested. When the Frogs neared the winner's circle, however, they became, as Fort Worth and West Texas, his.

He participated in every pep rally. Once, before a big game with Southern Methodist University, the Dallas school and traditional rival of TCU, Amon taunted students and team members, "Give 'em hell, but do it in a good Christian spirit." A school official later spoke and said his definition of Christian spirit probably did not "jibe with Mr. Carter's."

Instantly, Amon interrupted and defined his conception of Christian football: "Knock 'em down. Pick 'em up, dust 'em off and ask 'em how they feel. If they can answer, knock 'em down again."

As TCU's locker room and pep rally activist, Amon expounded on his theory that losing a football game was detrimental to the future of Fort Worth. To help the Frogs understand the seriousness of their role, he resorted to bribes. In 1931, Texas A & M had a standout team. TCU merely was adequate. Neither school could score in the first two quarters and at halftime Carter charged into the locker room.

"Men!" he shouted. "If you win, I'll give $1,000 to the athletic fund! If you tie, I'll give $500!"

He sweetened the deal: "... and I'll give every player a watch!"

Encouraged by Amon's intense and passionate speech, and perhaps some bit of youthful avarice, TCU knocked off the Aggies 6-0, and each man received his watch. Wee Horned Frogs substituted for numbers around the dials.

Shepherding his team to victory after victory, Amon guarded against the players' complacency with lectures stressing the Frogs' vulnerability. "You guys don't want to be like Lot's wife, so proud of your past you've got no future," was one rebuke. He even ordered the *Star-Telegram*'s sports department to write stories "playing up" the Frogs' opponents.

He gave the TCU teams expensive Shady Oak hats and threw banquets for them. When TCU won its first Southwest Conference football championship in 1929, the hero was a sophomore fullback, Harlos Green, who kicked an extra point to tie SMU, giving the Frogs a clear conference title. Amon collected Green's magic shoe and had it bronzed and mounted.

With the impetus of a conference championship, Amon was able to sell the community on supporting construction of a new football stadium seating forty thousand fans. The publisher personally sold $500,000 worth of bonds, and the concrete arena was named—no surprise here—Amon Carter Stadium.

Amon, said Nenetta, "went crazy" when TCU was winning. He strutted and yelled, whooped and stomped his purple and white Justin handmade boots with Horned Frog designs cut into the heels. And he would lead the band through rousing numbers, sometimes even the "Amon Carter March," written especially for him by director Don Gillis. TCU's band played swing music in the mid-1930s, and Amon's baton led it across the nation. He hauled the band on train trips and, at each destination city, Amon's influential friends provided motorcycle escorts and sirening fire engines as the whole entourage marched to its hotel, band out front, led by the strutting, big-hatted cowboy.

In San Francisco to play Santa Clara University, the team and band and Amon marched down Market Street to the Mark Hopkins Hotel where Amon was guest of honor at a welcoming banquet. He joshed, joked, and bragged of his TCU Frogs' great football ability until the audience began yelling for him to put his money where his mouth was. Grinning slyly, he commanded the hotel staff to bring out a "number two washtub, right out front here, and you fill it up. I'll cover anything you bet." The huge tub overflowed with money—tens of thousands of dollars, estimated witnesses—and Amon guaranteed every bet. He won it all on TCU's victory.

When TCU played Fordham in New York, Damon Runyon trailed the Texans from the train depot to city hall for an Amon-staged pep rally, then on to the polo grounds. Runyon wrote that Carter "went in for the yip-yip-yippy business . . . especially in the early stages when Texas Christian whipped a score over on Fordham faster than you could say Wojciechowicz. Between the football halves, Mr. Carter, in person, led the band in a parade about the field and upwards of 25,000 inmates . . . cheered the imposing figure. The field was muddy. Mr. Carter's high heels sank to his fetlocks in the ooze at every step."

TCU lost 7-6, and Runyon recorded Amon's reaction when a woman fan asked for an autograph. She inquired, "Well, how did you like it?"

"I didn't like it, Ma'am."

"Oh, don't cry about it. It was a wonderful game."

"I'm not crying, Ma'am. And it was a wonderful game. But you asked me how I liked it and I tell you I didn't like it. I still don't like it. In West Texas, Ma'am, truth always comes first."

That evening Amon appeared on Robert Ripley's national radio program, extolling TCU's swing band. "Well, Bob," explained Amon, "Believe It or Not, we've got the biggest horns of any college in the country and how we can blow them."

The bass horns were Amon's idea. He wrote TCU's president, Dr. E. M. Waits, "On the subject of the band, I would like to see about 75 pieces for next season, supplemented by a couple more bass horns. With all the brass SMU has, we are certainly not going to let them get away with six bass horns to our four."

Dallas again. Always Dallas. Amon led the TCU band one year in a pre-Cotton Bowl game parade, and the marshal placed SMU's band out front. Amon, furious, threatened to take his TCU band home. "Fort Worth never gets behind Dallas," he shouted. The marshal explained that the bands were arranged in alphabetical order, and Amon relented.

From the mid-1930s, TCU dominated the conference and became an innovating force in American football. Coached by Leo "Dutch" Meyer and starring, first, the inimitable Sammy Baugh, then the micro-quarterback Davey O'Brien, the Horned Frogs became an aerial show. They threw footballs as no team ever before, and Meyer declared in a *Saturday Evening Post* article, "The Southwest is just now being recognized, footballically speaking. . . ."

In 1938, TCU was undefeated and Dallas promoters of the three-year-old Cotton Bowl were joyous, confident that the Frogs would play there New Year's Day. They would have the nation's number-one bowl game. Well before the season's conclusion, Cotton Bowl supporters were visiting TCU, offering, rumor had it, fistfuls of money and other enticements, including a new automobile for Coach Meyer.

Politely, the Frogs refused all offers. Tempers began rising in Dallas.

Amon was busy. With two games remaining, TCU's name popped into national sports columns urging that it be selected as visiting team in the Rose Bowl against the University of Southern California, the probable host school. Runyon wrote, "We have half a notion to write those Rose Bowl people . . . and tell them that if they want the greatest show they have ever seen in all their born days they are suckers if they do not invite Señor Amon Carter, the Hidalgo of West Texas, and the Texas Christian University football team to play in the bowl on New Year's Day."

Backstage, Amon spent seven hundred and forty *Star-Telegram* dollars for more than one hundred telephone calls to California, eliciting private support for TCU's Rose Bowl invitation. He contacted every sports writer and publisher in the state. At the behest of C. R. Smith, American Airlines executives called on Norman Chandler of the *Los Angeles Times*. Amon enlisted W. R. Hearst, who sent down an order to Frank Barham, publisher of the *Los Angeles Herald Express*, to "help get TCU in the Rose

Bowl." Carter wired California Governor Frank Marrian and the USC president, signing, without authorization, the name of Texas Governor W. Lee O'Daniel.

In the beginning, Amon's letters to newspapers promised "3 or 4 thousand" Texas fans for the Rose Bowl, brought there on *Star-Telegram* chartered trains. At the end he was estimating "25,000 TCU supporters."

"Frankly, we can't blame the Trojans for preferring as soft a spot as possible," he twitted, daring USC to take on the Horned Frogs.

As selection time neared, Amon grew fidgety. Walter Winchell revealed on his Sunday-evening radio program that Duke University would be invited to the Rose Bowl, and TCU would play in the Cotton Bowl. Amon angrily telephoned Winchell on the air. After a commercial break, Winchell, subdued and chagrined by Amon's mad spell, admitted to his audience that "nothing is sure yet for the Rose Bowl."

The Rose Bowl selection committee, under siege by Amon's sales blitz, delayed its announcement one day, but in the end named twice-beaten Duke as USC's opponent. Amon had failed.

Enraged, he telephoned columnist Bill Corum, who was drinking at Toots Shor's in New York. Corum, who said Amon "had on his six-gun voice," recorded the publisher's tirade: "It's a shame!!! It's a shame!!! Let me tell you it's a downright outrage, a reflection on the fair name of Texas and an insult to the greatest football team that ever walked in cleats. Our boys will play any two teams in the country on the same afternoon."

Dallasites chortled, and prepared to receive the Horned Frogs on New Year's Day. Suddenly, TCU announced it had accepted a bid to play Carnegie Tech in the Sugar Bowl. Dallas exploded, and pointed its trembling civic finger at the one man it held responsible for the defection.

"The boys just wanted to take a little train ride," alibied Amon.

What followed was the most vitriolic get-Amon crusade in the long Dallas/Fort Worth feud. The theme seemed to be that stealing a business was one thing, but robbing the Cotton Bowl, messing with football, was high treason, a heinous crime, and committed not just on Dallas but against all of Texas.

"The news that Brutus had stabbed Caesar couldn't have been more unbelievable," gasped columnist Eddie Barr. Amon "manipulated the Frogs out of town" and was a "small town poo-bah," Barr raged. Letters to the editor called for a boycott of Fort Worth, its citizens, its products, and especially Amon Carter, who responded caustically: "Sour grapes just naturally grow in the shade of sour dispositions."

Amon was the "publicity-mad Fort Worth publisher," said the *Dispatch-Journal,* most vituperative of the Dallas newspapers. It printed a cartoon captioned, "The Bowl Weevil," which depicted Amon's head on a football body. The vicious insect gnawed on a stalk of cotton. Sports columnists mused that Amon "with money for everything else" should build a stadium of his own and call it "The Stockyards Bowl."

The *Dispatch-Journal* published a page-one editorial explaining Amon's great sin: "The spleen against Dallas which Amon Carter has cultivated in his overwhelming devotion to Fort Worth sometimes blinds him to common sense and the opportunity to do something beneficial for the state . . . [this] narrow small-town conduct will live long in the memory of Dallas, we fear."

Amid all this vociferous babble, Davey O'Brien won the Heisman Trophy, annually given by the Downtown Athletic Club of New York. Earlier he had been named recipient of the Washington Touchdown Club Trophy and Philadelphia's Maxwell Trophy—all symbolic of the greatest football player in America. O'Brien, the Frogs' minute quarterback, was 145 pounds and five feet and a couple of handshakes high, as Amon described him. He was a "pony-built, piano-legged boy" who threw nineteen touchdown passes and led TCU to its undefeated season and ranking as America's number-one team.

O'Brien and Dutch Meyer were in Amon's office when word came via *Associated Press* that the little quarterback had won the 1938 Heisman. Immediately, Amon telephoned the Downtown Athletic Club president in New York. O'Brien and Meyer could hear only Amon's side of the conversation: "Listen, this is Amon Carter down in Fort Worth. We're bringing our boy, Davey O'Brien, up there to get your award. What kind of thing is this? Is it a little affair? We're not coming if it's something small . . .

[pause] . . . Get Jack Garner. Will LaGuardia be there? . . . [pause] .
. . OK. OK. I'll call 'em. See if the president'll come. . . . [pause] . . .
OK, I'll call him, too. What kind of entertainment you having? . . .
[pause] . . . That's no good. I'll get Paul Whiteman."

Amon hung up, called Whiteman and received the band-
leader's acceptance, then placed a call to the White House and
left word for FDR. Having fully arranged the Downtown Athletic
Club's award program, Amon turned his attention to getting
there. He chartered an American Airlines plane for the quarterback, O'Brien's mother and uncle, TCU coaches, the team's cap-
tains—Ki Aldrich and I. B. Hale—and Texas Lieutenant Governor
Walter Woodul.

The plane swooped off to New York and landed at Floyd Bennett Field, where thirty men on horseback (Staten Island Sheriff's
Guard members, reported Corum) and a Knickerbocker stagecoach drawn by six white horses were awaiting the Texas group.
Amon placed Woodul and Meyer inside the coach. On top, he sat
O'Brien beside him, picked up the reins, called to his white
steeds, and away they went.

Thousands of usually blasé New Yorkers gawked that day at
the sight of cowboys and a stagecoach in lower Manhattan. Amon
drove straight down Wall Street, waving his hat, shouting "Hooray for Fort Worth and West Texas," saluting friends along the
way. O'Brien sat beside the exuberant Amon, embarrassed.

The convoy halted at city hall, where Mayor Fiorello LaGuardia
presented keys to the city to every Texan and posed for photographers with O'Brien and Amon. Then Amon drove the coach on to
"21" restaurant, where he hosted a luncheon.

Back in Dallas/Fort Worth, the tirade against Amon slowly
abated. Texas Tech played against, and lost to, the Galloping
Gaels of St. Mary's University in the Cotton Bowl while TCU beat
Carnegie Tech 15-7 in the Sugar Bowl. Eleven hundred fans filled
three *Star-Telegram* trains to New Orleans, and the Amon-led
Texans paraded on Bourbon Street, danced barefoot in Jackson
Square, drank Ramos gin fizzes in the Roosevelt Bar, ate at
Antoine's, and had themselves a high old time in the Crescent
City, courtesy of Amon G. Carter, who hated Dallas and loved to
lead a band.

Years later, City Editor John Ellis sat in the Worth Hotel coffee shop, adjacent to the *Star-Telegram,* awaiting breakfast. Outside, a Shrine Circus parade passed on Seventh Street. There were marching clowns and elephants, roaring motorcycle teams, high-stepping majorettes, and loud bands.

The waitress served Ellis his eggs. She heard the noise and wondered aloud, "What's that?"

Without looking up, Ellis muttered, "Just Amon comin' to work."

Amon shares a laugh with Texas Congressman Sam Rayburn at the Touchdown Dinner in honor of the outstanding football player of 1938, Davey O'Brien of TCU, January 9, 1939.

Newspapers can be more fun than a quiet girl.
—A. J. Leibling, *Press*, 1961

The *Star-Telegram* 'Family' is somewhat a homespun affair. Most people grew up on the staff.
—Amon, July 16, 1943

It used to be the only way to get fired was to shoot the managing editor. But you had to kill him. Wounding wouldn't do it.
—Cal Sutton, news editor, *Star-Telegram*, 1966

Everybody talks about the weather, but only the *Star-Telegram* does something about it.
—Alf Evans, newspaperman, *Star-Telegram*, 1969

I went to the *[Star-Telegram]* and asked for a paper route. The circulation manager explained that you just don't ask for paper routes. They're inherited, handed down in the families, with waiting lists!
—Pat Boone, entertainer, 1963

Early in his life, James R. Record began to harrumph. It was, probably, an unconscious mannerism, but he nevertheless practiced a modified Colonel Blimp harrumph. They were in character, the harrumphs, pained phonics of a shy man. They scaled the mountainous boundaries of emotions, being whatever he wished them to be. He issued angry harrumphs and joyful harrumphs and morose harrumphs, harrumphs for sympathy, harrumphs for enthusiasm, harrumphs that scolded, praised, and condemned.

He harrumphed because it was not within his nature to yell or cry or even laugh loudly. He was a gentleman, and gentlemen never betrayed their feelings. He was formal in all ways, precise and reserved, as aloof as the headmaster of a good prep school. "A kindly schoolmaster," said a reporter of James Record.

JRR—his memo signature—was shy. That was the wellspring of his eccentricities. He kept himself away from his newsmen to maintain a dignified and proper relationship, and no one except his immediate family called him anything but "Mr. Record." To the family, he was "Ferdinand," the gentle bull who enjoyed sitting on the porch of his ranch house near Throckmorton in West Texas gazing, as someone once wrote, "across the pasture at the cattle and the trees, and smelling the grass and breathing the pure air."

Because he was shy, his reporters learned to communicate with him by lengthy memo. JRR could not abide long involved discussions and refused to entangle himself in them. He used an open newspaper to end what he considered unnecessary talk, holding the paper between himself and the speaker, screening his face. Once a question was asked and answered or a statement made, JRR snapped the paper as a period to conversation. If the talk continued, Record snapped the newspaper again, louder, then louder, slowly swiveling his chair. "A persistent talker ended up talking to Mr. Record's back," remembered an observer of the ritual.

He opened each conversation, whether in person or over the telephone, with "All Right!" accenting the last word. For outsiders who wandered into the office, his greeting was "How do?" They were expected to say their piece, quickly, and leave. His punctuality was maddening, and amusing, to newsmen. He arrived exactly at seven o'clock each morning—by taxi; he never drove— deposited his jacket on a coatrack, collected a basket of notes from his office, and seated himself in the swivel chair near the city desk. At mid-morning he ate an apple. Precisely at 11:15 A.M. he stood, walked briskly to his office, put on his coat, and strolled to lunch, often waiting absentmindedly through green signal lights, walking on red.

Each and every morning, JRR's first question was "What's the weather?" Weather was his passion, a fetish to be served, and JRR hailed the weather each morning with the piety of a pharaoh greeting Ra. Weather was important, even vital, to the *Star-Telegram* and JRR because weather was the most significant factor of life in West Texas. A good weather story within the *Star-Telegram* was more notable and momentous than one about war, plague, the rise and fall of kings, even a bloody triple ax murder. Weather, especially rain, dictated how life was lived out there on the dry plains, and the *Star-Telegram* reported daily on what readers could expect.

West Texas weather was, if nothing else, versatile. Temperature extremes ranged between -23 to 120 degrees in one six-month period. Tornadoes struck Waco, Lubbock, Wichita Falls, Dallas, and hundreds of lesser towns; sightings of twenty tornadoes in a single day were common. There were sandstorms— called "Panhandle showers"—that stripped paint from cars, blistered faces, and stung eyes, and when combined with rain and wind, formed pellets of mud flung like machine-gun bullets. There were "northers," those sweeping winds of sudden cold as intense as the *buran* of the Siberian steppes, and spectacular summer storms of dreadful booming thunder, lightning like doomsday firebolts.

All of that happened on an annual schedule, but without very much rain. As assorted as West Texas weather was, its grab bag of climatology held little precipitation. When rain happened it was an event, an occasion for fanfare, and the *Star-Telegram* celebrated the rare phenomenon with great bold headlines: "MILLION DOLLAR RAIN IN WEST TEXAS!" and "BENEFICIAL RAIN SOAKS RANCHES."

Conversely, drought—the evil season of rainlessness—was, from all accounts, a stranger to the newspaper. By JRR's edict, the word "drought" could not appear in the *Star-Telegram*, and neither could West Texas be described with the adjectives "desolate," "wilderness," "parched" or "barren."

Flem Hall once traveled by train to El Paso for a basketball tournament. Stuck for a column, he wrote of West Texas, of the land, the stark beauty of the desert. Somehow the column slipped by JRR and was printed. When Hall returned, Record was waiting with the offending column. He confronted his sports editor.

"Where is it?" demanded JRR, thumping his forefinger on the newspaper. "Where is this 'desert?'"

"Between . . . B-B-Big Spring and El . . . Paso," stammered Hall.

"There's no desert in Texas! There's no desert in Texas!" declared Record in a frigid voice. "That's West Texas 'ranch land!'"

Because West Texas was not, to JRR, a desert, no droughts could occur there. The Sahara had droughts. Bir Misaha, Egypt, had droughts. Sharangad, Mongolia, had droughts. And New Mexico. And Oklahoma. But West Texas had "prolonged dry spells"—the only phrase Record would accept to explain the rainless condition. Wink, as it did in 1956, could receive only 1.76 inches of annual rainfall but its predicament was not drought; Wink was having a "prolonged dry spell." Within the pages of the *Star-Telegram* the great dust bowl of the 1930s never blew over the Oklahoma state line into West Texas. Out there, it was nothing more than a tempest in a dusty tea cup.

During that 1930s drought, a national magazine published a story picturing a small West Texas town as deserted and blowing away with the sand. *Harrumph!* JRR would not tolerate such ignorance. He immediately dispatched a team of reporters to the town to clear up the misconception that West Texas was a wasteland. The single story multiplied into a year's worth of articles, as each Sunday newsmen found something optimistic to write about this and that dusty hamlet.

Because rain was crucial to West Texas, and thus to the *Star-Telegram*, JRR established a network of special rain reporters. Gauges were distributed in the eighty-four counties of West Texas. The rain reporters were expected to monitor precipitation within their areas and immediately relay the amounts to the newspaper. Gauge readers were paid one dollar per report. In

Fort Worth, real reporters were given gauges and told to monitor rainfall amounts at home. Often that meant a predawn hike in a heavy downpour. Herb Owens, soaked with an early morning rain, reported poetically:

> As this wretched day was dawning,
> Out I stumbled, stretching, yawning,
> Through the muck and mire that lay without my door.
> Toward a gauge so distant mounted,
> That my steps I never counted,
> For I feared that I would get there, nevermore.
> But I reached my destination,
> Read the o'ernight accumulation,
> And am now reporting, swiftly true,
> .42

West Texas rain did not always fall softly but often splashed down in a rush, creating havoc among those poor folks who had prayed for help, but not that much. The newspaper, never wanting to be the messenger of bad news, softened deluges into something like gentle spring showers. In 1930, there was a general cloudburst in West Texas, and the *Star-Telegram* welcomed it with a bold headline: "HEAVY RAINS ARE BENEFICIAL TO TEXAS PASTURES." The story began with news that the rains meant good crops and well-watered cattle and hope for the future. Only persistent readers found deep within the story other aspects of the kindly rains: water rose eight and a half feet into Childress homes, "tore out bridges and left highways impassable." An Amarillo man was washed into the Canadian River. A mail plane crashed in the storm. Rock Island Railroad track was swept away, stranding trains and passengers.

Those Pollyanna rain reports caused Alf Evans to compose and thumbtack to the office bulletin board a joke headline: "BENEFICIAL RAINS DROWN 7."

Even into his eightieth year, when the *Star-Telegram* had become less preoccupied with weather and rain, JRR had to know the forecast and telephoned the city desk daily for a morning report. It was one of the ironies of his life that when drilling for precious water on his Throckmorton ranch, he struck, instead, oil.

The *Star-Telegram* was more than just a newspaper; it was three newspapers. First, there was the hard-core newspaper with a superb reporting staff that could cover a breaking story as no other in Texas. It was that essential *Star-Telegram*, carefully protected and separated by JRR from its other missions, that uncovered scandals in government, reported verbatim murder-trial testimony, collected and published first all names of the generation of children killed in the New London school explosion, tracked murderers and thieves, editorially stumped for mandatory fire escapes on public buildings, highway safety laws, reform in Austin and Washington. That *Star-Telegram* was a real newspaper and, by all examples, an excellent one. The pure-news *Star-Telegram* reported accurately and in-depth all that went on around it, from crimes to sports to governmental processes to farm and ranch news. It was a solid newspaper, and even Amon Carter kept his hands off. Not once in a half-century did he even attempt to keep a friend's name out of a hard news story, and his friends often asked it of him. Its editorial pages, conservative in all matters, were never intellectual, never campaigned for philosophical concepts but for more practical things like highways and parks and zoo elephants.

Leafing through those brittle, yellowed pages reveals an innocence of the era and of journalism. There was a wide-eyed, gee-whiz quality. World events were explained as they related to Fort Worth and West Texas. Whenever possible, wire stories were localized with the insertion of a paragraph providing the Texas angle. "If there was an avalanche in the Swiss Alps," exaggerated a reporter, "we would write a local story saying it couldn't happen here and why, quoting experts."

However exacting the fundamental *Star-Telegram*, no yellow and absolutely no by-god blue journalism was practiced. JRR would have none of either. He would not permit the word "rape" within *Star-Telegram* pages. The accepted euphemism was "attacked" (or, alternately, "assaulted"), which might have puzzled some readers, as in a story of the 1930s: "[Miss Mary Smith] was held up by two men Tuesday night and robbed and beaten. She suffered a broken jaw and minor bruises. She was not attacked." (JRR's legacies died hard. "Rape" did not appear in the

Star-Telegram until 1967. The word did not find a spot in evening-edition headlines until the early 1970s.)

The second *Star-Telegram* was Amon's alter ego. It boosted and swaggered and bragged, ever spreading the message of optimism throughout the land. Amon's *Star-Telegram* could post an eight-column banner headline on a busy news day: "BUSINESS GOOD: MONEY PLENTIFUL: BUILDING AT ITS PEAK IN WEST TEXAS." It could publish as many as 204 columns of type in ten days on the Fort Worth Fat Stock Show, scooting all other legitimate news onto back pages. It published regular pages devoted to "Texas Development" and a series on Fort Worth's "Self Made Men" and sections on the city's "Best Houses, Streets and Businesses."

That *Star-Telegram* was a chamber of commerce publication, and Amon used it like blaring trumpets and klieg lights on those he wished to impress. In 1928, Fort Worth was host to the West Texas Chamber of Commerce's annual convention, and the *Star-Telegram* pulsated with pride over the high honor. "WEST TEXAS CHAMBER OF COMMERCE IN FORT WORTH MEETING" crowed the newspaper on page one as delegates convened. The story went on to instruct its rural cousins from the West how to behave in the big city. "Visitors who find themselves in trouble through ignorance of local laws will be dealt with lightly," it promised. Under the heading, "Good Things to Remember for Our Auto-Driving Visitors" was published this list of reminders: "Don't drive over a fire hose"; "Don't drive your car down the center of the street"; "Don't allow bicycle riders to hang onto your car"; and "Don't argue with the traffic officer—if he has made a mistake, the court will right the wrong."

If delegates minded the condescending lecture, perhaps they were placated by reading about themselves. Throughout the week, the *Star-Telegram* turned over its major news columns to all details and every uttered word of the convention. Daily, there were pages of pictures and printed speeches and stories on those speeches. The newspaper even grouped news from West Texas on two adjoining pages to enable delegates to have a convenient reference for news from home. Regular readers who cared to learn of important matters in Kansas City, where Republicans were selecting a presidential nominee that week, had to search among the boosterisms. In Amon's opinion, the West Texas Chamber of Commerce was of far more value to Fort Worth than the GOP, and possibly he was right.

JRR worshipped Amon and felt his publisher could do no wrong. He also knew Amon's mind. Record kept to the party line, which is probably why once he filled the bottom of page one with an eight-column photograph of 108 visiting undertakers—the journalistic equivalent of stacking a clutch of angels on the head of a pin.

If Amon meddled in editorial business of the second *Star-Telegram*, it was with the idea of improving the stories to suit his version of the news. When Bell Helicopter Corporation began construction of its new production plant in Fort Worth, Lawrence Bell, the firm's president, delivered an inaugural speech of pure chamber of commerce gushings. Before publication, Amon inspected the Bell story. He found a statement with which he did not agree and reached for a copy pencil. "Hell, he didn't mean to say that," Amon grumbled, and changed Bell's direct quotes to please himself. On another occasion Amon was sorting and selecting pictures for a page to memorialize visiting oilmen. JRR was at his elbow. Other editors were near, waiting. Among the final group of photos were two pictures of the same man.

"Mr. Carter, we have a policy against running a person's picture twice on the same page," instructed Charlie Boatner, a city editor. Amon was amused.

"I never heard of such a policy, have you, Mr. Record?" Amon asked.

"No, Mr. Carter," replied JRR, who had made the rule.

That boosteristic *Star-Telegram*, which could banner during the Scopes Trial such breathless intelligence as "WEST TEXAS BUYING POWER TREBLES IN 10 YEARS," often camouflaged the first and real *Star-Telegram* and critics forgot that underneath all that puffery breathed a real newspaper.

The third *Star-Telegram* was a playful little thing, serious as all get-out but nevertheless a frivolous package slipped between the hard news and the squishy chamber messages. Because for so long the *Star-Telegram* was the only acceptable reading matter in West Texas, and because much of its circulation was out there in the provinces, it became a kind of family album for western sub-scribers, a yearbook and almanac of memories and homemaker hints and livestock advice. Removed from its city format, the third *Star-Telegram* would have made a serviceable little weekly newspaper for Muleshoe or Chillicothe.

The *Star-Telegram* spread into eighty-four counties of West Texas, and well beyond—as late as the 1940s, twenty-five hun-dred papers were delivered daily in Roswell, New Mexico; the home edition of the morning paper was delivered two hundred miles beyond El Paso, more than seven hundred miles from its presses, and closer to Los Angeles than Fort Worth. JRR often bragged that the newspaper was read in eleven hundred Texas towns, most of them in the West. To service this immense cos-mos of a circulation area, JRR organized a network of six hundred correspondents. And he regularly dispatched Amon's army of reporters to forage for news on the prairies. News out there was not what it was in Fort Worth. International anxiety was mean-ingless in West Texas. What really was important was: Could Bossy live on mesquite beans and cactus pods, and will the tur-key plague in Cuero spread to San Saba?

Those legions of correspondents were there to report on the notable events of their communities, and the *New York Times* with its Balkan intrigues be damned. Thus, the third *Star-Telegram* was brimming full of such one-inch stories as "Mem-bers of the First Baptist Church of Lampasas have completed plans for the building of a parsonage" and "Plans for the opening of cotton picking season in West Texas are being perfected" and "Twenty-eight rattlesnakes have been killed on a farm less than eight miles from Childress." Of such piddling matters are news-paper circulations and fortunes built.

There were full-page layouts headlined "HARRY VETCH EXPERIMENT IN RISING STAR" and detailed accounts of "MELON BLIGHT IN PARKER COUNTY" and lists of new teachers in Cooke County, art exhibits in Seagraves, parade reports from Stamford. With neither shame nor favoritism, the third *Star-Telegram* pub-lished pictures of grandchildren visiting in Floydada, of "the first Girls' Tomato Club in Comanche County," of a new crematory in Abilene, a rising young store executive in Colorado City, little girls who won dancing contests in Lubbock, and every bride between Amarillo and Zavala.

Sophisticated Fort Worthians may have been startled to find in their Sunday *Star-Telegram* a page of "NEWS AND SUGGESTIONS FOR THE HOG BREEDER" ("Don't let sows get constipated—see to it their bowels are kept in good working condition"), but without those imperative tidings the newspaper would have been of little use to West Texans. Such attention to the essentials of West Texas life was repaid with fawning loyalty. When JRR's newsmen went out there, they found themselves hailed as celebrities. Frank Reeves's name was known by every farmer and rancher for five hundred miles in all directions. Flem Hall was a more famous sportswriter than Damon Runyon. Reporters covering banquets were introduced along with visiting senators. Silliman Evans once went to Pampa for a story, and the town threw him an appreciation dinner.

The third *Star-Telegram*, as trivial and amusing as it seems in retrospect, was substantial stuff to the readership it served. Any newspaper could, as the first *Star-Telegram* often did, change the course of state governments, but only the third *Star-Telegram* and Amon Carter could improve the discomfort of farrowing sows. Content of the bucolic third *Star-Telegram* was evidence of what Amon felt was necessary for newspapers: public service.

From the beginning, the *Star-Telegram* burrowed into the lives of its readers, campaigning for more city parks as early as 1909. It was the patron for such traveling curiosities as a mechanized miniature model of Jerusalem, and sponsoring godparent for automobile shows, home shows, quilting bees, ranch and farm shows, vacation shows, bird-watching tours to the Texas gulf coast, more than two-score cooking schools, and group vacations to Europe, the Orient, and South America. To promote art, it distributed appreciation courses and portfolios of Old Masters while undiscovered authors were given their opportunity with Scholastic Writing Award programs.

At Amon's request, JRR formed the Fort Worth Zoological Association and served as its president (Bess Stephenson was drafted as secretary). *Star-Telegram* news space was used to obtain animals for the zoo. Through public subscription, giraffes were bought by the inch and the foot, and elephants by the pound. The zoo became a daily assignment, and cute animal pictures plagued page one for forty years. There was the Free Milk and Ice Fund and the annual state Golden Gloves Tournament. Goodfellows began in 1912 as a Christmas season drive to provide toys for poor children. JRR insisted that the names of all contributors be published on the front page—a decision that often consumed more than half of page one in December.

When disaster came, the *Star-Telegram* was there immediately as a community vehicle for relief funds. It gathered $335,000 in 1949 when Fort Worth suffered flooding, raised $18,000 for victims of a Texas City ship explosion—where there was no circulation or readership—and $18,000 for Olney, $50,000 for Waco, and $37,000 for San Angelo, all of which were struck by tornadoes.

The newspaper fought for more and better highways, and almost single-handedly forced the establishment of Texas Tech in Lubbock at a time when politicians believed West Texans weren't worth educating. It politicked for state parks, and higher crop and beef prices. Amon became president of an association wanting a national park in the Big Bend area of West Texas. Amon and the newspaper collected public funds with which to purchase 750,000 acres, and he and Bascom Timmons delivered the park land deed to FDR on a propitious date—June 6, 1944; they waited while the president monitored reports of the Allied invasion of Europe.

Because of the area it served, the *Star-Telegram* had no choice but to become more than just a newspaper, and its first purpose—that of providing comprehensive news coverage—suffered. Amon had very little real feel for journalism, but he understood that the public-service and boosterism commitments of his newspaper greatly harmed its professional reputation. As Jimmy North explained in a letter to publisher Ted Dealey, "He [Amon] has said in family councils that the *Dallas News* is a much better paper than our own." The *Dallas Morning News* could be a newspaper; it had no critical need to elevate the lives of poor dirt farmers and ragtag ranchers, or to bring hope where none existed.

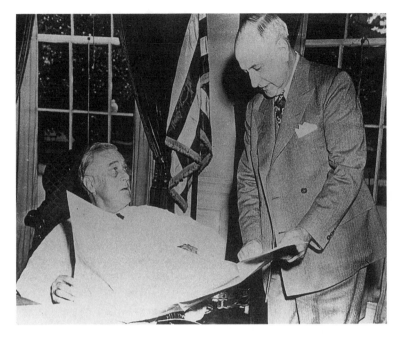

Amon presents deed for Big Bend National Park to President Franklin D. Roosevelt, June 6, 1944.

For most of fifty years, the *Star-Telegram* owned West Texas, but slowly circulation and influence diminished because, ironically, Amon's boosterism of the region succeeded. More people came. Good local newspapers flourished. The *Star-Telegram* held rights to the most popular syndicated features, comics, and press wires in the western half of Texas. But Amon gave up the monopoly, mostly, explained Katrine Deakins, because he "thought it would help."

Times and technology changed, too. The morning edition was the West Texas newspaper, and the distances it was shipped slowed distribution. As long as readers were isolated they never knew the news was stale. Enter radio, especially the instantaneous worldwide news programs during World War II; West Texans discovered that their old friend, the *Star-Telegram*, was always late with the news. And after WWII, with the growing popularity of automobiles, bus and train schedules were curtailed and shipping the newspaper into West Texas, particularly into smaller communities, became increasingly more difficult. The pattern of newspaper advertising also changed as large, national firms began buying only single markets.

High school football is a good example of why the *Star-Telegram* moved out of West Texas. Considered a test of manhood by West Texans, football was a game with fanatical supporters. Entire towns closed their doors on Friday afternoons to watch the local high school teams play. Using its network of correspondents, the newspaper reported on as many as three hundred high school football games in the Saturday-morning edition. At least fifty games were staffed each week, the coverage filling five open pages. Then outdoor athletic field lights were developed. High schools began playing football at night. The *Star-Telegram* could no longer provide complete coverage in the Saturday edition. The correspondent network was turned over to the *Associated Press*, and soon every newspaper published what the *Star-Telegram* had developed and owned exclusively.

In a sense, West Texas grew up and no longer needed its sponsor, the *Star-Telegram*. Amon had promoted its growth, nurtured it to maturity; West Texas could go it alone, and did.

Jimmy North was a square-shouldered, blocky-built man with a dark, almost Indian face. A contemporary described him as "retiring, but breezy, gregarious, the kind of man who whistles in the morning." North, said another, "could do everything in the office better than anybody else, but rarely did." Without North, Amon often said, "We would be in a hell of a fix."

Jimmy North, as editor, did not often edit. He was overseer of daily operations and, with Bert Honea, ran the *Star-Telegram* while Amon fiddled with the world. North was a gentleman who began his memos to JRR, "My dear Mr. Record . . ." North rarely interfered with the editorial processes because those were JRR's responsibilities. He had a profound respect for the reporting staffs, but confessed to a friend that reporters were "an unbridled bunch." Mostly, Jimmy did not breach JRR's domain because when he did Mr. Record asked him to fire or discipline someone, and North disliked doing either.

Newspaper offices were never the frantic places portrayed in fiction. There was a sustained intense-but-leisurely pace to them, a hum rather than a roar, with brief periods of commotion during breaking news events. The *Star-Telegram*, with the cast of a Russian novel and the plot of *The Little Train That Could*, had JRR, who was not ordinary even in the extraordinary world of newspapering. JRR ruled two complete reporting staffs, one for each edition, and his eccentricities created a very unconventional habitat.

Most reporters and editors came and never left, remaining because there was stimulation, because the newspaper was quality and consequently so were they, and because no one would make them leave. Like Jimmy North, JRR could not dismiss his reporters without provocations that would have meant criminal charges in other businesses. Few of those discharged had to face JRR; he either foisted the distasteful duty on North or assistant editors. JRR fired Gotcheye, a copyboy thief, with a stern lecture and a week's pay, but the experience was traumatic, and he moped about the newsroom for weeks. Reporters who deserved firing were pushed into a corner like stacked cordwood, left out of general pay raises and ignored until they understood their predicament and left voluntarily. The no-firing policy left few openings for new reporters. Still, the *Star-Telegram* was known as a newspaper where an itinerant reporter could find "temporary" work because gentle JRR could not deny a job to any man who needed one.

The *Star-Telegram* was not unlike one of those banana republic plantations where a benevolent padrone cared for his workers' every need. Amon gave his employees free insurance and bankrolled a generous retirement program with $4,500,000 of his own money. Christmas bonuses came every year. Once, in the 1930s, Amon was in New York when bonus checks were distributed. When he returned, he decided the bonus had been too little and issued another. During the Korean War, employees who went into the service were paid the difference between their military pay and the salary they left behind. Amon and Nenetta placed

$1,425,000 into a special fund that provided emergency assistance to workers. When a disastrous flood hit Fort Worth, many of its victims were *Star-Telegram* employees. The fund paid all of their losses. Amon often personally took charge of an employee's troubles. One reporter's son was born with a cleft palate. Amon found a doctor and paid for the expensive operation to correct the boy's disfigurement. The *Union Banner*, a local union publication, praised Amon as "perhaps the only employer in the United States who pays the entire cost."

Only the newspaper's backshop was unionized, and negotiations usually were left to Bert Honea. Once, though, Amon came to a contract discussion—dressed in a shabby, ragged suit and shoes with holes in the soles. Throughout its history, the *Star-Telegram* never had a strike or a serious labor problem.

In the newsroom, staffs were considered "family" and treated as such. JRR not only could not fire his people, he was reluctant even to reprimand them. The act of dressing down a wayward reporter distressed him and he rarely did it, but resorted to an assortment of excoriating glares, grimaces, and harrumphs that were as punishing as real scoldings. JRR's pantomimed discipline was as effective as heated words, and a disapproving stare from the managing editor usually corrected any problem.

JRR was a strict editor who wanted every detail in every story. Ida Belle Hicks, an amusement writer, was assigned to cover a new play. During the performance, a mouse unexpectedly ran across the stage. The audience roared. Ida Belle ignored the mouse. Next day, JRR read a review in the *Press* that contained an account of the rodent's appearance. He called Ida Belle to his desk and sternly lectured her, "Next time, mention the mouse. . . ."

JRR's life was filled with little crosses carved by the peculiarities of his staffs. George Dolan, temporarily promoted to assistant city editor, stood atop his desk to hand out daily assignments until harrumphed down by JRR. (Dolan later also was barred from taking obituary phone calls because the news unnerved him, and he giggled when relatives told of their departed loved ones.) Bert Griffith and Ned Record decided to welcome a new, sweet and innocent reporter, Bess Stephenson, to the *Star-*

Telegram family by escorting her to lunch at a nearby whore-house. Presley Bryant, the state editor—often called "The Terrible-Tempered Mr. Fang"—would, when angry, stand and slam his chair against a desk. JRR would rush over to examine the chair and desk for damage, then glare at Bryant. Bryant also wore ten-nis shoes in defiance of JRR's strict dress code, and daily vaulted the low fence dividing the newsroom from the elevator lobby. JRR grimaced but never spoke to Bryant of his offenses.

Byron Utecht was the first American reporter to ride with Pan-cho Villa. He was absentminded. Utecht lit one cigarette after another until a half-dozen burned in ashtrays. JRR, who refused to smoke in the newsroom, would snub out the offending ciga-rettes, then stand, hands on hips, harrumphing at Utecht.

Icky Pierce drank. Posted to the courthouse, Icky promptly went off to the nearest saloon and forgot his assignment. Late in the day, he telephoned the city desk to report that his absence was caused by the mob trying to spring their criminal friends from county jail. It was a near riot, exclaimed Icky. The city edi-tor immediately dispatched Alex Stedman to assist Icky with the big story. Icky tempted Alex into the saloon. Late that evening, Icky returned and was ordered to hurry with his mob story. Icky pecked out two sentences, stood uncertainly, and walked out. Editors read the sentences: "There ain't no mob. I have gone home." Next day, Icky and Alex were banished to the obituary desk where the latter uttered an immortal line: "The wages of gin is death notices."

Frank Reeves, a lean, gaunt man, a real cowboy who turned to photography and then to writing when ranch life became boring, ranged over West Texas as no other *Star-Telegram* reporter. He had a studied disregard for money and rarely filed expense accounts. He often misplaced his paychecks. The newspaper's accounting office would send frantic notes to JRR, urging him to force Mr. Reeves to straighten out his finances. At the end of the year, when accountants were trying to close their books, JRR would stand over Mr. Reeves while he completed expense accounts totaling thousands of dollars.

JRR, who disliked ostentation of any sort, often was irritated with his music critic, E. Clyde Whitlock, a balding cherub who played his violin for office Christmas parties. Mr. Whitlock was painstakingly methodical and a slow, forefinger typist. He sometimes fell asleep while writing a review. Whitlock loved language and his reviews were bewildering labyrinths in which multisyllabic words wandered across the page like bloated specters. Once, when an outdoor concert was rained out, Whitlock wrote that the cancellation was caused by "meteorological impediments." He reviewed Margaret Truman's concert in Fort Worth with the observation, "There are vocal faults, lacks and limitation but it is significant that they are amenable to amelioration under understanding guidance." JRR marked that column with a large "?".

Whitlock wrote his own obituary ("to run after my funeral") in which he called himself a "sesquipedantitarian" [one given to using long words], adding in a shaky hand, *Ave atque vale*—"Hail and farewell."

Bert Griffith's self-written death notice had a note attached, ordering "When I die, say I died—none of that 'passed away' crap." Dolan's obit asked that his creditors be designated as pallbearers. "They carried me through life," he wrote. "They may as well finish the job."

Boyce House was a breezy reporter who talked more than he wrote, and he was a prolific writer. On a rainy Sunday afternoon, in just four hours, he wrote *I Give You Texas*, a book that sold 225,000 copies. It was filled with all those Texas brags shouted by Amon. House had been editor of a weekly newspaper in Eastland, a small West Texas town, when he broke the story of Old Rip, a horned toad. Rip supposedly was cemented into the cornerstone of a courthouse. Thirty years later, the cornerstone was removed, and there was Rip—alive. Rip and House became famous, and went on the road, touring throughout the East. They stopped at the White House where Cal Coolidge ignored the nation's business for fifteen minutes while he inspected the Texas frog. A few months of fame and fortune later, Rip really died for good, was embalmed, stuffed, and laid to rest in a tiny, red-satin-lined casket. House came to the *Star-Telegram*, where he chittered on until JRR popped his newspaper like a machine gun.

Silliman Evans was without peer as a political writer in Texas, and perhaps the best reporter ever to work at the *Star-Telegram*.

But competent though he was, his arrogance irked everyone. He was jockey-sized and uncommonly preoccupied with self—pugnacious, dissolute, petulant, and dauntless—the perfect weapon to loose against the political shenanigans of Ma and Pa Ferguson. Because of the Ferguson stories, Evans was drawn close to Amon, and the reporter began to emulate the mannerisms of the publisher. He even switched to Amon's brand of cigars. Once, in Austin, as Evans and Bert Honea left a restaurant, Evans scooped up a supply of expensive cigars. Honea, who knew Evans's salary, asked, "You don't put those on your expense account, do you, Silliman?"

"Not as such, Mr. Honea, not as such."

Evans left the newspaper to become public relations director of Texas Air Transport and later American Airlines, then went to work for the Democrats. After the 1932 election, he was awarded the splendid title of Fourth Assistant Postmaster General. From that post he became president of Maryland Casualty Company, then, using Jesse Jones's money, purchased the bankrupt *Nashville Tennessean*. Within six months, the newspaper was making money. Successful as a major publisher, Evans bought a showcase estate and began staging parties for visiting celebrities. He gave expensive gifts and became a principal booster of Nashville. He named his son Amon Carter Evans.

And then there was C. L. Richhart. . . .

Rich was the playful breeze that blew through the *Star-Telegram* for more than a half-century. A little sunburst of a man, he was gnomic with prankish eyes and the soul of a gypsy. His irregular lifestyle gave him the complexion of a morgue attendant, but there was an infectious laugh, the breezy nervous energy, the perpetual-motion mind, the eternally optimistic spirit. He was never on time, neither for work nor assignments, was endlessly broke, ever happy, and always helping others—usually with *Star-Telegram* money.

"I always visualize Rich as an elf with the exhausted remnants of a cigar protruding from a plastic cigar holder clamped in his teeth," wrote Phil Record, who was a copyboy when he first encountered the irrepressible Richhart. "He looked as though he had gone into his closet blindfolded to select the day's wardrobe."

Early on, Rich both angered and bewildered the tidy, systematized JRR, who reacted rashly—he fired Rich. Amon interceded, and Rich's job was saved, and later he found an accommodation with JRR. No one could remain angry with Clarence Leon Richhart.

For Amon, Rich became a sinecure, of sorts, because the diminutive reporter, when not distracted, was competent and, said a colleague, "the best public relations man on the staff." But as did most everyone else, Amon at first tried to change Richhart. He surveyed the shabby clothes and unkempt appearance and ordered Rich to upgrade his wardrobe. Rich bought a suit off the rack at Washer Brothers—and charged it to Amon.

It was Rich to whom Amon turned when he wanted a train commandeered. After World War II, the French sent thanks for America's help. It came in the form of a Friendship Train laden with Gaelic exhibits. Fort Worth and Amon had packed boxcars with foodstuffs for European war relief in 1943; columnist Drew Pearson wrote that Amon delayed the Friendship Train while he had "Fort Worth, Where The West Begins" stamped on flour sacks. But the train was not routed through Fort Worth, an ingratitude that angered Amon. He commanded Rich to go get it. In Austin, Rich convinced French and Texas officials to send the train to Fort Worth. Afterwards, he promised, the train would be returned to its scheduled route. The train was delivered, and Fort Worthians were appeased. After a while, the French asked for their train back, and Amon said, "To hell with them." They had to come after it.

When not doing little things for Amon, Rich had the usual reporting duties, except that no one ever knew where he was supposed to be. The morning city editor once asked his counterpart on the afternoon edition, "Can I borrow Richhart for an assignment?"

"Borrow him? I thought he worked for you."

With a Bedouin's loathing for permanency, Rich belonged to no man, but flitted hither and yon, disappearing and reappearing with the suddenness of a spring breeze. Because he was ever late for work, Jack Butler wasn't disturbed when Rich telephoned one early morning. "Did you find those stories I left?" asked Rich. Butler said he did.

"Well," continued Rich, "I've run into a fellow who wanted me to go to a chuck wagon breakfast."

"OK, but I want you to check out a story and call me."

Long pause.

"From Stamford?"

"Stamford!" moaned Butler, visualizing the ranching community two hundred miles west of Fort Worth.

"I told you this fellow wanted me to go to a chuck wagon breakfast."

In the early 1950s, the *Star-Telegram* sponsored a community Christmas tree, and Rich was assigned to select the hundred-foot-tall fir from the New Mexico forests. He arranged for it to be delivered to Fort Worth. Outside Santa Fe, Rich met a guy on his way to Seattle. Having never seen Seattle, Rich said goodbye to the Fort Worth-bound tree and went northwest with the man.

Each New Year's Eve, Rich celebrated with a peculiar ritual. He ran through the newsroom ringing a cowbell, a noisy practice that disturbed night news editor Cal Sutton. One holiday season, Rich was sent to Mexico City on assignment, and Sutton anticipated a quiet evening. At midnight, the telephone rang. A deskman answered, and motioned to Sutton, "It's for you."

"Hello," said Sutton, and over the wires from Mexico City, he heard: "Happy New Year! (Clang . . . clang . . . clang)"

However unpredictable, Rich owned a gentle, sweet humanity that spread over everyone. There was the wartime Easter when Jack Butler was drafted into the Navy. His wife, Mary Lou, left to manage with one small child and pregnant with another, was spending a lonely holiday with Catherine Gunn, whose husband, Stanley, the *Star-Telegram* Pacific correspondent, had been killed months earlier. Catherine had two children. Neither woman was in a festive mood. Until Rich arrived. He came by taxi, with corsages for the wives and Easter eggs for the children, and, of course, the happiest gift of all—himself.

Reporters who learned of his generosity that Easter were sure he charged the taxi ride to the newspaper, plus, to be sure, a sizable tip. Rich, like Amon, always went first class on the *Star-Telegram*'s money, especially for the 1948 Employees Association picnic—not incidentally the last outing underwritten by the newspaper. The association was formed a decade earlier, and management agreed to fund an annual picnic. Amon believed the one thousand or so dollars were well spent, and the picnic always was a pleasant affair with hot dogs and potato salad and lemonade and softball games.

In 1948, Rich was elected president of the association, thus *maggiordomo* of the picnic. "I just lost my head," he admitted later.

The site he selected on the shores of Lake Worth had a beach and sports facilities and old pavilions. The buildings, Rich believed, were a little shoddy. He brought in carpenters and painters to spruce them up. A bog of quicksand was found on the grounds. He hired workmen to bridge the dangerous patch. He contracted for a caterer, Walter Jetton (later famous as Lyndon Johnson's favorite barbecue chef). Because the *Star-Telegram* operated in shifts, Rich declared the picnic would go on for thirty-six hours, so everyone could attend. And, of course, the workers needed transportation. A fleet of buses was chartered.

July 18, the picnic opened, and for the next day and a half association members marveled at what Rich had created.

There were fringed surreys to transport new arrivals over the quicksand bridge, speedboat rides and seaplane flights, a miniature train, goat carts (JRR puckishly drove one for the kids), wagons for hayrides, canoe-tilting contests and horseshoe tournaments, softball games, hourly drawings for door prizes, floor shows by the Flying X Ranchboys, square dancing, free liquor, and gambling at a pavilion outfitted as a casino. Bands played for dancing until after midnight.

According to published reports, the picnickers consumed three hundred pounds of barbecued beef, three hundred pounds of ribs, two hundred pounds of ham, seventy-five chickens, five hundred pounds of baked beans, seven hundred loaves of bread, and four hundred cases of soft drinks. Not all diners were association members or their families. Employees of other companies staging nearby picnics simply abandoned their nickel-and-dime day to join Rich's extravaganza. Off-duty policemen arrived and never left.

Amon was there. He played softball, danced with the ladies, and sang, off-key, "I'm in Love With the Man With the Handlebar Mustache." He appeared to enjoy himself.

Rich's surprise came at sunset of the second day. He gathered the picnickers at the lakeshore. Across the water, twilight exploded with a panorama of fireworks. Rockets soared and burst in sparkling showers, bombs shattered the night, blossoming fiery sky missiles spread fingers of reds and greens. A classic fireworks display. More was coming—Rich's finale.

There, above the lake, etched in fire dozens of feet high and, a reporter later wrote, "lighting up the night sky for miles around," was the flaming portrait of Amon G. Carter.

Onlookers were stunned, and within the silence was the astounded voice of Jimmy North: "Damn! What's next?"

The bill.

Rich's picnic cost twelve thousand dollars to produce, and Amon's *Star-Telegram* never again sponsored an employees' outing. When costs were assembled and totaled, a seething Amon summoned Rich.

"I guess what we ought to do," shouted Amon, "is make you a gawddammed vice president in charge of finances."

Legend says Rich answered, "I dunno. What's it pay?"

I didn't hire you to tell me I can't. I hired you to tell me I can.
　　—Amon, to his attorney, Abe Herman, early 1950s

It may be because I despise the publisher, but I cannot view him in any light but as a menace to the people of Fort Worth.
　　—Karl Crowley, unsuccessful Texas gubernatorial candidate, 1938

Mr. Carter never made a mistake. I always thought of him as the infallible man.
　　—James R. Record, managing editor, *Star-Telegram,* 1966

Amon Carter was the authority for Fort Worth and West Texas. His way, he believed, was the right way, the only way. That was that, and to oppose him was to experience a blast furnace fury that was sure to come. Amon brooked no interference. "There is only one white hunter on this safari," a contemporary said of Amon's singular role as authoritarian. Cross Amon, defy him, and one acquired an antagonist with a superb memory for old outrages and a fine aptitude for retribution. His was a low tolerance for slights and affronts and what he believed was ingratitude. He despised ingratitude, toward himself or others.

One year, a businessman refused to contribute to River Crest Country Club's employee Christmas fund. Amon never forgave the man, and thirty years later still ranted about the member's stingy ways. Silliman Evans, after becoming a Nashville publisher, was a force in Tennessee's Democratic Party. At the 1936 Democratic Convention, Amon still was campaigning for John Nance Garner as president and solicited Evans's help with the Tennessee delegation. Evans, who never wished to displease Amon, agreed to support Garner but privately continued to talk for FDR. Amon learned of the deceit and gawddamned Evans for his treasonous act.

Evans deeply regretted the loss of Amon's friendship, and for years wrote long fawning letters attempting to repair the damage. Amon was unmoved. "I've got my foot on his neck," he told Katrine Deakins. "I'm just gonna make him squirm." Amon couldn't abide a smart aleck.

The publisher was incapable of hiding his anger and confronted whatever or whoever riled him. "It has come to my attention," he wrote a man who gossiped about him around the Fort Worth Club, "that you, as a busy body [sic], have been devoting considerable time to the discussion of my personal affairs."

When a Texas & Pacific Railroad crew accidentally burned a portion of his Arlington peach orchard, Amon composed a sarcastic letter to J. L. Lancaster, the company's president. It read:

> I am the peaceful owner of a little farm adjoining the Texas & Pacific Railroad between Arlington and Fort Worth. I have lived on this farm for years and several years ago arrived at the age which made it impractical for me to do hard farm labor; so, I decided to plant a peach orchard. Since which time, I have been

pruning, nursing and tutoring these trees and about the time I had
them in good condition to bear fruit, and give me a sufficient
income to take care of my modest requirements, I find the big
Texas & Pacific Railroad comes along, carelessly, without thought
or consideration for its neighbors, with a [railway] motor car, and
sprayed oil on the grass on your right-a-way and set fire to it. As a
result, you have destroyed one hundred and seventy-nine peach
trees, leaving only four or five that might live, although that is
doubtful. Now, I have always been considered a fair man and want
to do what is right, provided what is right agrees with my idea of
what is right. In conclusion, please get your Directors together and
study this matter over and let me have a check, as I naturally
would prefer to settle a matter in this way than I would to bring it
up in the Court House here. In addition to all the financial loss, I
am heart-broken over having this orchard destroyed. It may be of
no consequence to a great railroad like the Texas & Pacific, but it
sure is an important matter to me. Now, please give me a personal
answer on this and do not send me form letter 8786 which usually
denies all responsibility, as I know damn well who burned up my
orchard.

Amon had another dispute with T & P over a dead hog. The
telephone company built a new line across his peach orchard,
near which he maintained a pigpen. Workers left a gate open,
and a sow wandered away to nap on the railroad tracks. It was
struck and killed by a freight train. He ranted at the Texas &
Pacific and received a $12.50 settlement. He then went to the
telephone company and demanded retribution for its careless-
ness, collecting another fifteen dollars. For years, Amon—owner
of a multimillion-dollar business—boasted again and again how
he pocketed $27.50 for a $25.00 hog, and how the telephone company compensated him for a sow already paid for by the railroad.

Amon always had trouble with railroads. The Southern Pacific
refused to extend its switching limits to Fort Worth. He told off its
president in a three-page letter, then sought out and welcomed to
town a competing line, the Katy, to freeze out Southern Pacific.
He indulged himself in a two-year fight with the Burlington
Lines. The Interstate Commerce Commission allowed the railroad to lease the Fort Worth and Denver, which ran from Dallas
to Texline on the northern fringe of the Panhandle. The lease,

Burlington's petition stated, would save $25,000 annually. To Amon, it meant only that Burlington's removal of Fort Worth and Denver's general offices from Fort Worth to Denver and its closing of maintenance shops in Childress in West Texas would leave 189 employees without jobs.

Amon dictated an editorial describing how Ralph Budd, Burlington's president, was attempting to sacrifice "The Fort Worth and Denver Railway on the altar of Burlington front office convenience."

"You, Mr. Budd, have cast the die," concluded the editorial, "with utter contempt for fair and decent treatment of both your faithful employees and old customers."

Amon forced the merger request into public hearings. After his testimony, the ICC denied the Burlington petition. Amon had won, but Amon was mad. He wrote to Budd: "As evidence of my sincerity, I am bringing up a boy . . . to carry on for me at the Fort Worth *Star-Telegram*. In my final papers to the young man, I am leaving everything discretionary with one exception, namely: The Burlington blitzkrieg against Texas. On this I have asked that he never relent in keeping the good folks of Texas continuously informed (through our newspapers and radio stations) of just HOW MEAN the Burlington has treated us 'country folks.'"

And still Amon was unsatisfied. He ordered that *Star-Telegram* papers no longer be delivered into West Texas by Burlington's new subsidiary, the Fort Worth and Denver, a loss of twelve thousand dollars monthly to the railroad. The matter should have ended there, but years later Budd came to visit Amon. "I want to apologize," the railroad president said. "I thought you were just meddling in our business, but after war came along we needed the shops here and in Childress. Without them we would have been in a mess."

Graciously, Amon thanked Budd, but as the executive left, muttered to Walter Claer, his oil office manager, "I still don't like that man."

As Budd, many who crossed Amon found the experience costly. Stanley Moore, the publisher's black chauffeur, wanted a shed built at his home. Amon agreed to pay for the small building and sent Moore to obtain an estimate from Cameron Lumber

Company. Cameron was the firm from which Amon's oil companies had purchased thousands of dollars of cement. Amon agreed to the price and the shed was built. The final bill, however, was double the estimate. Amon exploded. He ordered Walter Claer to stop buying cement from Cameron. Several years passed, and one day Amon told Claer, "You can buy from Cameron again. I guess they've been punished enough."

No affront, to himself or his city, was too small for Amon's attention. Returning from the airport with a reporter, he drove past the new Bell Helicopter plant. A large billboard advertising the Worth Hotel had been erected in front of the facility, blocking the view. "We've got to do something about that," he said, teeth gritted. Next day the sign came down.

General Motors's southwestern parts depot was housed in an old building west of downtown on Seventh Street, and Amon passed the shabby warehouse each day on his way to work. The structure and its faded sign offended him. Amon, who spoke only to presidents (he knew where power resided), wrote GM's chief executive officer, W. S. Knudsen, "That sign on your depot looks like a widow woman's boarding house." Replace it, ordered Amon, and GM did. An American Airlines sign over an airport counter irritated him. He complained, and the sign was lighted and lowered two inches. He demanded that the airline serve a chicken dinner between Fort Worth and Memphis, and it was done.

Amon could never understand why other men and companies did not support Fort Worth with the same fanaticism he and the *Star-Telegram* felt. Whatever Amon was boosting for the moment always needed financing, and the money came from the city's business community. He soaked the companies good—the involuntary contributions became known as "Amon Carter taxes." But not all firms would give him money, which annoyed Amon. He complained to the president of Western Union because its Fort Worth branch "never helped in civic projects." He wrote the manager of an ink company, "I've been doing business with you for twenty years and I know what's going on in this town. Every time we have a fund-raising campaign you don't give a penny. You're not going to get another dime's worth of my business."

When sufficiently provoked, Amon punished all of Fort Worth. In 1953, he and the *Star-Telegram* pushed hard for a city bond issue. Voters turned it down. Amon fumed. "To hell with them," he shouted to a reporter. At that time, the newspaper sponsored the annual community Christmas tree and, when the voters refused to raise their taxes, C. L. Richhart was in New Mexico searching for the perfect giant pine to place in downtown Burnett Park. Amon telephoned Richhart and summoned the reporter home, treeless. Fort Worth had no Christmas tree that year.

Amon once clashed with entertainer Arthur Godfrey, in Fort Worth on behalf of the Air Force Association. He and Amon were introduced at a reception and, at first, chatted amiably. They began speaking of their famous acquaintances. Godfrey dropped a name. Amon dropped one in return. Godfrey flung out another name. Amon countered with one of his celebrity friends. The contest reached shouting proportions, and Godfrey fled to a back room, not returning until Amon left the reception.

Douglas MacArthur arrived in Fort Worth, fresh from being fired by Harry Truman, to test his political popularity. He was to speak at Farrington Field—a high school football stadium. Sponsored by Scripps-Howard newspapers, including the *Fort Worth Press*, MacArthur was off-limits to Amon. The publisher, though, never strayed far from a visiting celebrity. The general and his wife entered the stadium riding in a convertible. Amon waited at the opposite end of the field. Reporters were astonished to see their elderly publisher sprint across the field, open the car door, and leap in beside the startled MacArthur. Amon joined the general in waving at the huge crowd. That evening, MacArthur was guest of honor at a Fort Worth Club dinner. For more than an hour he refused to enter the banquet room, where Amon had seated himself at the head table, because of his anger with the publisher.

When writer Alva Johnston first contacted Amon about an article for the *Saturday Evening Post* in 1938, Amon was flattered and suggested it be done in two parts "like the one given Mr. Chrysler." Johnston replied that the magazine editors wanted one story in one issue. Amon sat still for the interviews. Johnston then furnished him with a first draft of the story. Amon griped to Jimmy North that Johnston had made him "look like a playboy showman . . . and ballyhoo artist." Amon proposed that the story be rewritten with heavier emphasis on Fort Worth's eminence in America. Johnston balked. On Amon's behalf, North wrote Johnston suggesting that the article be canceled. Amon would pay Johnston for his time and trouble, and the story could be rewritten at a later date. Johnston refused and prepared his story, "Colonel Carter of Cartersville," for publication.

At the last minute, Amon wrote the *Post* editor complaining that "Col. Carter is a hell of a name to hang on me." He asked the editor to insert ". . .Where the West Begins" into the title. The magazine ignored Amon, and soon America was laughing at the divertissements and antics of the consummate cowboy. Amon fumed and fussed over the injustice of it all—didn't anyone understand that the cowboy was not real, that he was only a plaything, an imaginary character from childhood dreams, a fantasy

Cowboy Amon fronting *Saturday Evening Post* and *Star-Telegram* mastheads, September 18, 1939.

icon of the Texas plains? No, apparently no one understood that, and Amon grouched that he was "unknown for anything else."

Of all Amon's feuds—and they were legion—the best known was with H. C. Meacham, Fort Worth department store owner and mayor. They were longtime friends who fell out, though exactly why still is unknown. Several versions of the feud's origin are remembered: (1) the men bought a ranch together and quarreled over mineral rights; (2) Meacham reneged on paying his share of the ranch; (3) Amon used more than his half of the land; (4) they argued over the favors of a woman; (5) they argued about the division of a case of gift liquor; or (6) they disagreed over payment of a planeload of illegal liquor flown to Fort Worth from Mexico. Whatever the reason, their close friendship became hatred.

Until the friendship ended, Meacham's store published at least ten pages of advertising each week in the *Star-Telegram*. Then the storeowner campaigned for mayor, and the newspaper editorialized on its front page against his candidacy. Meacham was elected anyway, and he told his department managers, "There will never be another ad in the *Star-Telegram* as long as I live." And there was not, an act that, according to some sources, cost the newspaper as much as $100,000 annually. Meacham's loss was greater. Left only with the small-circulation *Press* in which to advertise, the store underwent a severe decline in sales. Bankruptcy loomed.

Meacham died in December 1929, and the Monday after his funeral the store's advertisements reappeared in the *Star-Telegram*, just in time for the Christmas rush.

Meacham's death did not end the feud, however. Within the pages of the *Star-Telegram*, the city's airport was called "Municipal Airport" rather than its official name, Meacham Field. That policy continued for eighteen years until 1947 when Amon suddenly—and with considerable irony—married Minnie Meacham Smith, second daughter of his old foe.

Not all of Amon's enemies were created by personal affronts. Several came to him because of the newspaper. Two were acquired on a warm afternoon in 1934. That day, a pair of motor-cycle patrolmen stopped on Highway 114 between Fort Worth and a suburban community, Grapevine. The men noticed a black Ford sedan with yellow wire wheels parked on a side road. Inside, the officers could see a man and woman necking. They approached the car, and the couple fired shotguns, killing both officers instantly. A farmer in an adjacent field saw everything. The Ford sped away.

The *Star-Telegram* bannered the senseless killing, its headline telling of the "INTENSIVE MAN HUNT FOR CLYDE BARROW AND HIS CIGAR-SMOKING WOMAN COMPANION, BONNIE PARKER." The outlaws escaped a posse of hundreds of lawmen, and where they disappeared to was a mystery—until Amon heard from them.

Bonnie and Clyde had driven to Decatur, forty miles north of Fort Worth, and hid out in a tourist court. They bought a *Star-Telegram* to read of their crime, and then Clyde got mad. He wrote Amon a rambling, profane, almost illegible, illiterate-though-chatty, threatening letter, dropped it by the post office at 7:30 P.M., April 3, and then disappeared again with Bonnie. The letter read:

> The postman may not find you at home but you will get this let-ter just the same. And you better think, decide and make up your mind and not let your Editor make another remark about Bonnie like you did the other day. They called her a cigar-smoking woman. Another remark about my underworld mate and I will end such men as you mighty quick. I know where you and your reporters live. Isn't every girl in Fort Worth cigaret feign [?] and whore they all lie around in cars night after night. . . . And those dirty sons-of-bitches came out to that by road [to] stop us from fucking. All I regret was that the third cop [cruising a hundred yards ahead of the slain officers] wasn't there while our guns were hot. Men and women are out in Dallas every day and night screwing and the department never sends a policeman after them. . . . You rich bas-tards go to church and are dirty rascals same as other robbers. You and your friends take whiskey and Fort Worth girls to Lard's ranch in New Mexico. Bonnie and I are not married and we fuck when we please too. And I am going to take up for her and she will take up for me. We may go back to that farm house near Grapevine [and]

pump that family full of lead for reporting us. But we'll drive to the Brazos River near Breckenridge[100 miles west of Fort Worth].

Say boy can't robbers get away fast in cars these days. I'm glad this country is different from what it was when Jessy James lived here.

If old lady [governor] Ferguson puts out a reward for us we will steal her out. . . . Now and then I do something extra. I cause tragedies by writing to married women and sign some man's name there her husband is acquainted with. Then he does a little shotting vice versa [?] Sometimes make the letter sound very nasty. Men ought to abuse lots of women because they don't respect the men in the city or country either. . . . Well, I must stop writing. We'll be seeing you soon, [Signed] Clyde Barrow."

The letter terrified Amon. Until the couple's ambush and death in Louisiana, Bonnie was never again called a cigar smoker within the pages of the *Star-Telegram*. Police provided protection to Amon and his family until the threat of Bonnie and Clyde was past.

Clyde's letter was the most menacing Amon ever received. The others just came from ordinary enemies. Karl Crowley was a solicitor general of the U.S. Post Office Department in Washington until he quit to run for governor of Texas in 1938. He lost badly, particularly in Tarrant County where he received only 690 of 35,936 votes, probably because of a front-page *Star-Telegram* editorial that in part declared, "Crowley gives the impression in Texas that Washington officially does not go to the outhouse without first asking him." Crowley, furious with Amon, wrote a letter to a Washington friend. A copy of it was sent to Amon. The Crowley letter said, "With reference to the skunk, Amon Carter, I want to say that the rank and file of Democrats are willing to make an open war on him. I consider him the most evil and pernicious influence on public affairs in the state of Texas. I do not think he should be allowed to own a newspaper, much less have a monopoly on radio in Texas."

When angry, Amon wanted immediate retribution, and his reactions rarely were temperate. There was the time he was embroiled in a local political squabble, and dictated a letter outlining the many shortcomings of men with whom he disagreed.

Seven hundred copies of the letter were mailed. His attorney, Sidney Samuels, read the letter too late, and declared it libelous. "Those men can sue you for every penny you've got," advised Samuels. Amon telephoned Charlie Boatner, his police reporter, at 9:00 P.M. and ordered him to "get those letters back."

Boatner protested. "Mr. Carter, you can't do that. You can't get letters back from the post office after you've mailed them."

Amon insisted, and because he was Amon Carter the postmaster helped Boatner. The men searched until 3:30 A.M. to collect all seven hundred letters.

Amon's little disputes did not often erupt into print and certainly not in Fort Worth. Outside, however, his influence and power diminished with distance. The *Amarillo Globe News*, for reasons unstated and now forgotten, published an editorial titled "Amon Carter: Little Emperor." The anonymous writer—who claimed he attempted to interview Amon and was refused—snorted indignantly, "As Editor, Politician and Cow Town's official greeter, you have shown an offensive disregard for such human weaknesses as breeding, intelligence and education. . . . Vengeance is mine, sayeth *[sic]* Amon Carter!"

At a distance of 350 miles, the Amarillo newspaper was safe enough. In Fort Worth, Amon was unassailable. Even the opposition *Press* took only light jabs at him. Amon's grasp on Fort Worth's municipal and political arms was firm. His dominion was the smoke-filled back room, usually the Fort Worth Club.

"What are you going to do about that industrial problem?" a reporter once asked a chamber of commerce official.

"I don't know," the man replied ruefully. "Amon Carter hasn't told me yet."

However offstage Amon was, no question ever existed about who ran Fort Worth, and nothing he did not want printed ever appeared in the *Star-Telegram* or even the *Press*. At a small Shady Oak dinner party, U.S. House Speaker Sam Rayburn stood to talk and indicated he wanted his remarks off the record.

"There is no reporter present, I believe," Rayburn said to Amon.

"There is," the publisher replied, "but he and I work for the same newspaper."

Byron Utecht folded his notepaper and tucked away his pencil.

A mature Amon in his souvenir-and gadget-crammed *Star-Telegram* office.

Shady Oak often was the site of political gatherings at which Amon made the schedule. The bar always closed thirty minutes before dinner. At one affair, Amon fired his pistols to signal the bar's closing, but a few minutes later he noticed Edgar Deen, Fort Worth's then-mayor, still drinking. Amon summoned James Wood, a policeman regularly hired for parties, and ordered, "Officer, go over there and tell Edgar that gawddammed bar is closed and unless we need a new mayor, to get the hell over here right now." Deen, Wood remembered, actually ran to Amon.

Amon's catalog of those with whom he feuded was thick with politicians, many of whom felt they had more to do than please the publisher. There were Governors Ma and Pa Ferguson, Sterling, Allred, and O'Daniel, Congressman Jim Wright, and the usually omnipotent Lyndon Baines Johnson. Amon wrote John Nance Garner that Allred was "thoroughly lacking in sincerity, being almost a feather for every wind." W. Lee O'Daniel, believed Amon, "managed his public affairs with a lack of dignity."

The political *sturm und drang* around Amon was never so tumultuous as in 1952 when he bolted the Democratic Party to support his old friend, Dwight Eisenhower, for president. Amon's position that year was not a revolutionary one. Many Texans campaigned for Ike, but Amon Carter had helped push the former general into the Republican Party, and there were Texans who could not forgive the publisher for that.

A local attorney wrote a disapproving, but cordial, hate letter about the matter to Amon: "You have no doubt aided in throwing Texas to the Republicans, but I feel sure that even you cannot be fully pleased with the tactics used in accomplishing the purpose. I want you to know that the writer will welcome the day when your death is announced and will upon such event feel that Fort Worth at long last has been blessed to rid itself of the worst enemy the city has ever had. I trust that I may soon enjoy this pleasure."

Amon wanted to publish the letter, but Jimmy North, with a cooler temper, refused.

Amon entertains Ike, Margaret Truman, American Airlines President C. R. Smith.

Amon's support of Ike also placed him in opposition to Lyndon Johnson. The publisher was never an enthusiastic Lyndon supporter, but his friend, Sid Richardson, liked and campaigned for LBJ and urged Carter to help the young senator from Texas. Curious about Johnson, Amon ordered Boatner and Sam Kinch, the Austin bureau chief, to "check him out." The reporters researched LBJ for six months and produced a book-sized report. Amon read it and declared, "Nothing there I wouldn't have done."

Amon was instrumental in having his neighbor, Fred Korth, become a Lyndon campaign manager (Korth later was appointed secretary of the Navy); Amon and still another Fort Worth neighbor, John Connally, advised and gave financial assistance to the future president. Shortly before taking his Senate seat in 1948, LBJ wrote Amon: "You did so much in so many ways that I could never fully express my appreciation. When I steered too close to impetuous and intemperate action, you pulled me back. When a firm hand was needed to steady the ship, you supplied it. . . . I just hope that I can use the opportunity to do as much for Texas— in the same impersonal spirit—as you have done. I will always look to your counsel to keep me pointed in the right direction."

That, of course, was before Ike became a Republican in 1952. A confirmed Democrat, LBJ stuck with the party and, as a contemporary said, "the britches were split." Johnson explained his predicament with Amon to Booth Mooney, his administrative aide. "The *Fort Worth Star-Telegram* always was for me 'till last year," Lyndon said in 1953. "Strongest paper in the state and my best supporter. But when I was committed to [Sam] Rayburn to introduce Adlai Stevenson when he appeared in Texas, Amon Carter called and asked me—no, he didn't; he told me—not to do it. I explained about my commitment and said I'd have to live up to it, and I did. Now old man Carter won't even accept my telephone calls. He even scratched me off his Christmas list."

Lyndon continued: "I'm gonna keep trying, Booth. First thing tomorrow morning, I want you to write a letter to Amon Carter for my signature. . . . Make it warm and friendly, but sad because of the difference that's come between us. Tell him I'm the same Lyndon Johnson I've always been. Tell him I'm working for Texas just the way he is and we can get a lot more done for the people—and for Fort Worth—if we work together. The way we used to. Really pour it on, Booth, and let's see if we can get through that hard old head of his."

Amon ignored the letter.

Amon took his feud with Lyndon Johnson into the hereafter. In his last few days of life, Amon summoned his son and daughter, Sid Richardson, and Katrine Deakins to his bedside. He discussed his estate and the newspaper and what he expected of the children. As a footnote, Amon said, ". . . if the paper ever supports Lyndon Johnson for anything, I'll turn over in my grave."

By the time he broke with LBJ, Amon's influence and power were waning, partly because he was old and sick, but mostly because everything had changed after World War II. Fort Worth had young men unimpressed and unafraid of Amon Carter, unwilling to do his bidding merely because he wanted it.

The new era probably arrived with a 1954 congressional election in which Amon's pet incumbent, Wingate Lucas, was challenged by Jim Wright, the young mayor of nearby Weatherford and a former *Star-Telegram* correspondent. Wright had ambitions beyond the mayoralty of a small town and knew Amon could help him. Wright attempted to speak to the publisher at a ceremony honoring General William Hood Simpson, a Weatherford native and war hero. After the speeches, Wright approached Amon, "I'm Jim Wright, Mr. Carter."

Amon looked disinterested.

"You don't know it, but I used to work for you," continued Wright.

"Well, that's nice," said Amon, and turned away.

Embarrassed, Wright promised himself he would never "risk a second dose of that treatment." Wright entered the congressional race against Lucas.

The *Star-Telegram* virtually ignored the young politician. He resorted to buying time on Amon's television station. No matter what he did, however, the newspaper would not provide equal space for his campaign. Wright recalled a rally at which a thousand people came to hear him speak. A *Star-Telegram* reporter, Bill Haworth, was present. Not a word about the speech was printed.

Before the election, the newspaper published an editorial supporting Lucas and criticizing Wright for not offering "well-defined ideas," and for not having commented on the farm program, taxation, federal spending, or other important issues.

The following day, Wright paid $974.40—all he had—for a six-column advertisement in the *Star-Telegram*. It was, the headline read, an "OPEN LETTER TO MR. AMON G. CARTER—You have at last met a man, Mr. Carter, who is not afraid of you. . . who will not bow his knee to you . . . and come running like a simpering pup at your beck and call."

Wright charged that he had taken stands on issues in greater detail "than your private errand-boy congressman," but the *Star-Telegram* had kept news coverage of his statements "well concealed."

"This is a new day," wrote Wright. "New blood and new minds and new thoughts, fresh from the people themselves, are needed . . . it is unhealthy for ANYONE to become TOO powerful . . . TOO influential . . . TOO dominating. It is not good for Democracy. The people are tired of 'One-Man Rule.'"

Perhaps they were. Jim Wright, who in the 1980s would become Speaker of the U.S. House of Representatives, easily defeated Lucas.

The old order, and Amon, were dying.

War is delightful to those who have had no experience of it.
    —Desiderius Erasmus, 1466-1536

Most everybody can get results when kindly encouraged, but give me the man who can get there in spite of hell.
    —Framed epigram in Amon's office

From now on, all sabotage of any nature should be answered with a sharp bayonet or a good old Texas forty-five.
    —Amon, in a letter to FDR, December 8, 1941

December 7, 1941. Pearl Harbor bombed; Amon furious.

Within hours, Amon and America were at war and, oh, what a glorious thing it was. For a short while.

Honolulu's ashes still were smoldering when Amon raised his shield and sword, marshaling forces. Immediately, Amon fired off a lengthy special-delivery letter to President Roosevelt, telling FDR how he wanted America's war run: "The disaster at Pearl Harbor, as tough as it is, may be a blessing in disguise. It certainly unified the country overnight. [You] . . . silence those god-dammed isolationists and America First sons-of-bitches, Lindbergh, Wheeler, Bennett, Clark, Nye and Fish. If they open their mouths again they should be put in concentration camps."

To Texas Senator Tom Connally, Amon wrote, "This is the greatest time of crisis since Valley Forge."

Amon was sixty-two, too old for duty in the trenches, so in the beginning he stayed behind to rally the home folks and to ready his newspaper troops. On December 8, he telephoned Washington, pulling strings to have his reporters accredited as war correspondents. He told Jimmy North to select his best men and get them ready to ship out. And, by the way, tell them to write only about Texans. From that moment, World War II became the exclusive copyrighted property of the *Star-Telegram*. Within its pages, readers were led to believe Texans—especially Fort Worth and West Texas Texans—were the only barriers between the enemy and victory. All others were but spear-carriers in the drama.

There were to be enough Texans at war to fill any newspaper. Ten percent of the population, the largest of any state, joined the armed services. Texas A & M furnished more officers than any other university, including West Point. Seven hundred thousand Texans were "over there" fighting for America's freedom, the *Star-Telegram* editorialized, and that was as it should be because everybody knew Texans were the most patriotic, most heroic, the bravest of all Americans, capable of whipping every Jap and German with bare fists and a peach orchard switch, and before breakfast.

Readers were urged to return their used *Star-Telegrams* to the newspaper office and have them mailed free to servicemen anywhere in the world. The newspaper paid the postage. The *Star-*

Telegram even sent a few copies of its rival, the *Press,* because the war, after all, was an emergency, and we had to pull together. An endless line of mothers appeared in the newsroom with photos of their sons and daughters in service. Carter's newspaper published all pictures, some as many as a half-dozen times—when he or she was inducted, at the first training station, when they were promoted, for overseas assignment, in times of valor and decoration, and finally, at death.

Amon became Texas's largest war-bond customer. The *Star-Telegram* conducted a running campaign to boost sales of bonds among its readers. Its newsboys sold 4,742,016 war savings stamps, more than any other group in the state. Rationing came. Food, gasoline, synthetics, tires, liquor. *Is This Trip Necessary? Use It Up, Wear It Out, Make It Last, Do Without.* The newspaper called on Texans to sacrifice luxuries and comforts, even essentials, to support "our boys." Amon bought nylon stockings on the black market for special gifts because one, after all, could sacrifice only so much.

W. Lee O'Daniel, the flour-peddler-turned-governor, stumped Texas, ostensibly to arouse patriotic fervor among the masses. Actually, he promoted himself, and Amon was furious that O'Daniel would play politics with the *Star-Telegram*'s war. The governor traveled about in a state limousine, and Carter seized on the Cadillac as a reason to publicly censure O'Daniel. The governor was making an "abusive use of auto tires," Amon dictated in a lengthy editorial. North refused to print the broadside. Not because of the tire issue. The general tone, North protested, was a bit overwrought, notably the opening paragraph: "W. Lee O'Daniel is the agent of Hitler in America."

For support, North called in Sidney Samuels. The natty lawyer read Amon's editorial and smiled. "Mr. Carter, you can't print this," he advised." It's libelous."

"Are you telling me what I can or cannot print in my own newspaper?"

"No, I'm only telling you of the consequences if you do."

"You write it, then," ordered Amon, "and make it legal."

Samuels's version was publishable, but bloodless; Amon wanted blood.

"Do it again," the publisher shouted at Samuels, "and don't be so gawddammed Christian."

A proper rendition of Amon's charges was never agreed on, and North vetoed any editorial criticism of the governor's four-plies. Angry but undeterred, Amon bought—it is remembered that he paid cash, in one hundred-dollar bills, banging each one on the desk as he counted—a full-page ad in his own newspaper to say what he wanted to say about O'Daniel. That is, he said what he wanted to say the way Samuels wanted him to say it—bloodlessly.

The war, at first, was going well, Amon thought. He kept up his correspondence with Washington. He wrote the president on behalf of osteopaths, urging that they be accepted for service as other doctors, and soon they were. He asked Texan Jesse Jones, the secretary of commerce, to have FDR persuade the Canadian government to send its fliers for training in Texas as "they did in the last war." The West Texas Chamber of Commerce raised $128,000 in defense bonds, and Amon wired the good news to Roosevelt, adding, "and there were no Lindbergs [sic], pacifists, isolationists or fifth columnists present. They do not thrive in West Texas." He pressed Frank Knox, the Navy secretary, to name a ship *Fort Worth*: "Of course, I figure Fort Worth rates a battleship. If you find a real strong, tough, high-spirited, fighting craft that will give the enemy Hell and never run up the white flag, name it after Fort Worth."

FDR sent the publisher photographs of his meeting with Winston Churchill in Casablanca. And the president returned his diamond-studded belt for cleaning and repairs. The president asked that another hole be added, and Amon worried that Roosevelt was working too hard and losing weight.

Amon offered his counsel, by letter and telegram, to Dwight Eisenhower, a Texan, to Admirals Chester Nimitz and Bull Halsey, another Texan. To Hap Arnold, commanding general of the Army Air Corps, Amon suggested that all American Airlines pilots and planes should be drafted for a massive bombing raid on Tokyo. Arnold replied that he would think it over.

Carter's dream of having a battleship named for Fort Worth, as was done for other sovereign states, was never realized, but Lieutenant Johnny Van Dyke, a *Star-Telegram* employee, wrote that he was bombardier on a B-29 named the *Amon Carter* and had just concluded a raid on Wake Island aboard the plane.

The plane came off the assembly line of Consolidated Aircraft Corporation's Fort Worth facility—"the bomber plant," as it became known. A whole town grew around the factory as West Texans moved in to work for high wages. It was White Settlement, but called "Liberator Village"—a place of ricky-ticky houses and open sewers named for the light bomber put together rivet by rivet in the mile-long windowless factory on Fort Worth's northwest corner.

Actually, a mile and twenty-nine feet. That extra ten yards was Amon's lagniappe to Texanism.

Amon, as did many in 1939, knew war was coming. He and FDR had discussed the country's entry into war, and Amon had scouted ahead for the president in England during his trip with Pan American Airways. War was inevitable and the country began putting up its defenses. Among plans were government-financed aircraft factories, and Amon meant to get one for Fort Worth. As chairman of a committee to bring the plant to the city, Amon prepared—actually *Star-Telegram* reporters, as usual, did the work—a tome of praise. Fort Worth offered to Consolidated special tax incentives, a waiting, eager workforce, an existing seaplane base on Lake Worth, and the availability of regular American Airlines flights for easy movement of executives. The site, wrote Amon, was adjacent to an existing airport and runways could be extended for military aircraft.

R. H. Fleet, Consolidated's president, bought Amon's pitch. Major General George Brett, acting Air Force chief, did not. Brett preferred Tulsa. The men argued by telegram:

Maj. Gen. George H. Brett
War Department
Washington, D.C.
13 Dec 1940

Retel if Fort Worth comes through with its promises Stop We prefer it as location

Cheerio
Consolidated Aircraft Corp.
R. H. Fleet

....

R. H. Fleet
Consolidated Aircraft Corp.
San Diego, Calif.
17 Dec 1940

Fort Worth not under consideration in present project Stop Please furnish today result of Van Dusens trip to Tulsa Stop It is urgent that action be taken today.

Brett

....

Maj. Gen. George Brett
17 Dec 1940

Result Van Dusens trip Tulsa unsatisfactory Stop We think Fort Worth site ideal.

Fleet

....

R. H. Fleet
18 Dec 1940

Request you submit your plans and estimates on Tulsa location at once.

Brett

....

Maj. Gen. George Brett
19 Dec 1940

Your telegram reminds of Henry Ford statement that customer could choose any color he desired just so he chose black.

Fleet

....

R. H. Fleet
19 Dec 1940

Choose any color you wish but you are still going to choose black.

Brett

General Brett announced Tulsa as the site of the new aircraft factory. An apoplectic Amon beat his fists against the wall, and exploded by telegram to FDR that Tulsa did not deserve the factory. Fort Worth had the best offer, best site, climate, size, and existing facilities, raged Amon. "It seems almost a crime against national defense to permit the rejection of this site as against Tulsa," he declared. FDR retreated to the position that Tulsa was an army decision and he could not interfere.

Amon, always the kind of man who would call on Noah's flood to fill a bathtub, blanketed Washington with angry telegrams to congressmen and senators, administration executives and old drinking buddies. He signed many of the wires with Governor O'Daniel's name. And he went back to FDR with a final compromise argument: "Why not allocate to Tulsa the possible additional plant to be built?"

January 3, 1941, Senator Morris Sheppard wired Amon: "War Department announces plants for both Fort Worth and Tulsa." Next morning the bi-city selections were made public and Amon messaged Roosevelt, "Bless your heart. Thanks for your timely and friendly help." He sent another telegram to Sheppard asking assistance in having the president's son, Captain Elliott Roosevelt—"A clean-cut, double-fisted six-footer"—assigned as military overseer for the plant's construction. And still Amon asked for more. A month later, reported *Time*, he was back on FDR's doorstep seeking a personal favor, after which he boasted to Harold Hough, "Well, I got my extra."

"Extra what?"

"My extra feet. That Tulsa plant was going to be the same size as ours. I couldn't have that."

The factories, and another in Georgia, were to be identical. Amon demanded a change. Army architects added two more support columns and twenty-nine feet to the Fort Worth plant to appease the publisher. Fort Worth had the world's largest and longest aircraft plant and the first with a fully automated assembly line. At the height of the war thirty thousand people worked there, and Amon bragged that his city had the highest per capita income in America.

The *Star-Telegram* was fully mobilized for war. Phil North, Jimmy's son, became a public relations officer on General MacArthur's staff. At least eight women joined the WACs, and dozens of men spread out to all service branches. As other businesses, the newspaper soon had a manpower problem. Jim Record—very, very reluctantly—began hiring women reporters, as many as seven in one month of 1942. He needed reporters, whatever their sex, so he hired women and hoped for the best. Soon they were everywhere and JRR would look out on his feminine crew and harrumph morosely. The few remaining men called the new order, "JRR's Harem." To underscore the seraglio theme, women reporters arrived at one office party dressed in harem costumes, complete with diaphanous pantaloons and bare stomachs. JRR blushed. The women danced as they believed haremites might, and during a lull in the entertainment, C. L. Richhart, who had planned the party, played his trump—a black porter dressed in the costume of a palace eunuch roared into the city room on a motorcycle, circled desks (and a harrumphing JRR), and disappeared down the hall.

Christmas parties were traditional, and the one time each year when JRR put aside his guardian dignity. He would smoke cigars in public and sip his toddies; he even financed the third floor bar from his own pocket. The arrival of so many women changed the party. For one thing, the men drank more and more until JRR finally banned liquor.

What ended the drinking was an incident at the pencil sharp-ener an hour after one party had finished. JRR intended to put a new point on his copy pencil. He looked down. At his feet was a comatose male reporter, supine on the floor, head in a wastebas-ket. Harrumph! "Somebody take care of this," he ordered, wag-ging his fresh pencil point at the body.

And sex—there are wonderful legends of quick-groping trysts on back stairs, between file cabinets in the morgue, and at least once on the roof. Whether true or not, the stories bothered JRR. Mr. Record was not a man who wanted sex mentioned within his hearing. He even refused to explain Bar Mitzvah to a new young woman reporter because it concerned puberty.

Martha Morris, pretty and blonde, was hired for the morning staff. A male reporter proposed he and she become acquainted between the morgue's file cabinets. Miss Morris retorted, "Get lost!"—a devastating 1940s put-down. The man complained to City Editor Cullum Greene that Martha had been rude to him. Greene told JRR, who summoned the wayward girl to his desk. JRR scolded her, said he understood she was not "being nice" to the male reporter. He lectured her on the war, on the shortage of competent male newsmen, and the necessity of keeping the few who remained, and how other women were out there waiting for jobs on newspapers. He suggested she be "a little nicer."

More amused than angered, Martha cocked a hip and asked coyly, "Mr. Record, just how nice do you want me to be?"

Suddenly realizing what the conversation was about, JRR stood and back-pedaled, blushing, blustering, "You . . . you know Cullum. . . . He's just . . . an . . . an old hen! Don't think anything more about it!"

Later, still in shock from actually having discussed sex with a female, JRR reached to file a story on the copy spike—a stiff sharpened metal wire mounted on a lead base—speared his hand clean through between the thumb and forefinger. *Harrumph.* Women bewildered JRR.

The heavy ironic cross of women reporters wore on Jim Record. One editor had become a heavy drinker, often arriving drunk to work, reeling and thrashing about with a hand over one eye because he could not focus his vision well enough to see with two. With no male replacement for the editor, JRR pretended the drunk was not drunk. North could not, and suggested something be done. Reluctantly, JRR threatened the man, "If you don't stop drinking, I'll fire you."

"No, you won't."

"Won't! . . . *Harrumph!*

"You can't find anybody to take my place."

True enough. The man stayed on, one hand over an eye, and JRR ignored him.

Star-Telegram employees who went to war were considered "out of the office." Amon Carter had loaned them to America. He kept them on the Christmas bonus list, and the newspaper was mailed to them daily. In return, they were expected to file an occasional story on their experiences and on any other Texans they found in war zones.

Meanwhile, the real *Star-Telegram* war correspondents sought everywhere for Texans. "Any Texans here?" was the commonly phrased question they asked in foxholes and tents, bars, CQs, and barracks from Bougainville to Bordeaux.

On his way to the Pacific, Stanley Gunn spent an evening at the San Francisco Press Club. A local reporter, envious of Gunn's assignment but astounded by its narrowness, asked, "You mean you're just going to write about Texans!"

"Who else is worth writing about?" answered Gunn, smiling.

Gunn, Sam Kinch, and Charlie Boatner went to the Pacific. Flem Hall left behind his sports beat and sailed to England. Robert Wear joined Hall in England, after D-Day covered France and Germany, and finally went into the Pacific. The *Star-Telegram* had more men—Boatner, Kinch, and Wear—on the battleship *Missouri* as witnesses to Japan's formal surrender than any other news-gathering organization.

Stanley Gunn was not there at the end.

Tall and thin, a contemplative pipe-smoker, Gunn was late to the war. He had been editor of the *Austin Tribune* when it folded in 1943. Record immediately hired him, and Gunn went off to the Pacific. He was dead in four months.

As other *Star-Telegram* writers, Gunn composed folksy, newsy little stories about Texas boys. The stories told of the soldiers' lives between battles, of their recreations, their hobbies, their thoughts of home. He even found one pair of Texans who had labeled their island foxhole "Shady Oaks *[sic]*, Where the West Begins." He had the men send photos of the sign to Amon.

Decades later, the correspondents' stories seem like personal notes to families of Texas servicemen. They wrote, too, real letters to parents, telling of visits to sons and daughters, half a world away. After the war, JRR reminisced in the *Star-Telegram*'s employee publication of the eleven-page letter written by Gunn to a mother. She had asked Gunn to try and find her MIA son. He never wrote a public story of his search. It was a private matter between him and an anguished mother.

In October, 1944, Gunn went ashore at Leyte with the first wave of American troops. He and seven other newsmen commandeered a house in Tacloban, capital of the Philippine island.

World War II hero General Jonathan Wainwright (third from left) is honored by Amon and others, December 17, 1945.

Before dawn, Japanese planes attacked the town, and wing bombs fell into the correspondents' house.

Associated Press reporter Asahel Bush was killed instantly. John Terry of the *Chicago Daily News* was mortally wounded. In the silence after the bombing, Gunn cried out, "I'm hit. Can you help me? Help me out of this hole."

John Walker of *Time* reached for his hand. A flashlight beam fell on Gunn. There was no hole. In shock and pain but conscious, Gunn helped wrap his mangled legs in a towel. He was taken to an evacuation hospital. Gunn underwent a four-hour operation, and died. Arthur Veysey of the *Chicago Tribune* later wrote of Gunn's last hours.

As the *Star-Telegram* correspondent was carried into the operating room, he raised himself on an elbow and looked into the masked faces waiting for him.

"Any Texans here?" he inquired. Then he smiled, and quietly closed his eyes.

16

Texas being practically three times as large as the British Isles in no way dampens our enthusiasm for the British people. They're just fine folks, as near Texans as they could be not having been born there.
　　—Amon, speaking on a BBC radio broadcast from
　　　London, October 1942

That's the stuff, Cowboy . . .
　　—Amon, in a 1943 letter, recalling the last conversation
　　　with his MIA son

When told of Stanley Gunn's death, remembered Katrine Deakins, Amon Carter wept and cried out "oh, gawddam."

It would have been like him to grieve for the wasting of young Gunn's life, and surely the loss of the newsman reminded Amon that his own son might never return home.

World War II was the lowest period of Amon Carter's life. He had depressions and doubts of his own worth, was uncharacteristically moody, emotional, and indecisive.

Nenetta, the second Mrs. Carter, said the war years took away, for the first time, his buoyancy, the resolution he held against every obstacle. He was never the same again. For the remainder of his life there was a delicate bitterness in Amon Carter, and it was within the period from 1943 until his death that most of the small, mean memories of him were made.

The reason was the son he worshipped, Amon Gary Carter Jr., whom he affectionately called "Cowboy."

Young Carter was twenty-one as war began, a University of Texas student who earlier graduated from Indiana's Culver Military Academy, and was called into service as a second lieutenant, May 1942. The son had a physical similarity to the father, accented by the same early balding pattern. Each was squarely built and compact, energetic. Amon had depthless pride in the youngster, and was preparing him to assume the empire's mantle of authority. When the boy was ten, the publisher had put him on the street selling newspapers. A year later he arose at 3:00 A.M. each day to deliver a home route. Summers, he worked as a copyboy, and later in the photography and advertising departments. The publisher established the Amon Carter Junior Scholarship at TCU, given annually to the newsboy with the best grades among Fort Worth's graduating high school seniors. On young Carter's eighteenth birthday, Amon wrote a long letter of congratulations, telling of his pride in the boy's accomplishments, of the dream that "you can step into my job." Amon lectured, "Courtesy is the cheapest as well as the most valuable assets [sic] one can possess."

The new lieutenant was sent for training to Fort Knox, Kentucky, and the father visited, timing his arrival for the Kentucky Derby. Amon gave his son a used pocketknife for which he demanded payment of one cent because of "the old superstition that you must never give away a knife, but sell it."

Late 1942, young Amon was ordered to Ireland for advanced training as a field artillery officer. The elder Amon immediately asked for credentials as a war correspondent, ostensibly to review Allied morale but actually, of course, to visit his son.

By the early 1940s, Amon Carter was an internationally famous man. His exploits among the high and mighty had been recorded and reported widely by syndicated newspaper columnists and in national magazines, on radio and in motion picture newsreels. His cowboy impersonation had been seen, cheered, and applauded all over America. The 1936 Frontier Centennial had registered Amon's name as familiar as any Hollywood star or Washington politician. So, when he went off to play war correspondent in Ireland and England, the real war correspondents there reported on him.

The *Associated Press* noted that he landed safely in Belfast, mid-October 1942. Amon cabled Katrine Deakins that father and son were doing well. Amon amused himself by dining with local dignitaries and roaming the countryside. He mailed stamps for the collection of FDR.

A month later, he was in England, at the Savoy Hotel, playing celebrity for English newsmen. In his twangy prairie voice, he spoke to Americans on a worldwide BBC radio broadcast. He told his countrymen that their soldier sons were "very fit" and eager for action. He praised the British who "feel that no price is too high to pay for liberty," and urged deeper understanding between the countries, which he compared to a "span of thoroughbred horses . . . they need practice before they can run in double harness."

Amon ended the broadcast by saying he spoke as a father "who has a son over here."

On leave, young Amon joined his father, and they were entertained by British press titan Lord Beaverbrook, who later wrote that "Carter, Junior, is a husky, lively young man . . . ready to go to town against the Germans anytime." They visited Sir Dudley Pound, "Admiral of the Fleet and First Sea Lord of the British Navy," to whom Amon presented a silver five-shilling piece. The

Amon and friends share stagecoach at Fort Worth's 1936 Frontier Centennial.

Amon as the cowboy, complete with his golden palamino.

publisher also searched out other Texans, especially men in the ranks, and cabled their families that he had seen their sons and they were well.

The two Amons attended at least one swanky party with General Eisenhower, Lord Mountbatten, and "royalty." Later the publisher would tell of the evening, always chuckling "and Amon Junior was the only second lieutenant there."

Before they parted, Amon reminded his son of their agreement. *Editor & Publisher*, the newspaper trade magazine, earlier revealed details of the deal Amon proposed to his son: ". . . one hundred dollars each for every dirty Jap, one hundred dollars each for every Damn German and ten dollars for every Italian, plus a bonus of five hundred dollars extra when you get as many as twenty."

Shortly before Christmas, Amon returned home, having written no stories as a war correspondent. Belatedly, he made an entry in the guest book of Suite 10G at the Fort Worth Club: "10/3/42 . . . AGC . . . leaving for Ireland to see Amon Jr. Told Amon goodbye in Liverpool as he left for Northern Africa. He was all pepped up over getting into action. Good Luck, Cow Boy, from Dad."

The son had little opportunity to collect the proffered bounties, even the fire-sale amount posted for Italians. Young Carter was sent to central Tunisia, where Allied forces were finally encircling Rommel. North Africa and war, Amon Jr. thought, was somewhat boring. He wrote, telling of his unit's camp in an old Roman ruin and how the men passed their time playing blackjack—he won 2,500 French francs in one game. The only diversion was "Photo Joe," a German JU-88 observer plane snapping daily reconnaissance pictures.

His final letter was postmarked February 13, 1943. In the envelope, he sent samples of Tunisian money for his coin collection. Next morning, Valentine's Day, Amon Carter Jr. disappeared.

The elder Carter returned from overseas in a sunny mood, joking with Katrine Deakins that the war now surely would be a brief affair. His son had joined other Texans, and the Lone Star State boys would take care of things mighty quick. Amon was optimistic and happy. Then the letters stopped coming.

The two Amons, father and son in Newcastle, England, December 6, 1942.

His moods turned darker, at first angered, then dispirited, then hopeless, as the days passed. He became quieter, less active, and he had long periods of staring vacantly at nothing, his eyes filled with tears. Amon spoke often by telephone with Nenetta, who had moved to New York after their 1941 divorce. She remained optimistic; Amon fell into deeper depression.

A War Department telegram reached Fort Worth March 11. It described, in vague language, a North African battle and stated that Amon Jr. was presumed "missing in action." The *Star-Telegram* printed the terse announcement as a two-paragraph story on its front page, under a small photograph of young Amon in uniform. That was the first. For the next two years, readers followed the adventures of Amon Carter & Son through a series of letters, stories by wire services and war correspondents, and finally by the publisher himself as he invaded Europe to rescue his son from "those gawddammed Germans." The pair combined to become a kind of Texas-style civilian, clandestine Red Cross, and at all times young Amon was a symbol for every POW Texan.

After the momentary shock of the initial telegram, Carter reacted typically. He reached for Western Union pads and telephones and began contacting friends in high places. He cabled the International Red Cross in Geneva and a Red Cross field director in Tunisia. Major General James A. Ulio, Adjutant of the Army, wired sympathies and recounted the fighting in which Amon Jr. disappeared, added that American forces lost fifty-nine men during seven days, with 170 wounded and 2,006 missing in action.

Amon petitioned the White House for help, and on March 26, the President replied that he had made "repeated inquiries, and the absence of definite news does not lessen the possibility that he was taken prisoner." Eleanor Roosevelt sent a note of regret, as did all Texas politicians in Washington and hundreds of Amon's friends. Waiters at the Fort Worth Club signed a sympathy card. William Best, vice president of General Cigar Company, mailed a box of one hundred Robert Burns panatelas "to be saved for Jr.'s return." (They were never smoked; at Amon Jr.'s induction, Amon had given up cigars, vowing not to smoke until after the war when his son returned, but he never smoked again.)

The Texas House of Representatives unanimously adopted a resolution, which read in part: "Whereas, Lieutenant Amon G. Carter Junior, son of a distinguished Texas citizen, was among the first to enter the Armed Service in Defense of Democracy and American Ideals and proved his willingness to undergo any sacrifice to maintain those principles, and . . . he is an outstanding type of young American and Texas manhood, upon which depends the future of this country and civilization itself . . . resolved that the Texas Legislature extend to the father . . . its deep sympathy; and at the same time congratulations for the heroic participation of his son in the North African Campaign to drive out the Axis."

General Hap Arnold messaged Amon, "Don't give up hope. He is alive."

Amon didn't think so; he sank deeper into despair. Katrine arrived at work one morning to find a sealed envelope on her desk. The previous evening Amon had scribbled a long letter. He wrote on the envelope "To be opened if we do not hear from Amon Jr. [signed] A. G. Carter, March 19, 1943." Katrine did not open the letter for several years, long after Amon Jr. had returned home. It read:

Dear Katrine:

After talking to Colonel Sumerall this A.M.—I can't help but feel more discouraged regarding sweet Amon Jr. Somehow I can't help but feel we are not going to see him again. God love his sweet soul. He certainly deserved a better fate, still bless his heart, it was just what he wanted to do—and he would not have it otherwise. . . . While I was in England one of his superior officers told me they might send some of the boys back to this country to help train the new armored divisions and if they did he was going to send Amon Jr., claiming he was a good officer, etc. I made no comment but later, in conference, I did mention it to Amon Jr., and he said, 'Oh, Dad, I could not do that'; that he just could not go away and leave his gang—meaning the men and officers in the 91st Field Artillery. In fact, he was complaining about half the Division getting the lucky break in going to Africa with the first contingent for the invasion November 8. . . . Amon was in London with me at the time. All of these things merely go to show his spirit and of course

I was proud of him. . . . He told me in Louisville before leaving for
. . . Ireland—he said, "Dad, I think some of the boys that are holding back will be sorry of it before the War is over." Further, stating,
"I may not get back, but if I do I will have the satisfaction of feeling
I have done my part." Well, I was so proud of him I gave him a big
hug . . . although tears came to my eyes. . . . This statement he
made was the cause of my telegram of April 1, 1942 offering the
bonus for each German, Italian and Jap. Whatever comes, I will
always have the feeling I did everything possible to make him
happy, and including making a 10,000 mile trip to see and be with
him. . . . I would not have missed the trip for all the money in the
world. I have not given up hope but I must confess I am slipping. I
guess it is the first time I have ever been a quitter. One thing it has
taught me is how to pray, which I do each night. It just seems he is
too fine to have to go when they could take me instead. Still I can't
help but believe in the Lord and his wisdom in justice to all of us.
So, again I am fervently praying each day and night for this sweet
youngster to have a chance and come home to his loved ones. How
I wish I could take his place. It's been fine to find so many friends
take such an interest in his case—at least it has given me a chance
to find out who my real friends are at a time like this. I am writing
this to be sealed and only given to you in the event my premoni-
tion should prove to be correct. God grant that I am wrong. While I
know you and Carl [Katrine's husband] love and worship him, still
it is hard to let you know just how my heart aches. Ruth is an
angel. She and Bertice have been a great comfort as you and Carl
have been, not to mention sweet friends. I hope I am wrong.

May 3, a message from Amon Jr. suddenly arrived. He was in
Szubin, Poland, southwest of Danzig [now Gdansk], in Oflag 64,
as prisoner of war number 1595.

The Valentine Day fate of B Battery, Ninety-first Armored Bat-
talion, was later explained in a letter from Captain W. Bruce Pirnie, Amon Jr.'s commanding officer. Rommel had broken out of
an Allied trap, and before dawn young Amon and a sergeant were
sent to establish a mountaintop observation post. German Mark
VI tanks ("They looked like . . . huge long-nosed crabs") moved on
the battery's flank. Pirnie admitted he gave retreat orders and forgot to tell Amon Jr. and the sergeant.

For a day, the young Texan stayed in his position above Faid Pass as Rommel's army swept by them. Then he and the sergeant slipped out, hiking east, away from the German-held pass. They wandered for ten days, hiding at night in caves and ravines, shivering with the subfreezing temperatures. For food, they chewed the pulpy insides of cactus, much as Comanches did in early West Texas. Amon Jr. split the cactus pods with the one-cent knife sold him by his father.

February 24, early morning, the men slept in a clump of cactus. Bedouins carrying rusty shotguns prodded them awake. Amon tried to explain that they were soldiers in need of help, but the Bedouins—about thirty, including women—beat the men with sticks and fists. The women spat on them. They were stripped of their clothing, and later in the day, sold to a passing German patrol.

Amon was taken to Tunis, loaded onto a German JU-52 and flown to Capua, north of Naples, where he went into a cattle car filled with other captured officers being shipped to Poland.

Relieved that his son was alive, Amon Carter once again manned his telephone, seeking information about the POW camp. FDR sent aerial maps of the area to Carter. Amon wired the president and Senator Tom Connally that General Eisenhower should be ordered *not* to bomb Oflag 64, adding a lengthy denunciation of the Red Cross's inefficiency. Legend says Amon even attempted to telephone Adolf Hitler, but that tale apparently is another piece of apocrypha grown after his death.

And he created the quasi-clandestine, lend-lease, Texas-style, underground smuggling partnership with his son. Amon Jr.'s first letter listed names of other Texans in the camp, including John Jones, nephew of Jesse Jones, Amon's millionaire Houston friend and FDR's commerce secretary. Amon immediately telephoned the men's parents. Young Amon reported that the prisoners were short on food, warm clothing, and blankets. Carter dispatched a supply of everything needed to the POW camp.

Excerpts from young Amon's letters were printed in the *Star-Telegram* as names of other Texas prisoners were ferreted out and passed on to Fort Worth. He began searching camp records of all

POWs, notifying his father, who then would contact the men's parents. At one time, Amon was corresponding with more than two hundred Texas families. Amon Carter's pipeline to Poland, free of governmental red tape, operated much more quickly and effectively than the military or Red Cross.

Amon Jr. was among the first twenty prisoners in the camp, arriving as it was being converted by Polish laborers from a youth correction institution known as Stalag 21-A. He became parcels officer, and began the Carter-to-Carter pipeline, using at one time a covert paramilitary organization in neutralist Portugal to pass through large shipments.

In addition to serving as the Polish branch of the Carter POW relief business, young Amon also published the camp's confidential and clandestine newspaper. Several times weekly, he was sent to the Szubin rail station to collect mail and packages. He befriended a Polish girl who worked there. Each night, she listened to British broadcasts in the Polish language, then wrote the latest war news in German on tiny scraps of paper. She left the notes in a wastebasket. Amon Jr. rescued the news from under the gaze of German guards, and sneaked it back into camp, where the messages were translated and copied on toilet paper. POWs passed the toilet tissue *Star-Telegram* from hand to hand.

German guards, generally benevolent to their officer prisoners, were intrigued by the endless flow of packages from Fort Worth. One group approached Amon Jr. with a request: "You have a rich father. Can you get a piano for us?"

By January 1945, the prisoners of Oflag 64 knew war was ending, knew Germany had lost. Still, they were unprepared for the panic created by approaching Allied armies. One early morning, the Russians suddenly were in the next valley, and German guards began marching the POWs toward Berlin. For more than a week and one hundred miles, the men were herded along in snow and freezing weather. In a small village near the German border, their guards abruptly deserted. The Americans begged food and wine and were celebrating when a troop of Latvian SS soldiers arrived. Once again, they were prisoners. The SS troops commandeered a train and loaded the POWs into boxcars, packing the men so tightly they could not sit. Amon Jr.'s feet were frostbitten. February 3, the train moved into Berlin as Allies sent more than twelve hundred bombers over the German capital while the Americans, huddled in the train cars, watched the bombs fall.

After the raid, the prisoners were moved to Luchenwalde, twenty-five miles from Berlin, and imprisoned again. Then the guards fled before the approaching Russian army. Soviets replaced German guards, and the Americans remained captives.

Amon Carter knew none of this, knew only that the Polish connection had been severed. No letters, no news. Silence. Washington inquiries failed. The old sorrows returned. Amon feared the worst. By April, he was in Europe.

The opportunity came in the form of a tour sponsored by Allied headquarters. General Eisenhower asked for a small group of publishers to "inspect German atrocities, the war damage *and prison camps* [italics added]."

Amon already had determined he was going to Europe, come hell or high command, and he telephoned his Washington bureau chief, Bascom Timmons. He ordered Timmons to get him on that plane to Europe. Timmons replied that the request was impossible; every seat was filled. Carter told Timmons to contact General Barney Giles, the Air Force chief coordinating statewide arrangements for the tour. Reluctantly, Timmons telephoned Giles.

"Impossible," Giles said. "The plane is full."

"I told him that. Now, you call and tell him."

"Hell, I can't tell him 'No.' He won't take 'No' for an answer."

Amon and seventeen other American publishers landed in Paris, April 24, 1945.

Nenetta, Katrine, and daughter Ruth thought Amon's pretense for going to Europe farcical. Each knew Amon. How could the man who blanched at the sight of blood, and who anguished over sick pets and tonsillectomies, endure the barbarisms of prison camps? They believed him too old and too despondent for the long trip, but each knew he would not be stopped.

Amon paused overnight in New York to visit Nenetta. Walter Winchell reported April 26 in his syndicated column that the publisher had been in the Stork Club and "sent over $100 to pay for 6 blind soldiers' night out because 'My boy is in a Nazi prison camp.'"

Before joining other publishers, Amon deposited $10,000 in a bank account for Ruth, then a student at Sarah Lawrence College in Bronxville. He told Nenetta, "I'm going to look for Amon Jr. If I don't find him, I'm not coming back."

Shocked, she admonished, "Yes, you are!"

"No," he said sadly, shaking his head, "I'm not."

The group remained in Paris overnight, then flew to Germany to inspect Buchenwald. Amon slipped away. With him was Robert Wear, the *Star-Telegram* correspondent, and following close behind were half the American reporters in Europe, sniffing at a magnificent human-interest story.

Meanwhile, the *Star-Telegram* received an *Associated Press* bulletin stating that Amon Jr. had been seen by two freed American soldiers and was "alive and well."

Amon was unaware of this as he and Wear moved across Germany. They stopped for days at General Omar Bradley's headquarters before moving to the command post of General William Hood Simpson—commander of the Ninth Army and a native of Weatherford, twenty miles west of Fort Worth.

About May 4, Amon and Wear were in a jeep near the Elbe River. They met Seymour Freidin, a correspondent for the *New York Herald-Tribune.* When introduced to Amon Carter, the correspondent tossed a handwritten note to the publisher. The note was from Amon Jr. He had given it to Freidin earlier that morning. The message told of his liberation April 22. Young Carter had asked Freidin to file the news with the *Star-Telegram.*

The American army had arrived finally at Luchenwalde, and when the Soviet guards refused to free the American officers, U.S. tanks broke through the front gate. Trucks transported the freed men to Eighty-third Division headquarters, where Amon Jr. joined Frank Conniff, a reporter for the *International News Service.* They drove toward General Simpson's headquarters.

Amon and Wear were mounting a jeep, preparing to resume their search, when young Carter called, "Dad, here I am." He

Amon embraces his son after Amon Jr.'s release from World War II POW camp.

slapped his father on the back and they embraced and kissed. Amon cried.

For a week father and son remained together. Then the army reclaimed the young lieutenant. With Wear and Bess Stephenson, who had left the *Star-Telegram* to become a WAC officer, Amon celebrated VE day in Paris. Young Amon was shipped home to America. His father rejoined the touring publishers, who had completed their atrocity inspections and had fallen into sightseeing. Amon—so elated was his mood—even filed several stories to the *Star-Telegram*—as the men moved down the continent.

Amon's war was over; his son was safe, going home. The publisher followed two weeks later. Back in New York he telephoned Katrine to report on the trip. Because of his gratitude for having his cowboy home, Amon issued a generous order.

"I want you to give a thousand dollars to every church in Fort Worth," he told Katrine. Pause.

"Even the colored churches?" *Pause.*

"They pray, don't they?"

"Yes, I expect they do."

"Well, gawddammit, pay 'em."

As news of Amon Carter Jr.'s deliverance from evil Nazi captivity flashed across the *Star-Telegram*'s front pages, and as the publisher's European reports arrived, a creaky little old lady made her way to the editorial offices and announced that she, and she alone, had effected young Amon's release.

"I asked God to save him, and He did," she declared, and demanded that the newspaper publish the fact of her providential miracle. Mary Sears, the society pages editor, dismissed the woman, sniffing indignantly, "Amon Carter makes his own deals with God."

At home, the publisher provided a practical means of showing Texas's involvement in the war. He ordered that all names of Texans killed in the fighting be printed because there should be a public record of the dead. The army list alone numbered more than fifteen thousand names and, in agate type, covered six full, open pages.

The publisher's postwar European reports mostly were dull accounts of how Texans once again had saved the world for democracy, but in a final story, he noted a side trip to Milan, where, he bragged:

I stood on Mussolini's balcony and gave a loud cheer for West Texas.

Amon directing a band.

Amon with William Knudsen, president of General Motors, playing "Let Me Call You Sweetheart" on the xylophone.

17

Always do anything Amon asks you to do. Just give him half as much money as he asks you for because he always asks for twice as much as he expects to get.
>—Father's advice to Fort Worth businessman Web
>   Maddox

Amon does my talking for me, and every time he does, he costs me money.
>—Sid Richardson, Fort Worth oilman, 1940s

He [Amon] was the last of the empire builders, and Fort Worth is his monument.
>—Billy Rose, Broadway producer, at Amon's funeral,
>   1955

It is Christmas, and Our Lady of Victory needs a new car. They will be by to pick it up. Send me the bill.
>—Amon, in a note to Fort Worth Packard dealer, Ray
>   Eisele, about 1948

Amon Carter was instinctively, often compulsively, generous, and no one will ever know how much money he gave away. He was the kind of man who never opened his own presents until late Christmas Day because he found too much pleasure in watching his family and friends open gifts he had given them. He gave money and things to everybody, anybody, in fits of philanthropy as spontaneous as they were anonymous, with a random casualness that defied all reason and certain documentation.

Amon could be, and often was, the bully of the block, but he was, throughout his life, a compassionate giver. A poor TCU student needed money for a holiday trip home. Amon heard of the boy's plight and paid for a train ticket. A family was seriously injured in an automobile accident, the father hospitalized for a year. Amon read of the family in the *Star-Telegram*, paid all hospital bills, supported the family, and set in motion a newspaper campaign to make safe the intersection at which the accident occurred. Neither the student nor the family ever knew the name of their benefactor. Two boys were injured when their speeding motorcycle overturned. Amon paid their medical expenses, anonymously.

He gave $1,500 to St. Francis Xavier Academy in Denison with the stipulation that no one ever know. His contributions to St. Joseph's Hospital included an x-ray machine, blood lab, elevator, and parking lot, and as Dr. R. J. White wrote, "They are daily used and enjoyed by hundreds of people who don't know where they come from, but I do."

Amon financed the first modern beauty shop in Fort Worth, and provided seed money for the crippled children's society. He regularly supported an old blind lady who sold the *Press* on street corners, and the widow of a bank president who died broke. He wrote a monthly check for expenses of a society widow left penniless by her late husband, and he supported two elderly black women who had no other source of income. A cement contractor, nearing bankruptcy, would have lost his home, but Amon saved it. The shanty of a black family burned; Amon repaired the house, gave the family six hundred dollars, and had Leonard Brothers Department Store provide furniture and household items at cost.

He gave a station wagon to a church federation that operated a children's home. He gave Jewish charities one thousand dollars each Christmas. He bought the old boarding house in Bowie at which he worked as a boy, kept it as a home for the landlady, Mrs. Jarrott, paid all of her expenses, paid for her funeral. Bill Ince, his childhood friend, died, and Amon gave the widow oil stock to provide an income for the remainder of her life. Never a church-going man, Amon gave an all-faith tabernacle to the community of Crafton, his birthplace, and paid $30,000 of the $45,000 needed to purchase a rectory for St. John's Episcopal Church in Fort Worth. An elderly couple would have lost their small grocery store but Amon bought the mortgage and gave it to them.

At one time, as he grouched in a letter, Amon supported thirteen relatives, several of whom found regular work at the *Star-Telegram*. In addition to the sixty dollars he provided monthly to the stepmother he despised, Amon also paid fifty dollars to an elderly uncle, forty dollars to his grandmother, and seventy-five dollars to his sister, Addie, a troublesome woman who endlessly asked for more money. He supported her children, paid for their educations, their weddings, and their homes.

He gave the county medical society a new building, and funded the school library at Montague High School in North Central Texas. He sold property in Amarillo for less than he paid for it to provide the town with the best site for a new post office.

Amon Carter, who seldom read anything but his newspaper, gave a rare book collection to TCU.

Cranky, cantankerous, irascible, grouchy old Amon Carter never missed a birthday of Pappy Waggoner's wife or Mrs. W. C. Stripling Sr. He always was there, smiling, with a kind word and a bouquet of flowers.

He provided generous benefits for employees, but there was more. He slipped them extra cash, always warning, "Now, don't say anything about this to the others." Jack Butler prepared to buy his first home, a step that required selling his car for downpayment money. Amon learned of Butler's plans and stopped him. First, he had Walter Claer investigate if Butler was getting his money's worth. Butler was not, Claer reported. Amon was selling some land to a developer. As part of the deal, Butler was given his choice of a free lot.

At Christmas, Amon gave a crisp, new, five-dollar bill to each rest home patient and orphan in Fort Worth. The money was given with one stipulation: it was not to be spent on essentials; it was for fun. One Christmas, Lena Pope, who operated the city's largest orphanage, used the money for badly needed linoleum. Amon was furious. He reprimanded her, then paid for the linoleum and replenished the supply of five-dollar bills for her orphans.

Orphanage directors and heads of other charitable organizations brought their lists to Amon shortly before Christmas. One year, a preacher asked for three hundred dollars. Next December, he wanted $350. Amon compared the lists and sent a reporter to find out why the preacher was dunning him for more money.

"He has ten more orphans," the newsman reported back.

"Pay him," said Amon, satisfied no one was cheating him.

That was Amon, too. Careful with his money. Though he lived expensively and well, and gave away millions, the pennies were tended like a flock of worrisome sheep. He never passed through the business offices without turning out lights and groaning over the high cost of electricity. A few months before Amon's death, LeRoy Menzing, then oil editor, was assigned to cover a Middle East petroleum conference. Amon generously told him, "Use my apartment on your way through New York. Throw a party if you want to and put it on the bill—but don't use the telephone. Those birds charge 21 cents a call. Look in the closet. There's a private line hidden in there. Use that one."

Once he escorted Nenetta and two friends to New York for a week. Always the superb host, Amon paid for everything —train tickets, meals, Broadway shows, shopping, entertainment. Before leaving his apartment, Amon gathered up the empty soda bottles, and lugged them eighteen hundred miles to Fort Worth, where he collected a few cents' refund on each.

Hospitalized with his first heart attack in St. Joseph's Hospital, he learned that a nursing sister was returning to Ireland for her first visit home in years. She was a small woman encased in an old-fashioned lace-up corset at which she tugged endlessly to

Amon and Amon Jr. (center) pose with the Fort Worth Fat Stock Show's grand champion bull.

ease the discomfort it caused. Amon instructed Katrine to buy the nun a new corset. The sister blushed, thanked Amon but said what she really wanted was long woolen underwear. Amon bought the underwear, and tucked money enough inside to pay for a plane ticket to Ireland.

Amon always bought the stock show's grand champion steer. Acting as auctioneer, he often raised his own bid or entered a money commitment for Sid Richardson.

"Sid Richardson bids $5,000," he would shout. "Anybody seen Sid today?"

Richardson was a barrel-bodied, taciturn, plainspoken man with a face of furrow-like wrinkles, one of the last of Texas's great wildcat oilmen. Most often broke, Sid was a fixture around the Fort Worth Club, where his bills went unpaid for years. When he finally hit his keystone pool in far West Texas, its reserves were valued at multimillions of dollars. "Luck did it," Richardson said of the strike, "I'd rather be lucky than smart 'cause a lot of smart people ain't eatin'."

With his bills paid, Sid, a lifelong bachelor, settled into the Fort Worth Club as Amon's close friend, confidante, political crony, and handy reserve fund for the publisher's various projects. Richardson always complained about the costs, but he paid.

Once Richardson was relaxing on an Atlantic cruise. Amon telephoned him and asked for a $37,000 contribution. Sid moaned, and began pleading poverty.

"Then I'll just charge this phone call to you," joked Amon.

"Like hell you will! Put me down for the $37,000."

Through Amon's exhortations, Sid paid one thousand dollars each year for support of 4-H Club members at the annual stock show. In 1945, Sid was vacationing at the Westward Ho Guest Ranch near Phoenix when Amon doubled the oilman's annual pledge. Then he wired Richardson the news, adding, "Unless I hear from you in the next five minutes, I will assume it is OK."

Sid's reply was terse: "Looks like you didn't hear from me in five minutes."

Another convenient cache of money belonged to old Pappy Waggoner, a multimillionaire with penurious ways with a dollar. Once Waggoner had his shoes polished and handed the shine man a two-bit tip. The man complained, "but your boys usually tip five dollars."

"They got a rich daddy, and I ain't," snapped Pappy.

When Amon was raising funds to construct TCU's new football stadium, a finance committee member approached Pappy and secured a thousand-dollar pledge. Proudly, the man bragged to Amon of the contribution. Amon snorted and said, "I'll show you how to raise money."

He telephoned Pappy: "I'm putting you down for $50,000. That'll buy a whole section. Your ranch brand is 3-D. I'll have 3-D put into the concrete in your section."

A *Star-Telegram* photographer once was assigned to take Waggoner's picture and the rancher/oilman held up a silver dollar.

"Here, take a picture of this," commanded Pappy. "It's one dollar Amon Carter didn't get."

As a member of the Democrats' national finance committee, Amon raised millions for his party, so much that in his January 23, 1933, nationally syndicated column, Will Rogers wrote: "I hear that Amon G. Carter, of Fort Worth, Texas, owner of the biggest newspaper in the Southwest, will take [Secretary of War] Hurley's place in the cabinet. Carter, from all I can gather from the 'inside,' will be the man that will draw that splendid Cabinet plum. Amon will make 'em a mighty fine man. He is mighty well liked by all Democrats and 50 percent of the Republicans (Well, I will say a dozen anyway). He would handle our army mighty well in peace and put us on a mighty pretty war if the occasion arises. . . ."

In the *Star-Telegram*, Amon added an editor's note to Rogers's column: "Thanks, Will, but your information is all wrong. The publisher of this newspaper never has accepted political appointment of any character and has no intention of so doing."

Amon, far more powerful and effective offstage, truly never wanted political office. During FDR's long reign, he had clear and easy access to Washington, and was considered the president's man in the Southwest. Amon and Houston's Jesse Jones, in fact, rustled so much government money for the Lone Star State during the Depression that Washington cynics spoke of Texas as the "star loan state."

Texas's national politicians—especially Senator Tom Connally—acquired reputations as "Amon Carter's rubber stamps." Not in a kindly way, Harold Ickes called Amon "the Horace Greeley of Texas."

Roosevelt was a good friend in addition to being a valuable source of Washington largess. Secret Service agents had standing instructions that *Star-Telegram* photographers would take pictures of FDR in Fort Worth whatever the orders in other cities. Amon's strong friendship with Roosevelt grew in spite of the publisher's frantic efforts to make a president of John Nance Garner. Throughout Roosevelt's three terms, Amon openly and continuously campaigned for Cactus Jack's ascension. Amon loved Garner, whom labor leader John L. Lewis once described as a "whiskey-drinking, poker-playing, evil old man."

America has never had a politician like Cactus Jack. With a hummock of graying hair brushed to one side, the waggling

Amon and John Nance Garner, 1933.

Andrew Jackson eyebrows, the bulldog jawline, John Garner was
a fixture in American politics for forty years. He was a county
judge in South Texas, then a congressman who, in his words,
"didn't amount to anything at first. For five or six years I just
answered roll calls and played poker." Washington never changed
him. He tucked pieces of cooked venison into his pockets, went
to bed each evening at nine o'clock, kept a dollar watch in the
vest of his off-the-rack suits. When the watch inevitably broke,
Amon bought another, and passed along the receipt proving the
timepiece cost no more than a dollar. Garner hated to dress, was

most comfortable in old jeans. He rose to the office of House Speaker, an ironic title because John Garner was a man of almost no words. Compared to Garner, Silent Cal Coolidge was as chatty as a debutante. In four decades, Garner made just three public speeches, none in the first twenty-five years. His last speech was in 1941 at of the U.S. Chamber of Commerce convention. He told the audience, "I'm not going to say a thing tonight that means a damn thing."

Elected vice president—asked for a comment on her son's new position, his mother said, "He's a good boy, it won't hurt him any"—Cactus Jack was surprisingly unchanged, and spoke only rarely with reporters—once to grumble his now-famous assessment of the vice presidency: "not worth a bucketful of warm spit." (Privately, Garner was a trifle more succinct, complaining the office was "not worth a bucketful of warm piss.")

When Roosevelt sought an unprecedented fourth term, Garner quit in disgust. He went home to Uvalde to sit on his front porch, and sip Amon's Shady Oak whiskey. Bascom Timmons, assisted by Bess Stephenson, wrote Garner's official biography. In 1947, Timmons reported a minor event in the life of the man who left the nation's second most powerful elected office for a principle. Old Cactus Jack, wrote Timmons, resisted all requests to write his political memoirs, carried his political files of forty years— the letters, memoranda, and official papers—to a small rise behind his home, and burned everything.

Amon kept Cactus Jack supplied with the necessities of life— cases and cases of the exclusive Shady Oak bourbon, cigars, jars of homemade pickles and marmalade, hand-tooled belts, and a special Shady Oak hat inscribed "Hooray for John Nance Garner and West Texas." When Carter visited in Washington, Garner would get a gleam in his eye and roar, "Amon! Let's you and me go into the back room and strike a blow for liberty!"—an invitation to nip from the whiskey reservoir.

Amon had Garner's portrait painted not once, but three times, and copies were hung in Austin and Washington. He hired Electra Waggoner Biggs to sculpt the craggy features, and busts were sent to the two capitols. A third went to Texas Tech, and a fourth rested in Amon's office near the lighted portrait of Will

Rogers—proof of the publisher's deeply held respect for the little man from Uvalde.

About the same time Pappy's granddaughter began work on Garner's bust, Amon commissioned her to sculpt Sid Richardson's head as a gesture of friendship. An attached plate was inscribed: "From One Old Bastard to Another."

By the late 1940s, Amon and Sid were involved in several political conspiracies, one of which was the pressuring of Dwight Eisenhower to run for president. Amon was unhappy that Ike chose the Republican Party as a vehicle to the office. His support of the general in the 1952 election was considered by recidivist Democrats as a treasonable act, but few of them understood the absolute necessity of Eisenhower being President. It was a matter of oil.

Sid met Ike when the latter was a young lieutenant and their friendship grew over the years. He introduced Amon to Eisenhower, and a 1950 entry in Suite 10G's logbook noted: "With best wishes to Amon in memory of an afternoon when his old friends Sid and Ike chinned with him through the problems of the world and quantities of good scotch."

In the mid-1940s, Texas oilmen were in a dither about rights to offshore petroleum deposits. Harry Truman vetoed a tidelands bill in 1946 that would have given Texas and other states clear ownership to all offshore oil. In April 1952, Amon wrote Truman urging him to sign a second bill soon to be passed: "Facts of history make the tidelands matter, insofar as Texas concerned, a moral as well as a legal matter." After passage of the bill, Amon again wrote Truman, noting that his 1946 veto still was criticized widely and that national defense requirements now justified Texas's retention of tidelands resources.

In Washington, Truman told newsmen he had written a "fellow down in Texas" that school children of other states would be the losers if the tidelands bill became law, but evidently the fellow "wanted all of this money to go to Texas. It is not going there if I can help it." Truman vetoed the bill, and Amon wrote still another letter—published in the *Star-Telegram*, it covered thirty-four column inches—attacking the president's veto and promising that Texas would fight until the issue was "settled in accord with the principles of right, justice and honesty."

Privately, Amon and Sid were priming Ike.

Four months earlier, Richardson and George E. Allen, a Democrat and former chairman of the Reconstruction Finance Corporation, sailed for France—Katrine Deakins said Amon "made Sid go"—to persuade Ike that he must return by April if he wanted the Republican nomination. They also enlisted the help of Billy Graham, the evangelist then on the rise to national prominence. Graham said in a 1970s interview that at Sid and Amon's urging he had spoken with Ike in Paris.

Ike came home for the nomination and offshore oil ownership became a campaign issue. Ike said he favored states' rights, Adlai Stevenson took the position that the matter had been settled by Truman's veto. Less than a month after Eisenhower's inauguration, reported columnist Drew Pearson, Amon delivered to the new president a copy of the 1849 Joint Resolution for Annexing Texas to the United States. The document, said Pearson, convinced Eisenhower of Texas's right to its tidelands. Four months later, Ike signed the bill. With offshore oil secured for Texas, Amon, said a friend, had smiled like a spinster who finally had scored. Amon and Sid formed a corporation to establish Eisenhower's birthplace in Denison as a state shrine.

Locally, anyone who ran for office courted the publisher, and those who did not get his support attacked those who did as "Amon Carter puppets." Within the empire, there were three candidates for state offices. Boyce House quit the newspaper to run—sans Amon's support—a losing race for lieutenant governor. Harold Hough campaigned for governor, but never very seriously. And then there was W. Lee O'Daniel. Amon hated the man.

O'Daniel was a flour peddler who emceed a daily WBAP radio show featuring the popular Light Crust Doughboys hillbilly band. Hough urged O'Daniel to test his political popularity, and one morning the flour salesman asked listeners, "How would you like me to run for governor?" Sixty thousand letters of support arrived at the station.

O'Daniel campaigned with the radio show band and a sound truck. He passed out flour sacks in which to collect donations and reportedly made a profit on his campaign. It was a good show. O'Daniel sang religious songs, read his poems ("A mother is a mother/wherever you find her/Be she a queen/Or an organ grinder"), recited his platform of "the golden rule and the Ten Commandments," and promised, if elected, to provide a thirty-dollar monthly pension for old folks. Voters knew a good demagogue when they heard one, and O'Daniel was elected. In early 1938, he took possession of the Texas governor's mansion, and while inspecting the home's screened porch, exclaimed loudly to reporters, "Boy, I can do some trick and fancy sleeping in here." O'Daniel muddled around for a couple of terms while Amon fretted over the condition of Texas's politics.

In Fort Worth, where Amon ran everything, being elected mayor or city councilman was mostly a ceremonial honor. The publisher presided over all grand events, like dinners and parades and groundbreakings. Especially groundbreakings. No dirt could be turned in Fort Worth without the exuberant Amon there wielding one of his special chrome-plated shovels, each engraved for the occasion—"Amon was born with a silver spade in his mouth," said Alf Evans of his publisher's groundbreaking mania.

As an emcee, Amon was a splendid speaker with an uncanny memory for names and details, but too often preachy and windy. *Time* told of one such introduction—Amon spoke so long that the speaker had no time remaining. Amon often joked that he once introduced William Jennings Bryan and left the great orator only three minutes to talk.

Amon emceed dinners and events all over America. He had a smooth, stammerless delivery and a limitless stock of appropriate stories and inspirational aphorisms with which to spread the gospel of Fort Worth and Texas. He described himself as a "peptimist," which he explained as a cross between an optimist and a pessimist: "A peptimist looks on the bright side of life, but always with a flashlight handy."

"There's a lot of difference between people and folks," he would tell audiences. Among his speech brighteners were: "You can't fill a sack that's full of holes"; "Eggs want to be smarter than hens"; "Step off the curb and watch yourself go by, and see what you think"; "Be polite to your customers, because the only fellow who ever made a success in business by driving his customers away was a taxi driver"; and "Abe Lincoln was not a great man because he lived in a log cabin, but because he was able to get out of it."

If his friends were unable to stop him, especially in the later years, he applied the adages to himself, his bootstrap beginnings, his celebrity and, after 1949, how he sold all those advertisements for the *Star-Telegram*'s centennial edition. In that year, Fort Worth was a century old, and Amon celebrated with a memorial newspaper edition—a 480-page behemoth printed on 1,578,000 pounds of paper. The October 30, 1949, centennial edition contained a record number of pages for Texas and the most advertising lineage—61,811 column inches—of any single newspaper ever published in the United States. Then sixty-nine years old, Amon personally sold 220 of the 271 full-page advertisements.

Characteristically, Amon sold his ads with the same subtle approach with which he collected cash for other projects. He telephoned friends and announced, "I'm putting you down for a full page." Around town, businessmen joked with one another, "Have you joined Amon's Full-Page Club yet?"

When the monster newspaper was ready for delivery, Amon shanghaied George Dolan—then a night rewrite man—to drive him about the city at 3:00 A.M. At friends' homes, Amon would hop out, trot to the door, and knock loudly. As the occupant sleepily opened the door, Amon would shove the twenty-pound newspaper into the man's arms and shout, "Here's your *Star-Telegram!* Don't call me about it not being delivered!"

At a final stop shortly before dawn, Amon ran to a door and yelled loudly. Moments later, the door opened cautiously to reveal a figure in a long, white nightgown. The man had a shotgun.

"You ol' sonovabitch!" Amon cried.

"Amon!" shouted the astonished man. "You ol' sonovabitch!"

They fell into each other's arms, giggling like schoolgirls.

If there was ever a man conspicuous with money, it was Amon. He was as flashy with it as a racetrack tout, a lavish tipper, an easy touch for a handout or a loan, a sure thing for a charity fund drive. Not that the money he gave away always was his own. Mason Lankford, a fireman's association president, once hesitantly asked for a small donation. Amon peeled off a hundred-dollar bill, then had Katrine telephone local business firms. Lankford's cause collected $2,200.

Amon kept his cash in fifties and hundreds, even one thousand-dollar bills, all folded into a metal clip he called his "money brassiere." He was forever sending Katrine to the bank for a fresh supply of hundreds, which he favored. Once he carried for months a $10,000 bill that he hauled out to impress friends and passing strangers.

Amon's gaudy theatrical way with cash was a personality trait of the cowboy. The cowboy flashed and lavished Amon's money on the world with the wastrel appetite of a small boy before a candy counter. The cowboy, in fact, kept Amon broke most of his life. Stony broke. Busted as a sharecropper. The cowboy treated Amon shamefully.

Except what he could borrow, Amon had little money to call his own. He always was drawn ahead on his *Star-Telegram* salary. His newspaper stock was heavily mortgaged. He often was months behind on grocery bills, payments lagged on automobiles, his country club debts mounted, Fort Worth Club charges went unpaid as other members complained.

The cowboy, that eternal prodigal playboy, was a classic spendthrift. Most of his life, Amon ran to stay ahead of the cowboy's creditors.

By 1916, when he and Louis Wortham owned controlling interest in the *Star-Telegram*, the cowboy had devised Amon's fiscal policy of borrowing from Peter to pay Paul (also Tom, Dick, and Harry). That year he borrowed $25,000 in "personal loans" and two years later, when the note was due, Amon paid by borrowing from another bank. The dollar relay was a perpetual race against insolvency. Wortham retired in 1922 to write an excellent four-volume history of Texas. Amon became publisher and majority stockholder, eventually owning 66²/₃ percent of the corporation, according to columnist Dorothy Kilgallen.

The remainder of the stock was spread among Jimmy North, Bert Honea, Al Shuman, Harold Hough, and James Record.

The newspaper's income supported Amon's outgoing lifestyle, his cowboy extravagances, the civic and charitable contributions; it was a fiscal treadmill that frazzled the nerves of penny-conscious Bert Honea. Alf Evans once described Honea's philosophy about money as, "It was fine to make, and bank at 6 percent interest, compounded, but a mortal sin to spend."

Honea, by necessity, became a genius at figuring out ways to beat the cowboy's spending habits and keep the *Star-Telegram* floating. Honea's firm grasp on the empire's fortune was one reason Amon did not buy the bankrupt *Washington Post* when it was offered to him in 1933. Amon told Bert he would have to move to Washington to run the newspaper and, recalled Honea, that "was when the deal fell through." Honea had no intention of leaving the *Star-Telegram* cash box in the cowboy's care.

Amon borrowed money only for important reasons, like to pay his income tax or to give it away. Often he mortgaged stock or land to buy his load of Christmas gifts—as much as thirty thousand dollars one year, said Walter Claer. At times, the money squeeze became unbearable. In the mid-1930s Amon went to New York to renew several past-due bank notes. Instead, the banks threatened foreclosure on the newspaper. Frantically, Amon telephoned Honea, whom somehow got blood from Fort Worth turnips and saved the *Star-Telegram* again.

When Nenetta asked for a divorce from Amon in the 1930s, there again was panic. Amon had mortgaged his stock and that owned by Honea, North, Hough, and Schuman. He had borrowed to his limit at every bank in Fort Worth, and several in New York. Even Katrine had co-signed notes to finance the cowboy's lifestyle.

Nenetta agreed to wait for a settlement. She waited because she was sure Amon would strike oil, which he had been seeking for two decades. His luck had to change.

Amon loved the gamble of wildcatting, but he had almost no success at it. A small $100,000 strike in 1920 began his quest for the big score, but for the next seventeen years he found only dust in New Mexico and West Texas. Amon became something of a novelty in the oil business, once being introduced to an audience as "the only big oil producer who has never produced." Word passed that Amon was unlucky and other wildcatters would not partner with him. After ninety consecutive dry holes—surely a record—Amon, alone, struck again in the New Mexico Mattix pool.

That strike gave him operating capital for wells in Gaines and Yoakum counties of West Texas. While the crews drilled, Amon fretted in Fort Worth, afraid that these were his final adventures into wildcatting. Days became weeks, which turned into months. The crew lived at a well site on the Wassom Ranch, and to save money they shot jackrabbits and stole corn from a nearby field. The ranch foreman threatened to have the men arrested for theft. The foreman's stinginess so enraged Amon that he bought the ranch of several thousand acres—with borrowed money, of course—and told the crew to eat all the corn and rabbits they wanted. The foreman was fired.

The men rewarded Amon's generosity by bringing in the Wassom pool discovery well in June 1937. Subsequently, Amon sold his holdings in the pool to Shell Oil Company for $16,500,000—to that time the largest oil transaction in Texas history. For waiting, Nenetta received, as her spousal share, 40 percent. She and Amon were divorced in 1941.

For the first time in his life, Amon was out of debt. Even the cowboy could not spend all that money, which pleased everyone, particularly Bert Honea, who knew that Amon no longer would have to rifle the *Star-Telegram* petty-cash drawer for pocket money. Amon's habit of taking from petty cash rankled Honea more than anything else. At the end of the day, Honea would find the petty cash short. He could not balance his books. He nagged Amon about the troublesome practice dozens of times, then the two men had a shouting argument.

"It's your money!" yelled Honea. "You can take it if you want to. But leave me a marker saying how much you took. My books never balance. Just leave me a chit, that's all!"

"All right, all right!" Amon hollered back. "I'll leave you a gawddammed chit!"

That afternoon Amon again raided the petty-cash drawer and, true to his word, he left a chit.

Honea read it:

> Dear Bert,
> I took it all.
> Amon

Amon was the most human man I ever saw.
　　—Nenetta Burton Carter, Amon's second wife, 1976

In a land of giants, he dwarfed them all. . . .
　　—Jim Wright, U.S. congressman, at Amon's funeral, June
　　　27,1955

His death closes a chapter in our history. . . .
　　—Lyndon Johnson, U.S. senator, at Amon's funeral, June
　　　27, 1955

I am a part of the heritage of Texas. Its pioneer spirit that peopled
the wide spaces and laid the foundation of a happy future comes
down to me in the strain of blood, and I wish to share it with
others who would make Texas their home and their inspiration. . . .
　　—Amon, in his will, dated August 11, 1954

The Amon Carter Museum faces the rising sun on ground sloping away to the east toward the river and Fort Worth's tiered skyline, dominating a place now called Amon Carter Square. Beside it, to the north, is Camp Bowie Boulevard, down which Amon took his daily, reckless, second-gear journey to the *Star-Telegram*. Opposite and slightly to the south are the Will Rogers Coliseum and Auditorium—"Amon's cowsheds." The bronze statue of the cowboy humorist astride Soapsuds is in front, looking west over Amon's museum to each sunset. Farther south are the Fort Worth Art Museum and Museum of Science and History and Scott Theater—a performing arts center. In front, beyond the Henry Moore impressionistic sculpture pieces and across a grassy field where children play on sunny days, is the Kimbell Museum, a repository of classical art endowed by another Fort Worth millionaire. Southeast above the treeline is the silvery dome of Casa Mañana, a musical-theater-in-the-round inspired by the 1936 Frontier Centennial original, which stood on the site.

Amon Carter Square is flush with culture—an irony for the many who felt Amon had none when he was alive.

His museum is a ruggedly handsome, limestone-faced, glass-fronted building designed by famed architect Philip Johnson. Its base collection is Amon's—no, it is the cowboy's—incomparable stockpile of paintings and sculpture pieces by Charles Russell and Frederic Remington.

The cowboy began assembling his artwork before Amon could afford such effete foolishness. In 1928, New York art dealer Bertram Newhouse showed the publisher six watercolors and an oil by Russell. All reminded Carter of his imagined *West* and he promptly signed a $7,500 note, paying for his new treasures in two yearly installments. He continued to buy Russell's paintings and sculptures, and in 1935 acquired his first Remington oil for $5,000. Will Rogers immediately offered Amon $10,000 for the painting, but Amon refused to sell.

In 1952, according to *Time*, Amon used his oil money to purchase the entire Russell collection housed in the old Mint Saloon of Great Falls, Montana.

Amon's art is the definitive representation of Western America, but the museum is much more. It was Amon's dream, but daughter Ruth's concept. He wanted a place to show off his western paintings; she gave him a museum of international repute by redefining her father's myopic vision of *The West*. Ruth understood that Amon had romanticized a frontier, and that America's frontier has changed with time, began, in fact, one step west from Plymouth Rock. So, the Amon Carter Museum is a museum of American frontier art, representing all periods. Its books and research facilities, collections of early frontier newspapers and photographs, are without compare in America.

Still, each January during the Fort Worth Fat Stock Show, the Remingtons and Russells and other artwork idealizing the traditional American West go up for the Texans who come to town. They drive in from the plains in their pickups and Cadillacs and roam the galleries communing with Amon's *West;* many are authentic cowboys, like brontosaurus out of time and space, leftover props from a long-ago synthetic drama.

The museum was a legacy from Amon, who specifically directed in his will that no admission ever be charged, merely one element of a remarkable document. The will—dated August 11, 1954—is a model of philosophical and practical humanity, so perfect in its phrasing and execution that hundreds of copies were requested by others with a philanthropic inclination. The will's thesis was written by the frail and scholarly Sidney Samuels—"Sidney had just enough body to hold up his intellect," remembered Nenetta. In Amon's name, Samuels produced a piece of legal literature, which begins with these words:

> Year in and year out, it has been borne in upon me [Amon] that money alone, nor broad acres, nor newspapers, nor stock, nor bonds, nor flocks and herds, nor estates of oil and gas hidden in the recesses of this planet can, of themselves, bear testimony to the fine quality of man or woman. . . . The grave is a democracy for all human kind. There is no rank in death—the pauper laid away in an unlettered grave carries with him as much of worldly goods as the rich man whose body is clad in silken shroud. Neither the winding sheet nor the shroud is lined with purse or pocket. The hand that in life grips with a miser's clutch and the ear that refuses to heed the pleading voice of humanity, forfeits the most precious of all gifts of Earth and Heaven—the happiness within the heart that comes from doing good to others.

The will is a blueprint of benevolence, a kind of written passing parade float with Amon at the reins, scattering gifts and trinkets to the crowd.

It left $100,000 each to son and daughter, $24,000 annually, free of all taxes, to the third wife, Minnie Meacham Smith Carter, $50,000 each to Katrine Deakins and a half-brother, Roy Carter, and $1,000 to Nancy Crouse, a blind news vendor who sold the *Press*. Nannie Moore, a black employee, and Monroe Odom each received $250. The fire and police associations got $10,000 apiece, eleven employees of the Fort Worth Club received amounts ranging from $100 to $1,000, and *Star-Telegram* carriers were granted $10 at Christmas and Thanksgiving. The Amon G. Carter Riverside High School was given $50,000, and a tract of land near Lake Worth was deeded to the YMCA as a recreational area. Sid Richardson's chauffeur got $250, and $200 went to a St. Joseph's Hospital x-ray technician. There were bequests for children of friends and employees, one hundred dollars for "Mammy" Korth, the "colored nurse" of Fred Korth, $25,000 for the city of Bowie, $500 for each surviving Chicken and Bread Boy, and sums ranging from $500 to $1,000 for sixteen *Star-Telegram* employees, none of them reporters or editors.

Almost a year passed before Amon's net worth was announced. The estate totaled $10,252,294.51, from which there was to be deducted various miscellaneous debts including $70,000 owed Sid Richardson. Even then, no one knew exactly how much money Amon had amassed in his lifetime because much of the wealth had been assigned to his children and other family members before his death. The estate's balance— $7,285,990.22—was handed over to the Amon G. Carter Foundation, which he and Nenetta endowed in 1945.

Amon, in death, was as generous to Fort Worth as he had been in life.

In the late 1940s, Amon, then a wealthy, aging patrician, put away the cowboy forever. He had outgrown the boots and chaps and blazing guns and other western paraphernalia that had by then become movie and novel clichés of Texas.

He settled in to live out his days as a dignified man of means, a fawning grandfather and generous husband to Minnie. She was a beautiful, slender woman with delicate features perfect for the jewels he lavished on her. They took long ocean cruises and entertained at home, becoming socialites of the first order in a Fort Worth society finally growing beyond its cow-chip origins.

In 1953, at 73, Amon still was a vigorous, active man, having very little to do with operations of the newspaper or the radio and television stations, but tending to his oil business. In that year, he had the first of his heart attacks—"A doozy of a coronary," said Ruth. He was at home and immediately Minnie rushed him toward St. Joseph's Hospital. On the way, police at a driver's license checkpoint stopped them. Minnie had no license and, for whatever reason, the police were not told of Amon's heart attack or the emergency of the trip. Amon drove himself on to the hospital, undoubtedly in second gear.

Amon was an abominable patient. He lay in the hospital bed for two months, grouchy and demanding, anxious to be up and about but fearful of the consequences. He alternated between despair and buoyancy. One reporter, Irv Farman, visited and Amon insisted on reading his get-well cards, mawkish verses and all. The last card he read slowly and with feeling, tears in his eyes, saying finally "and it's signed 'Ike.'"

Amon was furloughed with instructions that he must never again exert himself or become excited. His children and family and Sid Richardson escorted him home to a surprise. During his hospitalization, an elevator had been installed because doctors said he no longer could use stairs. Amon grumbled about the uselessness and expense of a private elevator. Sid explained helpfully, "But Amon, look how much easier it'll be to bring your body down."

Amon, of course, quickly dismissed doctors' orders from his mind, and after a period of further convalescence, did much as he pleased. And soon there was another heart attack, and another. Between attacks, he was impossible to control. He, said Katrine, even "bucked and pitched" until allowed to attend an American Airlines board meeting and publishers' convention.

Though frail and weak, he had moments when the old angers flashed. One day he crossed Taylor Street from the *Star-Telegram* to the Fort Worth Club and nearly was struck by an automobile driven by teenagers. He stood in the street, shaking his fist at the speeding car, yelling "You gawddammed little sonovabitches . . . ."

Mostly confined to bed, Amon would watch television—"Gunsmoke," not unexpectedly, was his favorite program—until after midnight, then telephone friends and associates. Harold Hough finally took his phone off the hook. Amon switched to James Byron, WBAP-TV's news director, complaining mostly that the station presented far too much Dallas news. Byron tried to explain that television was unlike newspapers. Newspaper circulation could be controlled; TV signals sprayed everywhere. Amon didn't like that.

He presided over opening night of the stock show rodeo in 1953 and later in the spring attended a special ceremony at the YMCA's Camp Carter. He read books for the first time in more than thirty years, and he bored visitors with an endless review of his life, which, depending on his mood, was either as the Book of Job or lighthearted as a fairy tale.

W. L. Redus, an editorial writer, sat through one of the retrospections in which Amon remembered being one of only three living men—Charles Lindbergh was another—to have a Pullman sleeping car named for him. Amon's name replaced Henry W. Longfellow, who was only a poet, not a cowboy. "I'm just happy it's not a baggage car," Amon said on the occasion. He reminisced about the bomber plant and the public health hospital and Chicago Pneumatic Tool Company, which he had sold on building a $4,500,000 plant in Fort Worth, and the regional headquarters of Continental, Pure, and Sinclair oil companies he dragged into town, and how, once there, he tended to their business. Sinclair regional officers declared they were moving to Houston, but Amon stopped that silly notion by telephoning his poker buddy, Harry Sinclair. Gulf Oil did move its regional offices from Fort Worth to Wichita Falls. Amon insisted Gulf return, and it did—an expensive lesson for the oil company.

He spoke of his honorary doctorate from Texas Tech—the first given by that high plains university—and of another from TCU, and most proudly of having his name on a school—"It's sorta nice to have your name on a high school when you never had the opportunity to go through one." One sultry May evening in 1951, Amon, with other Amon G. Carter Riverside High School graduating seniors, received his diploma. A sweating Sid Richardson, seated beside Amon during ceremonies, whispered in his ear, "You ol' bastard, if you ever graduate from high school again, you can do it in the winter or count me out."

He recalled the plaque at Meacham Field dedicating the air facility in his name: "The Matchless Texan—Amon Carter—Range Rider of the Air." And the *West-Texan*, a thirty-eight-foot twin-motored Chriscraft cruiser given him by the West Texas Chamber of Commerce. And that the Texas Legislature had declared him "Ambassador of Good Will" because, said House Speaker Homer Leonard, "If Texas has a press agent, you are it." And of the appreciation dinner given him by members of the Fort Worth Club, an honor he had delayed by one ruse or another for thirteen years until the banquet was given anyway against his wishes. Among the gifts was an oil portrait he professed to like, but actually hated.

In December 1954, Amon came to the *Star-Telegram* to sign Christmas bonus checks, but he was too weak to finish and Katrine, who could sign his name as well as any forger, had to continue. Nenetta saw him there and they spoke for a long time—of their children, and again, of the past. He attempted to dictate several letters, but his mind wandered, and Katrine stopped him. He was never again seen at the *Star-Telegram*.

By early June 1955, even Amon knew he soon would die and called Amon Jr. and Ruth, Katrine, and Sid to his bedside to discuss the estate, the museum he wanted built, and personal matters.

An evening or two later, about ten o'clock, Amon went into a coma. On June 19, Father's Day, he briefly awoke to ask, "Am I still here?" then lapsed again into unconsciousness. Four days later, with the morning *Star-Telegram*'s two-star deadline fast approaching, Herb Schulz received the telephone call, and announced to other editors around the city desk: "He's dead."

A frail Amon hosted Texas Governor Allan Shivers at the Fort Worth Fat Stock Show Rodeo in 1955, one of his final public appearances. Oilman Sid Richardson is on the governor's right.

The following day, on the floor of the United States Senate, Lyndon Johnson said, "Amon Carter was a man who stood in the main stream of the history of our times. He walked with cattlemen and kings, with crop farmers and with presidents . . . and such men are rare."

As news of Amon's death spread across the country, the *Star-Telegram* office filled with telegrams and messages of condolence from the famous men of America—Senators William Knowland and Alben Barkley and Stuart Symington, J. Edgar Hoover, Herbert Hoover, House Speaker Sam Rayburn and Governor Allan Shivers, Arthur Hays Sulzberger, publisher of the *New York Times*, Air Force Secretary Harold Talbott and Sherman Billingsley, owner of the Stork Club, Winthrop Aldrich, U.S. Ambassador to Great Britain, boxers Jack Dempsey and Gene Tunney, Eddie Rickenbacker and Samuel Goldwyn, Nelson Rockefeller and Bob Hope and Edgar Bergen, and another cowboy from *The West*, Gene Autry.

Eddie Cantor wired, "He gave so much of his heart, he had nothing left for himself."

Amon's, of course, was the largest funeral in Fort Worth history, especially at the grave site, where fifteen thousand people came to pay last respects. Services were at four o'clock because the cowboy said he wanted to be buried in the late afternoon, near sundown. Downtown stores closed. Flags were lowered to half-mast. The zoo closed, and the sheriff's office.

Reverend James K. Thompson, a Presbyterian, was in charge of the funeral, which by Amon's instructions was brief. Services were held in the First Methodist Church because it had the town's largest auditorium, and its pastor, Reverend Gaston Foote, a *Star-Telegram* columnist, led the eulogies.

Amon lay in a gray casket banked by flowers, including Billy Rose's floral tribute in the shape of a Shady Oak Stetson. The auditorium was filled, and speakers were set up in an adjoining banquet hall. Outside, many people stood on the sidewalk listening through open windows. Governor Shivers sat in the front row, as did Patrick Hurley, former secretary of war, and American Airlines President C. R. Smith. Harlow Curtice, president of General Motors, sat beside Monroe Odom, who left his pinewood crate long enough to attend his boss's last public moment.

Reporters who covered the funeral viewed the body before the casket was closed and noted that Amon was dressed in a dark suit and somber red tie. Nenetta saw a few soup stains on the tie. The newsmen seemed genuinely disappointed that Amon did not go to his grave with pearl-handled six-shooters strapped on, dressed in the familiar polo coat, chaps, purple-and-white boots, and Stetson. They saw Amon in the dark, formal suit and one supposedly commented, "It seems so undignified."

Thirty policemen on motorcycles led the procession from the church to Greenwood Memorial Cemetery on Fort Worth's west side. Graveside services were, again, brief. Designated pallbearers were too old and infirm to lift the heavy bronze coffin, and eight policemen actually bore Amon Carter to his grave. The deed done, one briefly touched his cap in silent tribute.

Soon, the fifteen thousand spectators left the cowboy and gravediggers spread dirt over the casket. A grave worker, by a quirk of circumstance that would have pleased Amon, was one of those tens of thousands of displaced West Texans in Fort Worth. The man had fled his barren little prairie hamlet for better things in the town built by the cowboy.

Finally, the cowboy was alone among a thicket of oak trees to savor that final sundown. It was—reported the *Star-Telegram*, which was rarely wrong about events out there in *The West*—a glorious sunset.

Pauline Naylor remembered Amon for me a month before she died. She was a puckish little woman wearing diamonds and surrounded by cats and her late husband's superb collection of rare books. As she spoke of the publisher and the cowboy and the *Star-Telegram*, she paused, and, smiling, said, "I'll bet Amon Carter was mad when he died because he wouldn't know how everything turned out." There is truth in that. Amon, the neurotic perfectionist, liked neat endings. Some of what happened would have provoked him into a spate of gawddams. The newspaper supported Lyndon Johnson—several times, in fact—but in 1955 no one had any notion that LBJ would become president. The *Star-Telegram* pulled away from West Texas, abdicating the plains kingdom to concentrate on a metropolitan circulation. In 1974, the empire itself was dismantled by a governmental order forbidding monopolization of a communications market. The television station went to LIN Broadcasting, and later became an NBC network-owned facility. The newspaper and radio stations were sold to Capital Cities of New York for an undisclosed price but one said to have been well in excess of $100,000,000. The *Star-Telegram* alone brought more than $80,000,000, then the largest amount ever paid for an American newspaper—a reasonable return on a dream begun over a pile of burning cow manure.

Capital Cities (Capital Cities/ABC, Inc., after merger with the national television network) moved the *Star-Telegram* into a futuristic world of bits and bytes, electronic editing, computer terminals, and banks of robotic-served printing presses. The newspaper had leaped from delivery by stagecoach to laser and fiber optics printing in a mere seven decades. In 1996, Cap Cities/ABC was merged into The Walt Disney Company, and the newspaper became part of the world's largest communications/ entertainment corporation. Less than a year later, Disney sold off all of Cap

Cities/ABC's publications, including the *Star-Telegram*, which was purchased by Knight-Ridder, America's second largest newspaper chain.

In early days of Cap Cities ownership—1981—*Star-Telegram* photographer Larry Price was assigned to cover a bloody civil war in the African nation of Liberia, and his work there received the Pulitzer Prize. Four years later, Washington Correspondent Mark Thompson wrote of a deadly design flaw in Tarrant County-built Bell helicopters, and the *Star-Telegram* won every major reporting honor in America, including another Pulitzer Prize—that one for "Meritorious Public Service," the most prestigious of all journalism awards. Each Pulitzer gold medallion carries the Latin phrase: *Honoris Cauis*. It means "honorable cause," which always was Amon's crusade.

Most of Amon's family and old friends and colleagues and employees are gone.

James Farley died a few months after I spoke with him of his experiences with Amon. Silliman Evans came to Amon's funeral. That night, in Suite 10G of the Fort Worth Club, he died in his sleep. He was sixty-one. Al Shuman died September 12, 1955, following Amon by a few months but fulfilling his vow. Shuman retired in 1932 and Amon, who did not believe in retirements, scolded him. Shuman said, "I'll outlive you." He was eighty-three. Harold Hough died January 4, 1967, after a half-century with the *Star-Telegram*. He was seventy-nine. Jimmy North died during a business trip to New York, October 16, 1956. He was seventy. James R. Record died July 1, 1973, in his sixty-sixth year at the newspaper. He would not retire and lived to see the newspaper he helped create become modern with computers and phototype and reporters hunched over keyboards that hummed with an electric energy not their own. At his funeral, he was described correctly as "a man who had no enemies." JRR's last day was clear and cloudless and hot, with a twelve-mile-an hour southwesterly wind. There was no rain. He was eighty-seven. Bert Honea remained on the job seventy-three years, daily checking the computer's accounting accuracy against the detailed, meticulous, handwritten ledgers he continued, because, he said at age ninety—when he still was shooting his age in golf—retirement was "for old folks who don't get around too good anymore." Capital Cities had offered Mr. Honea a lifetime contract. He refused, "I don't intend to spend the rest of my life at this place." But Bertrand Needham Honea did. He died May 13, 1979, last of the newspaper's management team. He was ninety-two.

After Amon's death, Katrine Deakins continued as board member of the Amon Carter Foundation and a trustee of the Amon Carter Museum, serving her frenetic boss's interests in absentia for the next twenty years as she had for the previous forty. Katrine, to the end, remained blunt-spoken and crusty and briskly efficient. I admired her. She died April 15, 1985. She was eighty-four.

Frank Reeves, who pioneered farm and ranch reporting in the Southwest, died February 4, 1975. He had refused to retire, returned to his desk, and continued writing. Editors surrendered, and let him do as he wished. Characteristically, Mr. Reeves forgot to cash his pension checks. The morning after his death, editors found in his typewriter the beginnings of a story memorializing the horse in the development of West Texas. He was ninety.

E. Clyde Whitlock died May 10, 1970. He had refused to retire and continued to write his multisyllabic reviews, often falling asleep in mid-sentence. He was eighty-four. *Ave atque vale*. Alf Evans died May 14, 1975. Though on pension, Alf Evans had not retired. He remained to edit religious news and prowl the hallways long before dawn each day in search of someone with whom to talk, to entertain with that wry, arched-eyebrow manner he had. In one of our last predawn conversations, he philosophized, "The trouble with life is, it's too damned constant." He was sixty-nine.

Clarence Leon Richhart entered old age as he had lived, indomitable, as blithe as an imp, forever irrepressible. He and his wife, Lucille, celebrated their golden anniversary, posing for family photos dressed in boxing gloves in the middle of a prize-fighting ring. She coldcocked him. Late in his life, the *Star-Telegram* published a series of stories about a fictional baseball team, the Fort Worth Strangers, and utilized Rich as the pictorial image of its aged manager, Leonard L. Leonard. The team became nationally famous, and one dinnertime across the country, there was Rich as

Leonard being interviewed by Walter Cronkite on the *CBS Evening News Show*. He was bent with age, his hearing almost gone, but he and Cronkite, and America, laughed together that night. Rich remained at the newspaper for more than fifty years, being, in his words, "only a reporter." He died in 1985. He was eighty-three. Rich, to no one's surprise, willed his body to a medical research center.

Nenetta Burton Carter never remarried but became a matriarch of Fort Worth society, living in a bright-pink home surrounded, in season, by thousands of brightly colored tulips. She had pleasant memories of Amon, and spoke of him as an old friend, but always with a rich and earthy assessment for the truth of him. As Amon, Nenetta was a philanthropist of major accomplishment and generosity, giving millions of dollars to Fort Worth. She died May 18, 1983. She was eighty-seven. Minnie Meacham Carter, Amon's third and final wife, never remarried, but involved herself in Fort Worth's performing arts, especially as president of the opera association. In the 1980s, she was stricken with Alzheimer's disease and spent the last years of her life at home in the Broad Street mansion. She died January 31, 1996, at age ninety-three, and was buried beside Amon.

As planned, Amon Carter Jr. was publisher after his father's death, and in many ways, became a better man. Amon Sr. was flamboyant, brash; the son, quiet and soft-spoken. Amon raged, the son smiled. Amon required a spotlight, the son was shy and retiring. Their styles were different, but the son, as the father, was an effective builder for his town. Amon Jr. was credited with bringing major league baseball—the Texas Rangers—to the Dallas/Fort Worth area and causing American Airlines to move its headquarters back, once again, to Fort Worth. From the end of his imprisonment during World War II until his death, Amon Jr., very quietly and illegally, supported his friends in communist Poland—the woman in the railroad station, an army sergeant who showed him kindnesses, a doctor who helped the prisoners, and the families of all. The Amon Carter underground smuggling business, begun in the mid-1940s, continued—generally unknown—for another forty years. Amon Jr. sent his friends clothing and necessities, luxury items and money, usually funneling the gifts through the doctor, who had some stature within the communist government. When I was preparing to visit Poland on assignment in 1981, Amon Jr. asked me to deliver a package to the doctor.

"What's in it?" I asked.

"Money," he said—several thousands of dollars.

"Isn't it illegal to take that much cash into Poland?" I asked. "They'll throw me under the jail."

He smiled and said, "It's not that bad. I spent two years there once."

I delivered the money—surreptitiously passing it wrapped inside a newspaper—in a dimly lighted coffeehouse around the corner from my hotel in Cracow. The doctor spoke passable English and was a thin man with a full beard and dark, wide eyes. He accepted the folded newspaper and said, "He [Amon Jr.] has never forgotten us. Many times, he has repaid the debt owed, but he has never forgotten us. He is a kind man." Yes, he was.

Amon Jr. died July 24, 1982. Heart attack, while driving on a Dallas freeway. He was only sixty-two.

Amon's daughter, Ruth Carter Stevenson, built her father and Fort Worth a truly grand and extraordinary American museum. From her position overseeing the Amon Carter Foundation, she became an essential philantrophist for the educational and artistic future of Fort Worth, including the gift of a unique block-sized downtown water garden. Maintaining other homes in North Carolina and Washington, D.C., Ruth became an influential figure in the American art world, serving the National Endowment for the Arts, the National Trust for Historic Preservation, and the National Gallery of Art. For a *Star-Telegram* story, when she was in her sixties, acquaintances, many of whom requested anonymity, described her as "extraordinarily thoughtful," "very direct," "impatient," "a very complex woman," even a little "meanspirited," all characteristics often used to describe her father. In the story, Ruth recalled Amon's lectures to his children about responsible "stewardship" of money and power, and spoke somewhat sharply of her father's decision to prepare the son, not the daughter, to rule the empire, declaring, "I'd love to think that we'd still have the paper if I'd been given a shot at running it." I think so, too.

The proof of Amon Carter in Fort Worth has lessened over the years. The cultural district of museums and theaters carries the official name of Amon Carter Square, though few residents know that. TCU's football arena remains Amon Carter Stadium, but only for official purposes; otherwise it is "TCU Stadium." Amon's school has become Carter-Riverside High; nevertheless a student professed not to know the origin of the "Carter" half of the building in which she was being educated. Suite 10G, where Amon entertained hundreds of America's most famous men, was designed away during a remodeling of the Fort Worth Club. Shady Oak Farm has become a housing development on the shores of Lake Worth. The *West-Texan,* Amon's elegant Chriscraft motorboat given him by the West Texas Chamber of Commerce, still cruises on Eagle Mountain Lake. It remains in the guardianship of the newspaper, used for corporate outings, and still is cared for, its bird's-eye maple veneer maintained to a shiny antique gloss by Boone Blakeley, as it has been for more than a half-century. On one early-morning 1990s Memorial Day cruise, Boone confirmed that it probably was on the *West-Texan,* in the middle of Eagle Mountain Lake, that Amon and Sid Richardson finally convinced Dwight Eisenhower to become a presidential candidate. Peters Brothers Hatters in downtown Fort Worth, operated by a grandson, Joe, continues to manufacture its version of Stetson's Amon Carter Shady Oak Western hat. The lighted portrait of Will Rogers in Amon's old office has been removed, along with the bust of John Nance Garner and all those engraved chrome-plated shovels the publisher used for groundbreakings. Capital Cities built a modern suburban printing plant and set aside space for a small company museum that contains one of Amon's famous hats and other miscellanea of his and the *Star-Telegram*'s history.

During a 1970s redesign of the newspaper, the masthead slogan, "Where The West Begins," disappeared from the front page. A decade later, during yet another design change, that old relic of Amon apocrypha suddenly reappeared. "Where The West Begins" remains in its rightful, traditional place, but the implied message seems less imperious and absolute than in the good old days. It seems, almost, quaint.

Today, Amon rests in a marble and granite mausoleum on a grassy knoll surrounded by large oaks. It is not Boot Hill, but it is a pleasant place to be. He was moved two years after his burial because, in his will, Amon bequeathed himself the mausoleum. Though never reported in the *Star-Telegram*, he set aside $100,000 for the memorial with instructions that it be inscribed suitably "to attest the love I hold for my fellowman and my devotion to the cause of the weak and underprivileged."

Above the mausoleum's door are these words: "His Life Made Charity As Real As Hope Itself."

Amon Carter requires neither apologist nor protector of his memory. There were too many of both. He was a piquant man with a generous hand and heart but one of angers and vanities, onerousness, ever immoderate and amazing. He was not a journalist, but he raised journalism to public-service perfection, and, in the process, raised journalism.

He left behind a widow, two ex-wives, two children, two radio stations, a television station, a newspaper, an uncountable number of oil wells, legacies, legends, lies, and . . . an imperishable cowboy.

His cowboy is with us still, hopefully always will be—a Texas personality famous for its extravagant, outrageous, whoopeeing ways. Whatever else Amon Carter may have accomplished, he consigned forever to the world the modern image of that big-hatted, booted, six-gunning, swaggering, blustering satire of a cowboy who practiced professional Texanism as a grand art and made all western clichés seem irreducible truth.

It fell to Alf Evans to pronounce the most valid epitaph for the cowboy. Paraphrasing humorist Frank Sullivan's thoughts on a dead friend, Alf said, "I don't know where Amon Carter is today, but wherever it is, the people there are having a good time."

And that's the way it was,
A long, long time ago . . .
Out Where the West Begins.